"I learned more in three hours at your seminar than I did in my two previous marriages."

Systems engineer, 47, Chicago

"It is surprising to me that men do not have as much arrogance about learning about money as they do about learning about sex. A man can always talk about ways to make more money, yet underneath the one thing he really wants to know how to do best is 'make it' with his partner."

Accountant, 51, Denver

"I had no idea how little idea I had—I thank you and my fiancée thanks you."

Novelist, 42, Santa Monica

"Thank you, thank you, thank you! Do you know what a goldmine you are? Every man, teenager, college student, whatever, should have access to your course."

Attorney, 32, New York

"After my brother and I had attended your class we could talk more freely—and not just in the way guys usually do. I think your message, about respecting our sexuality was the biggest one for me."

College student, 25, St. Louis

"It was the simplest of things, it was the ways you showed me how to stroke and touch my wife. I only wish I had known this forty years ago."

Recently married executive, 64, Beverly Hills

Praise for Lou Paget's Exquisitely Pleasurable Techniques

THE MEN SAY . . .

"I already knew five languages, but tonight after your seminar I now consider myself a cunnilinguist."

Executive, 54, Pasadena

"I had no idea this subject area could be treated with such grace and elegance while still delivering an informed and powerful message. You have a most unique seminar."

German documentary director, 58, Paris

"I saw the results of your presentation at my bachelor dinner. The next night, on the dance floor after our wedding, my friends and their wives were dancing closer, kissing and hugging more *and* the wives couldn't stop thanking me. Thank you!"

Publisher, 42, Indianapolis

"*Finally!* The information we guys have always wanted and women haven't told us. Anytime I can learn more about my woman and how to please her, sign me up, and it just hasn't been available like this before and it's good to get it from their gender perspective."

Radio talk show host, 44, New Jersey

"I read the *Kama Sutra* when I was fourteen or fifteen and it made about as much sense as Bobby Fischer's book on chess moves—and I could just see an old guy with a heart condition trying this stuff having a heart attack in the garage on the third day. Thank God we finally have you as a source of information."

Photographer, 47, Oakland

THEIR PARTNERS SAY

"Lou, this is G's wife, he did your seminar last week. And what can I say, I am yet another *satisfied* customer."

Author, 47, Manhattan

"We had adopted our first child and then we each did your seminar. Three months later I got pregnant and I want you to know my husband and I hold you completely responsible for our beautiful baby girl."

Singer/actress, 36, Encino

"You put the spark back into a forty-year marriage—something we had hoped for and can't believe has actually happened."

Retail executive, 63, Las Vegas

"I am amazed at how comfortable we are about talking about sexual things now. After the class my husband of fifteen years said, 'You know what, I really want to talk and we did!' We found out things we both wanted to do and try and had never had the courage to ask—are we having fun."

Producer, 41, Phoenix

"At first I thought he can't get better or know more; he was already a fabulous lover. But there was something about what he heard from you that gave him the permission or I don't know what that moved our sex life from good to great to amazing. We now connect sexually even better in our bodies and at a much deeper level in our hearts."

Full-time housewife, 52, Minneapolis

"It is almost embarrassing how obvious the results of my husband's seminar are on me. If one more friend asks me why I look so good—I'll just laugh and say my husband took a class."

Marketing executive, 28, San Francisco

Road Map to Ecstasy

Also by Lou Paget

The Big O
How to Be a Great Lover
How to Give Her Absolute Pleasure

Available in bookstores

RoadMap to Ecstasy

Totally Explicit Techniques Every Man Needs to Know

LOU PAGET

RODALE

Sex and Values at Rodale
We believe that an active and healthy sex life, based on mutual consent and respect between partners, is an important component of physical and mental well-being. We also
respect that sex is a private matter and that each person has a different opinion of what
sexual practices or levels of discourse are appropriate. Rodale is committed to offering
responsible, practical advice about sexual matters, supported by accredited professionals
and legitimate scientific research. Our goal—for sex and all other topics—is to publish
information that empowers people's lives.

Notice
Mention of specific companies, organizations, or authorities in this book does not necessarily imply endorsement by the publisher, nor does mention of specific companies,
organizations, or authorities in the book imply that they endorse the book.
    Internet addresses, telephone numbers, and product information given in this book
were accurate at the time this book went to press.

Book Design by Ralph Fowler

Library of Congress Cataloging-in-Publication Data

Paget, Lou.
    Road map to ecstasy : totally explicit techniques every man needs
to know / Lou Paget.
        p.   cm.
    Includes bibliographical references and index.
    ISBN 1–57954–701–X hardcover
    1. Sex instruction for men.   2. Women—Sexual behavior.
3. Men—Sexual behavior.   4. Sexual excitement.   I. Title.
    HQ36 P35   2002
    613.9'6'081—dc21   2002013171

2   4   6   8   10   9   7   5   3   hardcover

Visit us on the Web at www.rodalestore.com,
or call us toll-free at (800) 848-4735.

WE **INSPIRE** AND **ENABLE** PEOPLE TO IMPROVE
THEIR LIVES AND THE WORLD AROUND THEM

To my father, Kenneth Kane Paget,
the first man I ever loved with all my heart.

To all those who quest for
accurate information in the arena of human sexuality.

And for everyone who knows there can be
greater possibility and future in their own sexuality.

Contents

Acknowledgments   xix

Part I: Mapping the Body

CHAPTER ONE

The Kama *Lou* Tra   3
The Yin and the Yang

CHAPTER TWO

The Body Game   23
The Physical Side of Sex

CHAPTER THREE

The Mind Game   47
The Mental Side of Sex

CHAPTER FOUR

Get Her in the Mood   59
Mental Seduction

CHAPTER FIVE

Chart Her Erogenous Zones   81
Physical Seduction

Part II: Capturing the O

CHAPTER SIX

Debunking the Orgasm Myths   109
There's No Right or Wrong in Sex

CHAPTER SEVEN

Your Orgasm   125
Get the Most from the Tools You've Got

CHAPTER EIGHT

Her Orgasm   147
Going for the Unexpected

CHAPTER NINE

Manual Finesse   171
Let Your Hands Delight Her

CHAPTER TEN

Oral Finesse   199
Tricks of Your Tongue

CHAPTER ELEVEN

Nights of Ecstasy   227
Intercourse That Will Leave You Breathless

Part III: Exploring Uncharted Territory

CHAPTER TWELVE

Expand Your Tool Chest   257
The Beauty of Enhancers

CHAPTER THIRTEEN

Sex and the Spirit   291
Following an Enlightened Path to Ecstasy

Part IV: Healthy Ecstasy

CHAPTER FOURTEEN

Avoiding Physical Roadblocks   323
Medical Concerns That Impact Sexuality

CHAPTER FIFTEEN

Safe Sensuality   341
Keeping Yourself Protected

A Final Note   371

Resources
Where You Can Get the Toys   373

Bibliography   383

Index   389

Acknowledgments

Truly one of the best parts of writing a book is doing these pages . . .

The Support Team

As always some of my biggest and strongest has come from the ladies in my family: Dede, Katerena, Sherry, Lisa, Michelle, and Carolynn.

Jay Rosen, Frankly Speaking, Inc., marketing director, my business right hand. And he's great on the phone.

Tara Raucci, my ever-capable executive assistant, who hit the ground running.

To all who have been there through yet another tour of duty: Jessica Kalkin, Bernard Spigner, Maura McAniff, Kendra King, Raymond Davi, Bryce Britton, Priscilla Wallace, Sandra Beck, Alan Cochran, Christine Hildebrand,

Nance Mitchell, Morley Winnick, Eileen Michaels, Mark Charbonneau, Lilianna and Ali Moradi, Craig Dellio, Ron Ireland, Patrick Boyd, Flint Nelson, Paul Drill, Elaine Wilkes, Gwinn Ioka, Piper Dano, Matthew Davidge, Rhonda Britten, Rebecca Clemons.

The Review Team

Bernard Spigner, Matthew Davidge, Michael Levin, Marty Waldman, Rafi Tahmazian, Ron Ireland, Wayne Williams, David James, T. J. Rozsa, Jay Rosen, Craig Dellio.

The Creative Team

Billie Fitzpatrick: We did it again. And indeed the e-mails were equally as good this time around. Gretchen: for your patience through number 3.

Debra Goldstein: Dream agent, and so much more; and her support team Steven and Bodhi.

Lauren Marino: The book's Executive Producer, who sees it all and guides through the minefields.

Cate Tynan, assistant editor; Liz DeRidder, copyeditor; "J" the illustrator; and Wanda Knight, who keeps those books coming.

Mary Anne Naples and Mark Roy at Creative Culture, Chandler Crawford for all the international sales, and all at Broadway Books.

The Research and Development Team

Penelope Hitchcock, D.V.M.; Beverly Whipple, Ph.D.; Patti Britton, Ph.D.; Sherri J. Tenpenny, D.O.; Gary Richwald, M.D.; Joseph C. Wood, M.D.; Stephen Sacks, M.D.; Mitchell Tepper, Ph.D.; Bernie Zilbergeld, Ph.D.; Bryce Britton, M.S.; Jacquie Brandwynne; Dennis Paradise; Dan and Shay Martin; Mark Fishman; Jules S. Black, M.B., B.S.; Stephen Sacks, M.D.; Jacqueline Snow, M.N., C.N.P.; Eric Daar, M.D.

Road Map to Ecstasy

PART I

Mapping the Body

CHAPTER ONE

The Kama *Lou* Tra

The Yin and the Yang

You Asked for It

I've been curious about sex since I was a teenager, but it took me almost twenty years to gain enough confidence and knowledge to feel comfortable speaking about how to be a great lover. As a woman, my dilemma was that there was no apparent way to be both a nice girl and one that knew a lot about sex. When I realized I was curious about sex, I also realized that there was no safe, dependable source of information I could access. My girlfriends knew only limited amounts about sexuality. And sleeping around wasn't a reasonable or respectable option. So after I surveyed the porn magazines, the movies, and various books on the subject, including the *Kama Sutra*, *The Joy of Sex*, and *The Sensuous Woman*, I came up fairly empty-handed. No one source gave me what I was looking for: accurate, complete information about sex.

Consequently, I began talking, asking questions, and then sharing information about sexual experiences with my women friends. It was from and through them that I began to learn what works, what turns men on, and what doesn't.

Soon I found myself an amateur "sexpert," simply because I felt it was important and necessary that accurate, reliable information about sex be available to all women—whatever their age, background, or experience. I had gathered the stories and details of the women who had shared with me and began to assemble and present the information to focus groups, which then gave me feedback. To make a long story very short, that's how my sex seminars for women were born.

I can still remember when I first realized how frustrated *men* were about sex. The turning point was one particular night about four years ago. It was a Saturday in late May, and I had just arrived at a friend's house for a dinner party. I had been tied up in traffic on the freeway and was the last guest to arrive. I was already tired and had lost my enthusiasm for the party, and was making an effort to be polite, charming, and upbeat. I sat down next to a gentleman who looked to be in his early forties and introduced myself. We got to talking and he told me that he was a television producer. He then asked what I did. For a moment, I felt myself begin to blush, and then I went for it. I should not have felt embarrassed or hesitant to say what I do after having done it for three years at that point, but I had found myself already feeling a bit shy. I then said to him, as demurely as possible, "Well, I give sex seminars to women." Without skipping a beat, he looked straight at me and asked, "Well, do you give them to men, too? We need them!"

In an instant it dawned on me that men, like women, are not only curious about sex, but feel confined or restricted by what they know and do not know. The more I began to listen and talk to men, the more I realized that most men seem to think and feel that they are expected to *already* know everything there is to know about sex, as if the information is tied to their Y chromosome. The more I thought about it, the more I realized that men are acculturated to feel they should know *all* about sex—what works well, what feels the best—both for themselves and for the women they're with. Whereas it's all right for women not to know, many men feel enormous pressure to possess an encyclopedic knowledge of all things sexual. This is not only an enormous falsehood but also an unfair burden for men.

The solution to this problem is simple. First, men need to be granted the permission to ask questions about what they don't know or are not comfortable with regarding sex. Second, and perhaps more important, men need to realize that all women are different and therefore require different treatment. There is no possible way to know what works best for a woman without asking her. Finally, men need to realize that the onus of sex does not fall solely on them. Both men and women should be responsible for learning and then knowing about how to please one another. If these factors are in place, any man can become an expert lover.

So in the same way that I created the seminars to teach women about their bodies, men's bodies, and what the two can do together to experience sex in the most passionate ways possible, I began my quest to do the same for men.

The men's seminar is a group of six to ten men, introduced only by first name, not by surname or by what they do. At a big round table I distribute to each man an "instructional product," which is a life-size woman's genitalia made of a soft, fleshlike material and molded from a porn star. Without too much fanfare, I show the attendees what works for women and what doesn't—manually, orally, during penetration, how women most often reach orgasm, and what toys to use that will drive women wild in bed. This information is based on the data I've gathered from my field researchers.

The men who have attended my seminars have come from all walks of life—professionals, artists, athletes, doctors, mechanics, architects, builders, actors, producers, television executives. They have come in all sizes and shapes, education levels, and personalities. And they have all come wanting to know more about sex—specifically, how better to please the women in their lives. As one political consultant said, "Making love makes me feel manly, in the most basic sense of the word. There is nothing that makes sex with my partner better than knowing I can take care of her. So if there is information out there for me to experience that more and differently, then I want it." Referring to his wife, another seminar attendee, this one an investment banker from New York, put it this way: "We've been together ten years and I want to know how to make it more fun, more interesting." Another male seminar attendee, a photographer from Palo Alto, California, said, "Please, just tell me what works."

I hear not only yearning in these voices but a demand for the tried and true. A real estate developer from Philadelphia said in frustration, "I wouldn't ask her to do anything she doesn't want to do, but I'd love to know anything that is going to make our sex life keep growing. It is good, really good, but I want to make it better."

Becoming an Expert Lover

Giving sexuality seminars to both men and women has taught me a great deal about male and female sexuality and psychology. The information in this book, then, comes from my listening and observing and hearing the feedback that thousands of men and women have shared with me about what works, what doesn't, and what they're missing. Don't you want to know what women honestly want, like, and don't like? I want to be your special confidante, a translator and provider of women's hidden desires and wishes. Inside these two covers, I have assembled—for her benefit as well as yours— the most scintillating, most practical, and most reliable information out there. If you believe that one's sexual prowess is gained by being with skilled, sensitive, and informative lovers, think of this book as that one lover who will share all she knows—and she knows a lot!

Another way to think of me is as your coach. In sports it's perfectly understandable and acceptable to have a coach, as it is in business to have a mentor. While I don't pretend to be a doctor of sex, I do think that my so-called time in the field, gathering information from thousands of men and women, has enabled me to present you with what works best in the sex department for both women and men. I presume that you are tired of the same old, stale information that purports to give you the real goods but falls short. Rather, I think you ultimately want to know what works, what's going to warm her up, get her excited, and eventually have her scream your name in ecstasy. I will describe the tips to perfect your "game" and point out snafus that may hinder you. I'm going to tell it like it is, from the point of view of women, and I'm not going to spare you any details. I feel confident that, as your coach, I will not lead you astray, but rather will lead you down the path to mutual bliss.

This book is the first step in making you an expert lover. How does one become an expert? In order to transform yourself from a competent lover to one who can bring his lover to unparalleled heights of pleasure, you must not only learn the tried-and-true techniques of a master seducer, but also incorporate the insight that makes you open, willing, and ready to climb such heights.

Road Map to Ecstasy is about how to please women, pamper them, and thrill them—and how to achieve ecstasy for yourself. So I'm making another assumption here: that you, the readers, not only want to be at the top of your sexual game, but also care deeply and passionately about women. And although the women in your lives will be the direct beneficiaries of the treasure trove of information between these seductive covers, doesn't it make sense that by pleasing your partner, you will receive that pleasure back in spades? Sex, like other endeavors, whether they are career-oriented, spiritual, physical, or emotional, is about synergy. Specifically, if you please your partner, her satisfaction builds and bounces back to you, increasing your pleasure. As one physician from Seattle said, "There is nothing better than knowing I have taken care of her, that I made her feel great. That for me is what making love is all about." Another man said, "Like most guys, I do not want people knowing what I do with my wife at those most intimate moments. And even though women may talk about sex, we men don't or can't. But my male pride went into orbit when my wife told me that I had become the guy her friends wanted cloned and who they talk about in *their* locker room!"

SECRET FROM LOU'S ARCHIVES

The use of lipstick apparently originates from wanting to have the oral labia resemble the blood-flushed look of the aroused genital labia. In the animal kingdom this indicates to the male that the female is sexually ready.

In preparing and doing the seminars, I discovered that reliable or accurate sources of information about sex are still very limited. The typical sources men use to learn about sex are slanted and incomplete. Pornography—both magazines and films—is problematic for three main reasons. First, the majority of porn magazines and movies are created with the visual stimulation/fantasy factor as the driving force and are therefore often unrealistic. Second, because they "program" men to expect the unrealistic in sex, men are disappointed when women or their bodies can't or don't deliver. Third, because these movies and magazines are targeted to men, they ignore half the population (i.e., women), which means that what pleases women is not adequately or faithfully represented.

Although I have nothing against visual material that stimulates men, I think it's important to know that while some of these fantasies may work in your mind to get you excited, they may not work in real life. By all means, use these movies, written scenarios, or other forms of pornography to pleasure you and even your partner. I know one seminar attendee and his partner who loved to read each other some of the erotica stories in *Playboy*. He said, "Sometimes it just helps to get us in the mood." But when these scenarios are actually brought into the bedroom and acted out, many men and women are often surprised, frustrated, and ultimately disappointed when they don't work. Remember, these are actors—professionals—who are working on choreographed sets with props, editing, voice-overs, and special lighting, which all combine to create an unreal environment. If a fantasy story of one man making love with two women is a turn-on for you (and perhaps your partner as well), things may get a bit more complicated if you test such a scenario in real life. Real feelings are at stake, and no matter how open one or both of you may be in terms of your fantasies, you may end up getting hurt, the intimacy and trust between you and your partner forever severed. I asked a television talk show host what he felt was the basis for porn, and he said, "Minimal plot ideas with the aim to get the clothes off as soon as possible and get into the action, geared at men aged 17 to 37."

Another downfall of relying too heavily on porn and the fantasies they promote is that they tend to program men to expect a certain kind of turn-on. Again, the real world rarely meets this expectation. If your lover is unable to play out the fantasies as they are depicted or described in the movies or magazines, porn can actually distract and/or come between you and her. A good example of this is the frequency with which "deep throating," swallowing, or anal play appears in pornography. Again, while the images may stimulate or titillate you, many women cannot deep-throat and prefer not to swallow or be penetrated anally. Of course, there are women who love anal sex or the sensation of your semen down their throats. But from what thousands of women have shared with me, many women would rather not engage in these activities. Specifically, the gag reflex makes it nearly impossible to deep-throat. Again, the women in the films who are performing such feats are professionals, who do such moves day in, day out for the camera, not for a man they love or care about. Based on my seminars and research, I would say only 20 to 25 percent of women swallow, and although many women try anal sex at least once, most say it's too painful to be enjoyable.

In addition, I know of several people (a couple of men and one woman) who wrote for "personal-experience" columns in Larry Flynt publications. They admitted that the published scenarios are completely made up. When I asked one gentleman, he said, "Lou, it was great fun writing those columns. I had a great time!" Yet in response to my question about how much of the information was truthful, he said, "Not a word." The same writer also wrote a first-person column on how to seduce and have sex with women in different countries. He went into great detail on the clubs, bars, and lounges where one could get the best action across Europe. A minor overlooked fact, however, was that this gentleman had never been out of the United States in his life. You got it: He made it all up.

Porn producers are there to make money—plain and simple. Until the bottom line is negatively affected by marketing only to men, these publishers and producers will keep churning out what customers seem to want. Why consider what women want if they don't have to? That said, there are a few producers who keep the female market in mind. One of these more female-friendly producers is Femme Productions, headed by Candida Royale. *The Wise Woman's Guide to Erotic Videos*, by Angela Cohen and Sarah Gardner Fox, is an excellent reference guide.

Another source of misinformation about sex comes from that eponymous group called the "guys." In the seminars, men will often share the "helpful" information of friends. What they soon realize is that their friends don't know any more than they do; they just act like they do. As a rule, and many of you have probably already figured this out by now, the biggest talkers are usually the least informed. These are the locker-room braggarts who exaggerate in quantity and exploit the quality. As one man I know recalls, "This dude had eight guys listening to him brag about doing this married babe six times in one afternoon. Even though we knew he was full of sh—, we all were standing around like maybe some of that would fall off on us." Sound familiar?

Another gentleman I know stopped his 23-year-old

nephew's manly adventure story during the family picnic. When the nephew said, "Yeah, I did her eight times last night," the uncle said, "Okay, drop trou. Let's see it—that will be the proof. You should be so sore today you can't pee." As you can imagine, the nephew did not drop trou, but he did quickly drop the subject.

Sex as Performance

An indirect consequence of the problem with pornography is its dangerous reinforcement of sex as some kind of performance. Men look at the taut, muscular, never-aging bodies on-screen or in high-gloss print and automatically compare (and contrast) themselves. Although I know some of you can easily stand up to such scrutiny, I know even the most confident men may feel a bit put-off by the hard bodies displayed on-screen or in magazines. (The media do the same brainwashing on women when they use prepubescent girls to model and when they airbrush and retouch advertisements.) No wonder you guys associate sex with pressure! The media are constantly reminding you to compare yourselves to the alpha males in magazines. I understand that most males have the basic trait of competitiveness, but for these industries to manipulate this trait and use it to sell magazines or movies is just plain Machiavellian. Isn't this merely an exploitative business tactic of knowingly feeding the other side false information to gain competitive advantage? Best said, it is beyond unkind to force you to compare yourselves to false measurements and information.

Isn't a woman who really lets go and gets into sex a com-

plete turn-on for you? Well, the same goes for women. Women
don't want you to perform in bed. Nor do they necessarily care

---

Secret from Lou's Archives

*Always tell a woman what works, not what doesn't. Empha-
size the positive and she'll listen.*

---

how many times you can "do it" in one night. Rather, they
want you to simply enjoy being with them. If you are completely present, focused on her, and into what you're doing, a
woman will not only feel cared for, she will also begin to un-
leash her sexual energy. As one seminar attendee told me,
"The most satisfying sex happens in one long, slow lovemaking
session."

The Big O

I receive a lot of interesting, sometimes ludicrous questions
about sex, specifically about orgasms. But the questions that
most intrigue me are those that speak to men's and women's
uncertainty about orgasms. I remember one woman in particular who had been recently widowed after a 29-year marriage.
She said to me, "I don't know if I've ever had an orgasm. I
think I have, but I'm not sure. How can I be sure?" This same
feeling was echoed by a man who said that his girlfriend was
convinced that she had had an orgasm, but he felt sure that
she hadn't.

How can we be so uncertain about something so big? I see
sex not as a performance experience with orgasm as its ulti-

mate goal, but instead as a wide, meandering avenue toward pleasure—in whatever form you desire. An orgasm, of course, is a wonderful, satisfying state, but it should not be held up as the sole goal that drives your sexual experience.

First, women and men experience orgasms very differently. Whereas men can experience an orgasm in up to seven different ways, women can experience orgasms in up to ten different ways! Have you ever heard of a mouth orgasm? A zone orgasm? Breast orgasms? Both sexes can and do experience all of these types. The second factor complicating orgasm information is the very fact that men and women have very different sexual arousal cycles. From the starting gate, a couple trying to coordinate orgasms simultaneously generally faces very normal physiological challenges.

HISTORICAL AND HYSTERICAL FACTS

Throughout the ages, people have referred to sex in many different ways. Try these on for size:

- Come in and recognize her again (attributed to Louis XV)
- Fling one's spear into the future (Franz Liszt)
- Long conversation
- Disrespect for my person
- Tool (Lord Byron)
- Swive (Elizabeth I)
- Be overcome with sympathy
- Feel like a woman

The good news is that this book will give you much more insight into your own body, your partner's, and orgasms in general.

The Communication Conundrum

We've all heard it over and over again: Men and women communicate differently. The king of communication between the sexes, John Gray, goes so far as to say that men access love through sex, while women access sex through love or feelings. If you ascribe to this theory, it's no wonder that men and women often find they're not speaking the same language. Haven't you ever felt that you and the woman in your life are speaking similar but not identical dialects, requiring a translator?

I won't bore you with an involved sociological study here, but suffice it to say that since boys and girls are socialized differently, based in general on their biology and then later reinforced by societal gender roles, they tend to communicate differently, in almost opposing ways. As a result, in order to communicate successfully—whether the subject is sex or dinner—I think it's important for men (and women) to acknowledge the differences between them. For instance, when a woman doesn't feel she's been heard, she will withdraw—both emotionally and physically. She may be reacting to you. As one woman said, "I fell in love with my husband when I discovered he absolutely listened. I couldn't believe it when days later he would consistently repeat what I had said, and understood where I was coming from—amazing."

Women respond best to the more self-confident and self-assured men, and those are men who listen. If a woman comes to you with a question, worry, concern, problem, or simple story from her life, she may not be asking for your advice. Ask her up front if she wants you to just listen or, if she does want advice, listen first and then give advice. Often she quite simply wants to be heard, and your listening means that you care. However, as a man, you may respond by wanting to "fix" her problem. Providing a solution isn't what she wants, and she may think you're condescending. And if you constantly interrupt her while she is speaking, she will know you're not listening. Then she will withdraw, and where will that get either of you?

There are ways to communicate that you are listening to her: Make direct eye contact, touch her, and even gently nod your head. If your eyes are darting all over the place, chances are you're not really paying attention, and chances are for sure that she knows you are distracted. And as I said above, when a woman doesn't feel heard, she will withdraw, both emotionally and physically, or find someone else who will listen. This is not a threat, just a fact. It is extremely important to women that they feel heard. One of their biggest complaints is that they aren't.

In the sexual arena, some gender differences in communicating have concrete effects or consequences. On the one hand, women want you to know what pleases them sexually; on the other hand, they are often reluctant to share this information with you in a direct way. Although women may talk among themselves about sex, many tend to shy away from talking directly to men about sex. This contrast points not only to a built-in communication challenge but also to these differences between men and women.

From my work in the seminars, I've narrowed down the four main reasons women hesitate to share what we want with our partners.

1. If we say what we want, we will be judged either as sleazy or as sexual traffic cops.
2. We don't know what to say or how to say it. A graphic designer from Miami said, "I'd love to tell him, I just don't know how. I know the sensation, but it's hard to describe exactly what he's doing to me."
3. We are concerned that men will feel criticized and hear our suggestions as a message that they aren't good lovers.
4. We are worried that men don't really listen. One woman said, "Even if I tell him what I like, he doesn't listen. He just keeps doing the same thing."

The reason some women won't tell you what they want or how to do it is related to one of those old stereotypes, which still has lingering power on female psyches. Most women, especially those who are single, often still want to be thought of as "nice girls," and don't want to risk being perceived as having slept around. They are afraid that men will hear any kind of "I like it this way" as an indication of what worked with "another guy." If they risk introducing this information, they fear that their partner may feel alienated or angry.

By being aware that women are hesitant to tell you their likes and dislikes, you can make the task of finding out what your partner wants simpler and easier (and far more pleasurable) for both of you if you tell her that you *want* to know. You need to encourage her to feel free to tell you, even show you at times, the way she wants to be touched, kissed, or licked, perhaps. By opening this front door of communication, you immediately establish a potent force for her relaxation.

Also, gentlemen, please be aware of how you deliver information. If you and your partner are comfortable with the term "pussy" and its various derivations, by all means use it. But know that if a woman is uncomfortable with the way you may describe *any* piece of her anatomy, chances are she will be turned off, not turned on. My suggestion here is to start with the most politically correct terms and go from there. You may want to ask her what she prefers to call her body parts, in conversation and in passion, and then adjust accordingly. Let her set the level of frankness. In other words, she may enjoy and get excited by using "dirty" words.

After being with the same lover for a long time, you can anticipate what she wants as well as surprise her and explore with her, but if you're wondering how to please your lover consistently, then you need to communicate. There's just no way around it.

The importance of communication cannot be underestimated. Indeed, when you are conscious and aware of how you are interacting with her and how she is interacting with you, then all the other elements of sex will fall into place. As one male seminar attendee commented, "When you are with a woman, you have to be super, super aware. You have to forget about getting your rocks off and, instead, tune into her. The directions are right there for what she wants—you just have to pay total attention to what and how she reacts. She's like a schematic and you just need to adjust your hard-wiring." With that in mind, I have put together a list of typical differences between men and women that you might want to keep in mind as you prepare yourself to become an expert lover. These, of course, are generalizations, and are not true for all men and women, but as a rule, they may be helpful.

> ➤ Women fall in love between their ears and men through their eyes.
> ➤ Men tend to be visual creatures, coming alive at the mere sight of a bare breast. Women are more aural and tactile. They need to hear and to feel a man in order to get excited.
> ➤ Men often enjoy a fast rush to sex. Women prefer a slow buildup.
> ➤ Men are goal-oriented, tending to head for the charge of orgasm. Women love the route getting there, meandering and taking their time.
> ➤ Most men absolutely love getting a wet, slippery tongue kiss in the ear, but most women abhor this.
> ➤ Women respond to gentle, light touching. Men respond to deeper pressure.
> ➤ Women usually know when they are going to have sex, whereas men can be surprised. Women usually make up their minds based on how they've been treated. And often the thing that tips the tables isn't anything you are aware of. However, to put the odds more in your favor, I have written this book. The more you know, the better prepared you will be.

The Golden Parachute

Like any kind of project or endeavor, the more you put into sex, the more you and your lover will get out of it. Those men who say they have strong, wonderful, passionate love lives are those who approach sex with the same determination and gusto as they do their other goals, whether those goals are about their careers, artistic pursuits, humanitarian endeavors, or athletic interests. The consistent factor is focus. An oil executive from Arizona said, "When my sexual relationship and personal life are working well, I feel invincible in business. There is a direct correlation between being happy at home and being a success in my career." Again and again I've heard men say that when they are able to satisfy and fulfill their partner sexually, they feel better about themselves, more confident and energized in other areas of their lives.

In the same way that you plan ahead for your Saturday golf game, you need to plan for intercourse. In the beginning of a relationship, didn't you make more of an effort to seduce her? Well, don't forget this once you've been together for a while. No matter what your age or the status of your relationship, you still need to think ahead and make a commitment to your intimacy: Like your chip shot, your sexual relationship needs practice and concentration. I would bet that you have a long-term plan for your investments. How you take care of your money now affects its performance in the future. The same is true with your relationship: How you invest in your sexual relationship now pays off in the future. So you need to have a plan for it as well. And believe me, you'll see very real returns.

If you've never put into words how sex connects you with your partner, let her know. Don't assume she knows exactly how you feel about sex, intimacy, and connection. As one seminar attendee said, "I just assumed my wife knew how she turned me on. But after sex one time, she finally exploded and told me that she felt like all I wanted to do was f— her, and that I didn't love her. Nothing could be further from the truth, but I guess I thought she knew I loved her. Boy, was I wrong."

As you read through this book, I would like you to remember that I am sharing what I have learned and gleaned from the thousands of men and women I have encountered in my sexuality seminars. It goes without saying that all of these people attend the seminars in the spirit of mutual respect and wanting to learn how to be a great lover. And being a great lover is 20 percent technique and 80 percent openness, willingness, enthusiasm, and communication. That said, I want to thank you for being here. As I say to the men who walk through the door and sit down at an oval table among ten or so other men to hear about the techniques to best please ladies, it takes courage just to show up. But what you are about to receive may very well change your sex life forever.

The ultimate focus and goal of both the men's seminar and this book is to find and access your sexual soul. To give you the ideas, attitudes, and information that others say have worked for them so that as a lover, you can create a wondrous, playful, mutually enjoyable sexual relationship with the woman you love.

CHAPTER TWO

The Body Game

The Physical Side of Sex

Body Boldness

Most of the time, when we think about sex, we imagine it as an activity or expression of the body. From a purely physical point of view, the body is the vehicle through which we experience pleasure.

Nowhere is the importance of knowing and being comfortable with your body more crucial than with your sexuality. And yet, in my experience, many people don't really know what's happening with their bodies sexually. This is in part because sex is a private and intimate matter, and it's rare that we feel completely free and open about discussing this area of our lives. But I also think that our lack of knowledge or familiarity with our sexual bodies is a result of the conflicting messages and contradictory information we receive about sex. Without accurate information we are fated to remain in information limbo—not sure how to find answers to our questions or to share our experiences.

23

Do you have a sense of when your body is not responding sexually the way you want it to? Sometimes it's because of a recent cold or flu, or because you're feeling tired or over-stressed at work. Sometimes it's a result of a recent operation or other serious health condition. If your body isn't working, or you're unsure how it works sexually, then you won't be able to fully access your sexual pleasure. Knowing how the body is supposed to work sexually will at the very least give you a sense of what's happening and why. Then, if some part of you is responding slowly or not at all, you will be more aware and can take the steps to ask a professional.

SECRET FROM LOU'S ARCHIVES

Dr. Herbert Otto points out that most sexologists have concluded that sex is largely a learned response. Not only are most of our sexual behavior and response patterns learned, but the orgasm, as well as the possibilities of this event, is also learned. The implication is that what is learned is furnished by the society in which we grew up. The question then has to be asked: "What is the content of the learning about sex that defines the parameters of a person's sexual potential?"

The Phases—Twain the Two Shall Meet

In their pioneering work *Human Sexual Response*, Masters and Johnson described the physiological changes that men and women go through during sex in terms of a sexual response cycle. They arbitrarily divided this cycle into four phases:

1. Excitement or arousal
2. Plateau
3. Orgasm
4. Resolution

For the past twenty-five years, this part of their work has been widely popularized and accepted. However as Bernie Zilbergeld, Ph.D., points out in his groundbreaking book *The New Male Sexuality,* Alfred Kinsey is more on target: "There is nothing more characteristic of sexual response than the fact that it is not the same in any two individuals." In other words, there is no right or normal way to have a sexual experience. Your (or your partner's) response is the result of a complex interaction among many variables, including your age, your physical and emotional state, how turned on you are, what your partner does, and how you feel about her.

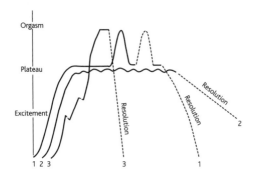

THE FEMALE SEXUAL RESPONSE CYCLE

Three representative variations of female sexual response. Pattern 1 shows multiple orgasms; pattern 2 shows arousal that reaches the plateau level without going on to orgasm (note that resolution occurs very slowly); and pattern 3 shows several brief drops in the excitement phase followed by an even more rapid resolution phase. Also note that, unlike in males, there is no refractory period in the female sexual response cycle.

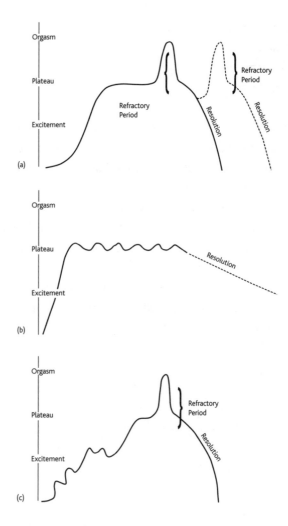

THE MALE SEXUAL RESPONSE CYCLE

(a) The most typical pattern of male sexual response. The dotted line shows one possible variation: a second orgasm and ejaculation after the refractory period is over. (b) Male sexual response in a situation of prolonged arousal at the plateau level not going on to orgasm and ejaculation. Note that there is no refractory period in this instance, and resolution occurs considerably more slowly. (c) Male sexual response pattern showing erratic initial arousal and a relatively brief plateau prior to orgasm.

The duration of copulation for a bee is two seconds; a cat, eight seconds; a brown bear, one to three minutes; and a worm, four hours. But the copulation winner is the mink, which remains in the coital position for as long as eight hours, say Richard Milsten and Julian Slowinski in their book *The Sexual Male*. Hence the expression "mink-like" behavior.

Another important sexologist, Dr. Lasse Hessel, presents a slightly different approach to men's and women's sexual cycles. He divides the act of making love into five phases, which he says, "is, of course, a very theoretical division, as the phases merge into each other, one after the other."

1. Foreplay
2. Sexual stimulation
3. Dilation (expansion of the upper part of the vagina in the woman and erection in the man)
4. Orgasm/climax
5. Relaxation

For Dr. Hessel, the distinction between foreplay and sexual stimulation is important because it underscores that becoming aroused with your partner is both a mental and physical activity. In foreplay, Hessel maintains, couples excite and prepare each other for having sex, using their own rituals or sexual code. This happens at a more mental and emotional level.

In the next phase, couples sexually stimulate each other by touching, kissing, or any other way that gets their bodies sexually aroused so that bloodflow to the genitals increases. In the third phase, bloodflow increases to such a degree that genitals are fully engorged with blood—for the woman, her vagina and clitoris are enlarged and aroused; for the man, his penis has become erect and his scrotum swells or lifts. The fourth phase is orgasm, and the fifth and last phase is relaxation, similar to what Masters and Johnson call resolution.

My point here is to show you that even though there are some universal patterns that indicate sexual excitement and the steps leading toward orgasm, many experts distinguish the phases differently, emphasizing their own particular point of view. I think what's important is becoming familiar with the general sexual flow so that you are comfortable with all aspects of your sexual experience.

Some questions to consider: How can you help your partner reach orgasm if you've rushed through foreplay? (Gentlemen, this is especially true if you haven't given a woman time to warm up.) And do you really want to push yourself toward climax when you're enjoying being touched, caressed, and fondled?

Dr. Hessel points out that "exciting and fulfilling lovemaking takes more than just knowing how to treat your partner physically in order for you both to achieve orgasm." Foreplay is at least as important and pleasurable as intercourse, and it is essential to remember that the same things are not necessarily as sexually stimulating for your partner as they are for you. Normally, a woman takes much longer to reach the same level of arousal as you do and you may have to restrain your own needs so that your partner can gradually build up her level of sexual arousal.

While many of us may recognize these differing definitions, my point is both to offer you a general framework from which to become aware of your own sexual cycles, and to bring to light the shades of gray when it comes to pinpointing an exact cycle that matches all women and all men. Matching, it appears from the research, is a rarity. Use the information as a way to become more aware of and therefore in tune with your own sexual potential.

Your Sexual Cycle

The main physical changes that occur in men's bodies during a sexual experience result from vasocongestion, or the accumulation of blood in various parts of the body. Muscle tension increases, and other changes (such as increased respiration and pulse rate) also occur. With orgasm, the muscular tension is released and bloodflow resumes its normal rate.

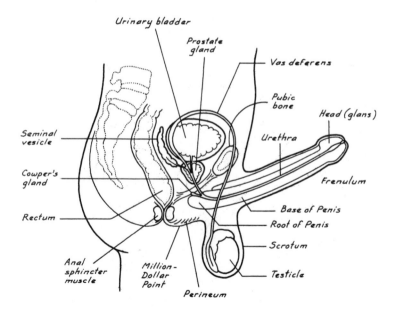

Male Genitalia

Male Physical Response

EXCITEMENT

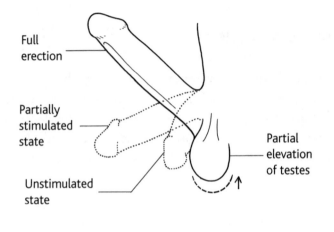

Full
erection

Partially
stimulated
state

Unstimulated
state

Partial
elevation
of testes

PLATEAU

Color deepens

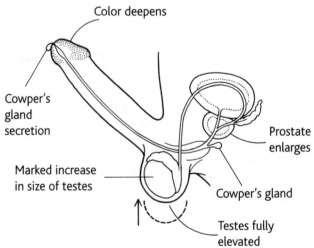

Cowper's
gland
secretion

Marked increase
in size of testes

Prostate
enlarges

Cowper's gland

Testes fully
elevated

ORGASM

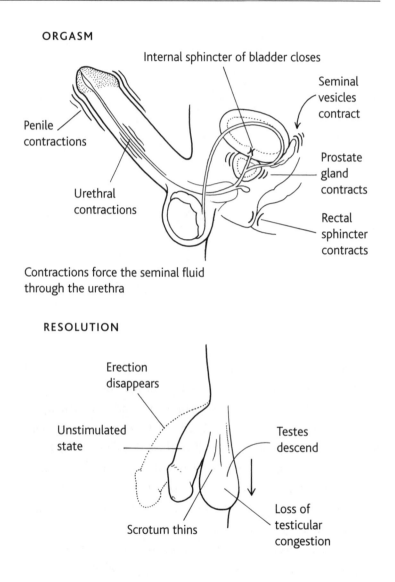

Internal sphincter of bladder closes

Seminal vesicles contract

Penile contractions

Prostate gland contracts

Urethral contractions

Rectal sphincter contracts

Contractions force the seminal fluid through the urethra

RESOLUTION

Erection disappears

Unstimulated state

Testes descend

Loss of testicular congestion

Scrotum thins

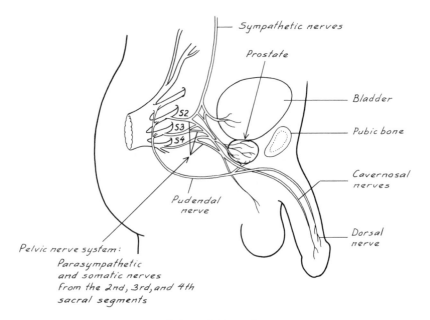

Male Sexual Nerve Arrangement

Arousal

Sexual response begins when you receive some kind of sexual stimulation: a touch, smell, sight, thought, fantasy, or anything that has erotic meaning for you—and given the range of ideas floating around in our heads, just about anything might have erotic meaning. As a result of this stimulation, the brain triggers an increased volume of blood to pump into various parts of your body, increasing the size of the genitals. As a result of this increase in bloodflow, the genitals become darker and even more sensitive to stimulation. It goes without saying that Mother Nature really knew what she was doing here.

Your penis, your lips, earlobes, and nipples all receive more bloodflow, making them more alert and receptive to touch or stimulation. Have you ever noticed that when your partner touches your arm while you are kissing or beginning to make love that you suddenly feel the hair stand up on end, as if suddenly your entire arm has become an erogenous zone?! Other areas also become aroused and change form. The scrotal sac, for instance, thickens and contracts, while the testes increase in size with the engorgement of blood. The testes are also pulled up within the sac until they press against the wall of the pelvis. It is the thin layer of muscle within the scrotum called the cremasteric muscle that does this. This elevation of the testes anticipates ejaculation and is necessary for it to occur.

SECRET FROM LOU'S ARCHIVES

According to Milsten and Slowinski, "it is known that testosterone levels are secreted in the male according to circadian rhythm, with maximal levels occurring in the morning and minimal levels at night. It is also known that serum testosterone levels decline with advancing age, beginning in the mid-forties. This is most likely a result of decreased rate of testosterone production in the testicles due to aging. In addition, size and weight of the testicles decrease with age. Seventy-year-old males can be expected to have approximately 50 percent of the testosterone concentrations found in men half their age."

Erection

An erection is really a study in fluid hydraulics. With each wave of stimulation, the brain signals blood to flow into the three main spongy tissue chambers of the penis. When these are filled (fully engorged), an erection occurs. The penis also has a regular cycle of nocturnal erections, which explains why you often wake with an erection. This doesn't necessarily mean you were having wild sex dreams; it's simply nature's way of maintaining good, healthy penis tissue.

SECRET FROM LOU'S ARCHIVES

During REM sleep, males—from one-day-old infants to men ninety or older—usually have erections. This means three to five-plus erections a night, each lasting from a few minutes to an hour.

In many young men, erection is almost instantaneous; they get hard as soon as they get any stimulation. With increasing age, however, it usually takes longer to get hard, and even direct stimulation of the penis may not be enough to make a man erect. As men age, their sexual reactions become more in line with those of women, especially in terms of timing. I've been told this is nature's way of leveling the playing field. Older men are more easily distracted and require more direct stimulation to become and stay erect. (We'll discuss medical issues such as impotence and premature ejaculation later, in chapter 14.)

Many factors can affect your ability to become erect, including anxiety, stress, or simply distraction. As one man put it, "When I am stressed about work, it is like my equipment doesn't work." Another man said this: "When I am angry, I can still get up to do the job. But I'm definitely not as there mentally." Strong emotion is a natural distraction to sex, especially if the emotion is caused by something outside the sexual or romantic moment.

Ejaculation

Ejaculation is a spinal reflex that releases the built-up muscular tension and reverses bloodflow in the body, draining it away from the penis and other engorged areas. Two distinct steps are involved in ejaculation: First the prostate, seminal vesicles, and vas deferens contract, pouring their contents into the urethra. The sperm mix with the secretions of the seminal vesicles and the prostate to form the ejaculate. The contractions are the beginning of the ejaculation. This is when men say they feel they're about to come. Masters and Johnson call this point of the phase "ejaculatory inevitability," because once the contractions begin, the process usually happens involuntarily.

SECRET FROM LOU'S ARCHIVES

Smoking directly and negatively impacts a man's ability to get and maintain an erection. It has also been shown to affect sperm count and ejaculation. My suggestion: Kick the habit.

During the second step of the ejaculatory process, the fluid is propelled through the urethra by contractions of the pubococcygeus, or PC, muscle. The semen may spurt several inches or even feet beyond the tip of the penis, or it may simply seep or trickle out. (Of course, I've noted in my research that many men have claimed great distance—"high jumpers" I like to call them.) The amount and force of ejaculate expelled are determined by a number of factors, including age, general health, and length of time since the last ejaculation. Anecdotally, it seems that the younger you are, the greater the distance your semen will travel. Also, if you haven't come in a long time, you will tend to have more semen built up, ready to be released.

Although ejaculation occurs in and through the penis, it is in fact a "total-body response," according to Dr. Bernie Zilbergeld. Respiration, blood pressure, and heartbeat increase as a man approaches ejaculation, usually peaking at the moment of "propulsion." But many men have reported (to me), "At that moment, I don't know anything else in the world except that sensation." Another male seminar attendee said, "Sometimes I think it is going to be a great one, and then it just sort of pffts out—there just isn't enough flow. Those are rather disappointing." While I understand his disappointment, this is perfectly natural and certainly not a reflection of his manhood or sexual prowess.

Resolution

After ejaculation, your body starts to return to its equilibrium, or prearoused state. For most men, this move (what Masters and Johnson refer to as the shift from orgasm to resolution) happens very quickly, hence the clichéd image of men falling into a deep slumber once they come. One man explained the feeling this way: "After I have an orgasm, every ounce of stress in my body is gone for the next twenty-five minutes."

What's really happening in the body is that after ejaculation, the blood flows out of the penis, which then returns to a flaccid (nonerect) state. Blood pressure, pulse, and breathing rates also return to normal. The scrotum and testes lose their engorgement, become smaller in size, and return to their normal position. The reason many men feel as if they could sleep is because of a deep state of relaxation—they've just built up and then released tremendous muscle tension, giving them overall body relaxation. Think of how you feel after a workout: Once your body is moved, manipulated, and stretched, don't you then feel an all-around sense of relaxation?

Her Sexual Cycle

Like you, a woman goes through the four basic phases from arousal through climax to resolution. However, her cycle is rarely in sync with yours.

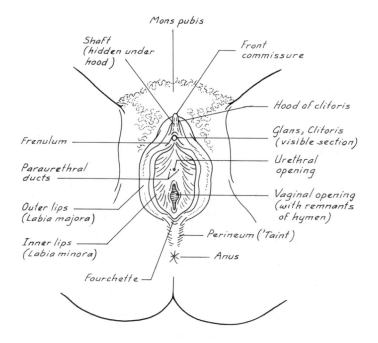

Female Genitalia

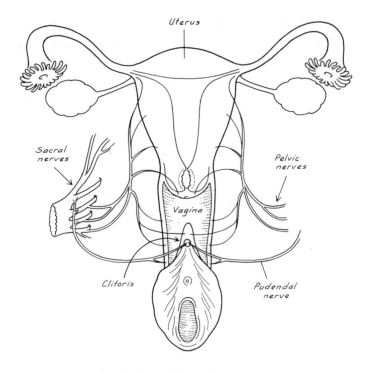

Female Sexual Nerve Arrangement

Arousal

When a woman is stimulated through kissing and touching, blood flows into all the structures of her pelvis, her vagina moistens, and her labia majora and labia minora begin to swell and become duskier in color. Her body also begins to lubricate. That is, the mucosal walls of her vagina start to exude fluid in preparation for intercourse. In this way, lubrication is one of the first signs of sexual arousal in women.

Physiologically, lubrication is identical to erection in the male, yet women often take much longer to lubricate than men take to get an erection. Women's bodies respond as they were designed to, but often men seem to be way ahead of them—you may be erect and ready to go while she is still getting warmed up. Although some women begin to lubricate within thirty seconds of stimulation—either mental or physical—not all women do. Some may take several minutes or not lubricate at all. So please don't use this as the only criteria for assessing whether your partner is ready.

HISTORICAL AND HYSTERICAL FACTS	According to Drs. Joel Block and Susan Crain Bakos, "women's increased ease with their bodies and confidence in lovemaking continues to grow after their thirties. And a woman's orgasmic capacity including the ability to have multiple orgasms is undiminished by age." However, a "man cannot be truly said to peak until he has become a good, even a great, lover with ejaculatory control and the ability to please his partner in different ways, and that is unlikely to happen at nineteen."

Sometimes women, no matter how aroused they may be in their heads, still may be dry and unable to lubricate. This can be caused by a range of things from medications (such as antihistamines, which dry out body tissues) to how hydrated she is. If she has drunk any alcohol during the evening, she may be slightly dehydrated, which will directly affect her ability to lubricate. This reaction is also caused by cigarette smoking or

(continued on page 42)

Female Physical Response

AROUSAL

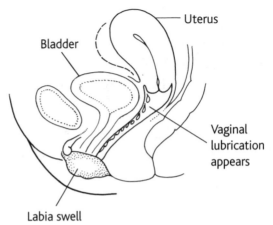

Uterus

Bladder

Vaginal lubrication appears

Labia swell

PLATEAU

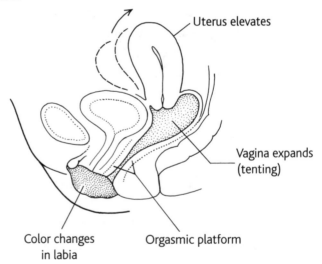

Uterus elevates

Vagina expands (tenting)

Color changes in labia

Orgasmic platform

ORGASM

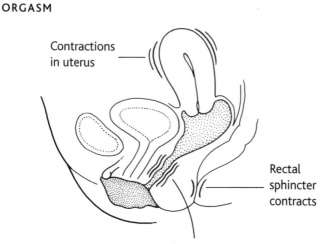

Contractions in uterus

Rectal sphincter contracts

Rhythmic contractions in orgasmic platform

RESOLUTION

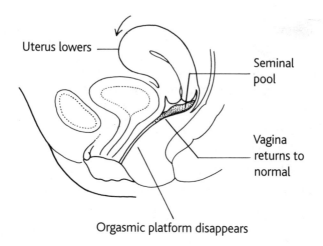

Uterus lowers

Seminal pool

Vagina returns to normal

Orgasmic platform disappears

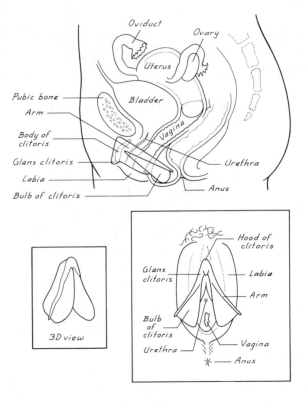

The Clitoris

by a lack of the hormone estrogen, which is essential for lubrication. In chapter 12, I suggest a number of wonderful lubricants that can be used for intercourse, manual stimulation, oral sex, and with toys.

The second stage of arousal for women is when the vagina elongates, ballooning in the upper third to make room for the penis, and the uterus has moved up and out of the way. Most women are unaware of this internal change, especially during intercourse when they become even more stimulated.

Orgasm

From a strictly physiological point of view, a woman's orgasm is marked by the muscles of the upper third of the vagina and the uterus beginning to contract. But a lot more is going on. This is what is happening in her body as she reaches climax:

1. Muscles tense and heart rate and blood pressure increase.
2. Nipples become erect.
3. The blood-engorged clitoris becomes erect and pulls under the clitoral hood.
4. The labia majora and labia minora enlarge and lubrication increases.
5. The vagina continues to expand and lengthen and breasts engorge slightly.
6. The clitoris shortens; the color of the labia deepens.
7. Muscles, including the anal sphincter, continue to tense and then contract, sometimes spasming.
8. Orgasm or release occurs (contractions increase to every .8 seconds).

Orgasms can be big or small, short or long, and as you will see in chapter 8, women can experience up to ten different types! Some women who have never experienced an orgasm feel that their lack of response is related to never having had the safety of a secure sexual relationship in which to explore how they like to be touched. Still other women feel they are anorgasmic (unable to orgasm) because they suffered some kind of emotional or sexual abuse. I'm sure that as our scientific insight into orgasm progresses, we will begin to understand more fully why some women are unable to have an orgasm. But please keep in mind that although orgasms follow a very concrete physiological course, they also possess an enormous emotional and psychological component. If your partner has not yet experienced an orgasm, encourage her to not give up hope. An orgasm is not only possible, it's probable.

HISTORICAL AND HYSTERICAL FACTS	The Dutch physician Regnier de Graaf first mentioned female ejaculation in 1672.

Female Ejaculation

Recent research has documented female ejaculation and actually analyzed the fluid that is emitted. The liquid was found to contain a chemical, acid phosphatase, which is only found in one other gland, the male prostate. Francisco Cabello Santamaria, a Spanish sex researcher, showed that the fluid ejaculated by women contained PSA, prostatic specific antigen. This finding came from a study in which the female subjects masturbated, therefore eliminating the possibility that a man's fluid may somehow have appeared on the scene. This finding also suggests the existence of glands along the urethra, the channel from the bladder, that produce the fluid for female ejaculation. Many women who ejaculate have found that stimulation of the clitoris produces this release. Other women feel the urge to bear down as they feel this swelling from increased stimulation in the vagina, which can also produce the ejaculation. Women describe the sensation of ejaculation as a pushing down and an overall bodily release. And some women say that this state is a much more intense and satisfying orgasm.

Is ejaculation necessary for good sex? No. Is it something a woman should be ashamed of? Absolutely not, although a woman may think that she has urinated because neither she nor her partner knows at the time what is happening. Most women who ejaculate explain that it occurs when they feel safe and free with a partner and that it happens only when they are certain that it will not be viewed with alarm. If you think your partner may ejaculate, try putting a towel under her hips. Then, if she ejaculates—or if you want to use massage oil or a vaginal lubricant—neither of you will have to be thinking about the laundry.

Resolution

The last stage of the sexual response is when all of the changes a woman experiences—from increased heart rate to pelvic bloodflow—subside. Women often feel a surge of energy following orgasm. In fact some women have said they feel more awake: "I am more in tune with everything. Unfortunately, this tends to happen at night. But otherwise, what a jolt!" Another woman said this: "Sometimes when we make love I feel so connected to my husband that it is like I want to be inside his skin. The feeling of coming and being that close to him is electric."

How Should We Define an Orgasm?

Masters and Johnson describe orgasm as strictly mechanical (i.e., muscular) and hydraulic (i.e., related to bloodflow). This definition neatly leaves out any psychological or emotional dimension or aspect contributing to orgasm. This is important to note because of the prevalent and pervasive effect of their research on other thinkers. If we think of orgasm in such a limited way, won't we also experience orgasms in a limited way? Other researchers who have a psychological point of view see orgasm as "peaking of sexual pleasure, with a release of sexual tension and rhythmic contraction of the perineal muscles and reproductive organs." I find both these definitions so pinpoint-specific that they limit the possible range of orgasms women and men can experience.

I would rather adopt a definition that includes a range of points, so that both the psychological (mental and emotional) aspects of orgasm as well as its physiological connections are emphasized. This is vital to being able to tap into your individual sexual pleasure—in whatever form that exists. Blending the two points of view encourages you to experience and take pleasure in whatever you wish.

Orgasms clearly happen in the body and through the body. However, for all their physiological reality, they also have a very real mental (both psychological and emotional) dimension. Want to know why the brain has often been called the body's most important sex organ? Just wait and see.

CHAPTER THREE

The Mind Game

The Mental Side of Sex

Turning the Tables on Performance Anxiety

We've all heard that the power or control of sex and orgasm is tied to our brains, which makes all kinds of sense, as our brain is our most powerful sex organ. We hear, too, that many men and women are stressed about sex and can experience a tremendous amount of performance anxiety when it comes to giving or having an orgasm. In my seminars I hear time and again how afraid men and women are to even try, for fear of being disappointed themselves or disappointing their lovers.

I say throw all this negative energy out the window. We've become a nation of people sexually trying to keep up with the Joneses, who live down the street and are having amazing sex every night of the week with awesome, transporting orgasms. Well, might I suggest we know it doesn't serve us to try to keep up with the Joneses relative to material possessions, so let's not do the same relative to sex.

Although I believe that there can be a serious side to sex, sometimes deep and life-altering, I think that if you focus too much on anticipating, controlling, or examining your orgasm, then you not only put enormous pressure on yourself and your partner to have one, you also take the fun and enjoyment out of it!

There are many misconceptions and myths about the negative aspects or limitations of sex that are still embedded in our culture and therefore our minds. The point of this chapter is to turn the negative to positive and give you the tools to better access the sexual pleasure you want. I've tried to keep the information simple, straightforward, and fun so you can accept, enjoy, and revel in the ecstasy you find.

The Role of Communication

Speak Now or Forever Hold Thy Peace

How can you expect your partner to miraculously pleasure you the way you like to be pleasured unless you've given her the information? Don't you want your partner to know how to do what works for you? And don't you want to know how to do the same for your partner? We can't read our partners' minds, so why expect them to be able to read ours? As one man from a seminar said, "I can't believe that I spent years expecting my wife to know what I wanted and how I wanted to be touched; it was like I figured if she really loved me, she would know what I liked and what I wanted." Believe me, in this case, love has nothing to do with it. You can't know through osmosis; you've got to communicate—either in words or through your actions. Remember Show and Tell?

| HISTORICAL AND HYSTERICAL FACTS | Death during orgasm is a fairly uncommon event. Factors that can contribute are alcohol ingestion, food consumption, and an extramarital partner. |

The key to achieving the best sex possible is for you to share as much as you honestly can with your lover. First you need to know yourself—what you like, how you prefer to be touched, caressed, kissed, or licked—then you need to share this information with your partner. Sharing need not be a conversation; it can be a physical motion or action. Also, for those of you intimidated by what you don't know and think you should know, keep in mind that although we are all born of sexuality, none of us is born knowing how to have sex. We all have to learn. And what works for one may not work for another. So as they say, every journey begins with the first step, and this may well be yours on the road to knowing yourself sexually.

Most women say that in order to share or be open with their partner, they have to feel safe. A woman from one of my seminars explained why even though she was attracted to a certain man, she was still unable to open herself up sexually with him. "He was charming, sophisticated, great looking, and French to boot. But I simply didn't feel safe with him. I knew he had been seeing another woman and even though he professed it was over, his actions didn't make me feel safe. I couldn't relax enough to consider even getting into bed with him. Could I imagine what he would be like? Oh yeah! But in reality it was too scary, too not okay for me."

Another married woman underscored how emotionally

complicated it feels to be honest with her partner: "My husband has always been the initiator in sex and I know there are things I'd like to try, but I worry he'll feel badly if I say I want to do something. I don't want him to think that he hasn't been good enough for me and then he could also think I have done something with someone else, when of course I haven't." I've heard many men and women speak of their hesitation to be direct about what they want. Afraid to hurt a partner's feelings, they sacrifice their own pleasure. But take a moment here: Don't you think if you bring up the idea of your pleasure in a "hey, let's have more fun" kind of way, your partner will be turned on rather than turned off?

You won't know until you try. Consider what one woman said: "I fell in love with my husband because he had the most open, nonjudgmental attitude that I had ever encountered. The more I got to know him, the more I realized he had this attitude in all areas of his life. What a gold mine! But what I remember best is the first time he told me, 'Whatever you want a man to do to a woman, I will do. Whatever you want to do to a man, you can do to me. Baby, if you want me to bark like a dog I'll do it—'cause I'm your man.' He said this to me over the phone—I got the shivers!"

SECRET FROM LOU'S ARCHIVES

A landmark 1986 study involving more than two hundred married women reached the following conclusion: ". . . sexual fantasies help many married women to achieve sexual arousal and/or orgasm during sexual intercourse, irrespective of their current sex life status."

Testing the Waters of Compatibility

I think in most relationships, especially those where trust and commitment have already been established, openness is the best policy. But sometimes it's also a matter of compatibility. Many of you say that you don't want to alienate your partner by asking for "too much" or say that by asking, your wife or girlfriend will feel pressure. Men are aware that they ride a thin line between wanting to ask for what they want and not offending their partners.

> ### SECRET FROM LOU'S ARCHIVES
> *Boredom is one of the biggest robbers of intimacy.*

Any man knows that the woman in his life controls the access to the "prize," and he has to remove as many impediments to that access as possible. One of these impediments is the fear of being rejected. One man described his situation by saying, "For me, the reason I hold back is if she rejects me one night, I'll never want to try again." We are all aware that there is a range of sexual activity and fantasy that is acceptable. And obviously you risk offending or hurting someone with your request. But if you are careful and considerate in how you suggest a certain position, toy, or fantasy, you'll have more chance for success or at the very least an understanding. Perhaps she'll say, "No, not tonight honey, but maybe some other time."

Another man expressed his dilemma this way: "I knew I would never again ask this woman to try one of my favorite things [he wanted her to use a small anal vibrator on him while she was performing oral sex]. After a year and a half, I learned in that one reaction she and I wouldn't make it. I thought she was it."

It makes total sense that revealing what you want sexually can make you feel wide open and vulnerable—this is one of the great paradoxes of wonderful, gratifying sex. To feel vulnerable is only normal; after all, it is not every day we are as we came into the world—naked—with another person exploring our body in ways we may never have before. The good part about vulnerability is that it flows both ways. You can have yours and your partner can have hers. Yet how you both react to something either can give each of you the space you need or shut both of you down.

Whether you are in a long-term relationship or a brand-spanking-new one, you both can benefit from the "sharing principle." I have witnessed in my seminars that those people who risk sharing this most intimate side of themselves are invariably rewarded by being able to create an even more trusting, passionate, and charged sexual relationship. The following is a great comment from a therapist: "Showing your vulnerability creates space for someone to see where they can move into and impact your life. If the space isn't there, they can't show up—be it emotionally, psychologically, or physically."

Fun Sex or Deep Sex? Are You and Your Partner on the Same Page?

On the road to orgasm I think it's important that you and your partner know where you both are coming from. Mother Nature didn't make us all alike (identical twins aside), so from the get-go, two people are not going to have exactly the same sex drives or attitudes. Even identical twins, like my sister and I, have very different preferences. If you're in a playful, let's-get-hot mood, and your partner is in a more relaxed, romantic mood, you might encounter a bit of tension. To further complicate this situation, the number of demands and stresses we all have to deal with on a daily basis underscores the need for couples to be up-front about where they are and what they need sexually.

The suggestions below will help you both clear your heads and at the very least give you a way of finding out what is going on with each other. At the very most, they'll help you see that you are both on the same page, and heading to the bedroom will never feel so enticing or exciting.

> ### SECRET FROM LOU'S ARCHIVES
>
> *Not sure what she really likes? Ask her to rent a video or buy magazines that give you ideas you can consider together.*

Open the Channels

When you think of orgasm as the one and only goal of sex, you greatly limit yourself to the overall sensations of sex. Specifically, as you will see in Part Two, in which I describe the seven different types of orgasms men can experience and the ten different types of orgasms women can experience, there is much more to sex than your old standby.

The more you involve your entire body in sex, the more likely you will open other avenues of pleasure and sensation.

One woman used this example: "There is something about how my boyfriend massages my neck that causes me to melt. He is good with his hands, but this is beyond! And if we go on to have sex, it feels bigger for me."

One man pointed out how important relaxation is to a woman when he said, "What I know about my wife is if she isn't relaxed enough, nothing is going to happen. If I start to give her a foot massage as soon as she sits down on the sofa after work, she is invariably turned on. She knows I care about her, and this works!"

SECRET FROM LOU'S ARCHIVES

Orgasm during lovemaking builds intimacy. Orgasm has a relationship-bonding power. After orgasm, men and women often feel closer to their partners, a feeling that has in part a physical basis. The chemical oxytocin, released in the brain upon orgasm and nicknamed the "cuddling hormone," inspires feelings of attachment. And women produce larger amounts of oxytocin than men do until midlife when the percentages are more aligned. —DRS. JOEL BLOCK AND SUSAN CRAIN BAKOS

Keep It Spontaneous

In the years that I've been giving sexuality seminars to hundreds—thousands—of men and women, the number-one comment I hear is how much they want the heat and spontaneity back in their relationship. Once the proverbial honeymoon is over, how can a loving, committed couple keep their sexual relationship playful, fun, and zinging with that passionate energy they knew in the early years of their courtship?

Anyone who has been together five months, five years, or forty-five years knows that both people need to work at keeping the sexual relationship new and fresh, and the biggest thing that keeps sex fresh is your attitude. Quite simply, you have to make intimacy and private time together a priority. You have to do this consciously. When you were dating, romance and getting it on were a natural priority. It was automatic. Later on, as time passes, and the two of you become more familiar with each other, you have to make a conscious effort, including scheduling sex.

Couples need to consciously set aside time for intimacy. Anyone who is a parent knows all about juggling timetables and the necessity of being organized. You have to stick to some sort of a timetable to keep all the machinery of a family running. The same is true for sex. By making it part of your day or week, you not only have sex, but you and your partner will connect better, and all other aspects of your life will likely fall into place. Couples without kids need to make the same consideration: Sex is a vital priority in your relationship. As one woman, a mother of three small children, said, "That, my dear, is why my husband and I have a date every Wednesday night and why my office doubles as our secret hideaway."

The threat of boring sex can freeze people internally. Sometimes women are so focused on pleasing their partners that they lose touch with their own sexual desires. Men are just as susceptible. When a man is more concerned with pleasing his woman, he can forget to access his own pleasure. My advice is to stay in your body. Stay with your own sensation. One of the biggest turn-ons for your partner is getting you turned on and knowing you are into it.

Don't Take It Home with You

Does this sound familiar? You've just had a long, hard day at the office. You have spent the last month or so on a project and when you present it to your boss, he shoots it down and gives you your walking papers. When you go home that evening, trying to get yourself in the mood for some tender lovemaking with your partner, you realize that nothing is happening down there.

Many of you are prone to taking outside stress (particularly when you experience any kind of failure) into the bedroom. Whether it's an ever-increasing workload or the stress of caring for children, these outside distractions can interfere with sexual desire. There's no doubt about it, work and children often get in the way of feeling up for sex.

HISTORICAL AND HYSTERICAL FACTS	Having your children sleep with you is the ultimate form of birth control.

We often rely on the age-old excuse "I'm too tired" to postpone or avoid sex. Admittedly, it is sometimes hard not to let the aggravations of the day get to you. But if you treat your sexual relationship with your partner as a sanctuary, a place that gives energy instead of takes energy, then you can overcome the excuses. Right before putting sex on the back burner, stop and think about how good you will feel afterward. Whether it's a place and time for you both to go a little wild, rekindle the romantic fire, or create a bubble of bliss, chances are you will feel revitalized, energized, and connected when you go there.

Openness, honesty, and tact are the three keys to good communication. And without strong communication, your chances for having mind-blowing sex decrease. So go for the gold! Share your ideas and fantasies with your partner in a tactful and respectful manner—who knows the boundaries you might cross together? This kind of sharing also increases your sexual confidence, which is so important to feeling sexy and desirable. Once you're in the right mind-set, the rest (of sex) will begin to flow.

CHAPTER FOUR

Get Her in the Mood

Mental Seduction

The Two Rs

Most of us divide sex into two distinct stages: foreplay followed by intercourse. Just like when we play a sport, we usually spend just a few minutes warming up, and then we feel ready for "the real game." I'd like to turn that particular formula on its head. First, in order to have great, fabulous, mind-blowing sex, you've got to have great, fabulous, mind-blowing foreplay. This is especially true for women, who can barely enjoy intercourse without first having foreplay.

So what exactly is foreplay? For women, foreplay has two essential stages. The first stage works on her brain, and the second, on her body.

In this chapter, I will show you how to seduce her mind. It's actually quite simple: First you romance her and then you relax her.

These two steps are simple in concept, but I cannot overemphasize how crucial they are to successfully getting her in the mood for sex so she can truly let go and let you bring her to the heights of pleasure. Relaxing and romancing combine two of the most potent forms of mental foreplay. The reason these two activities hold such sway is that they are controlled by our most powerful sexual organ: the brain (which, as I mentioned in chapter 3, also controls our sexual response).

Romance and Courtly Behavior

It has been my observation that the surest way to guarantee a man's ability to turn a woman on and drive her mad with desire is through good old-fashioned courting. I am absolutely serious—despite all those voices in your head and hers saying that she wants to be treated as your equal partner. While no woman wants to give up that mutuality, she does want to feel special and singular, and the best way to help her feel that way is by being a gentleman and treating her like a lady. After all, it is a very simple equation: Since there are fewer and fewer real gentlemen out there, those of you who adopt this courting policy will have a genuine market advantage.

In order to behave like a gentleman, you need to think like one. Again, it comes down to your attitude. If a woman feels you're being solicitous and caring, taking her pleasure and comfort into consideration, chances are she will hand you carte blanche. This is, of course, assuming you've already passed her litmus test.

Secret from Lou's Archives

A woman's litmus test is whether or not she can see herself underneath or on top of you.

One of the primary ingredients of courtly behavior is good manners. Sadly, many parents no longer teach their young boys manners, and many men have lost the habit even if they were taught early on in life.

What are good manners? Quite simply, they are nothing other than pleasant and respectful ways of interacting with others. Be polite, be courteous, and treat her as you know she wishes to be treated. There are certain social niceties that only a gentleman can perform. Please know this is not an exhaustive list but merely an outline, so feel free to add or subtract as you wish.

Open a door for a lady. This particular gesture often receives a bum rap, and yet for most women it is a lovely acknowledgment of how you think of her. Having said that, I must admit that I have had men tell me unpleasant tales of women sneering at them when they try this move. As a fully emancipated, independent woman, I find a woman's rejection of this masculine attempt at being courteous just plain sad. I love this social acknowledgment of my femininity and I believe that, deep down, most women enjoy being treated like a lady as well.

The historic rationale for a lady entering a room before a gentleman was not so enchanting or courtly. Supposedly in less-civilized, war-torn times women were quite literally sacrificial social lambs. Considered less valuable than men, they would be "tossed" through an unknown entry in order to test for enemies. This rationale then changed to women leading the entry of a man in order to introduce his wealth and status: The more beautiful and bejeweled the woman, the more important the man. In some social circles today, this attitude may not have changed all that much.

Open the car door. Have you heard the joke about being able to tell who the wife is by who has to climb the snowbank to get in the car? Suffice it to say that if you let the woman in your life know from the get-go that you'd like to open the car door for her, nine times out of ten, she will love and appreciate the gesture. If this is an entirely new ritual for you, it may take some time to get used to—for both of you—but I believe it may be a pleasant and rewarding courtly move to add to your growing repertoire. The mother of a male friend of mine from Louisiana will not get in or out of the car unless a man opens the door for her. This may be taking things to an extreme, but I give her credit for standing by what she believes in. If you have a low-slung car, you may want to offer your hand to help balance her as she gets in.

If the two of you are getting in or out of a cab, bus, or other public conveyance, you might also consider offering your hand or arm to help her alight.

Stand when a lady enters or leaves a room. Please note that this move is appropriate for social situations, not business. When I was in private school, we were expected to stand whenever a teacher entered or left the room. This was a very clear display of respect for our elders. However, in social situations, standing for a woman, even simply raising yourself from a chair, can be a wonderful gesture of consideration and civility. Men in the seminars have made such comments as, "When I do something so simple, it makes such an impact on her. I know she knows I care about her."

Pull out her chair. Like parallel parking, this move takes awareness, several front-and-back moves, and finesse. If she is returning from the ladies' room, you don't need to jump to your feet. Instead, gently pull out or slide her chair as she returns to the table. She will be doing the majority of the work, so you need not jump up behind her like a butler.

Take her arm or place your hand on the small of her back. Both of these moves can be used publicly and socially, and they are the least objectionable public displays of affection. Holding hands or draping your arm around her shoulders is more informal and therefore not suggested for public events. Rather, these moves are best saved for the weekend stroll, sitting in the movie theater, or at the table, where the intimacy is about the two of you.

Carry items for her. One woman related, "I remember my boyfriend telling me when we first met that he would carry all my packages when I went shopping. He didn't want me to carry anything but my purse. It took me a while to realize this was one of his unspoken ways to say 'I love you' and that he cares about me."

Then again, if a woman wants to carry her own bags, let her; it's her choice. But keep in mind that most women will welcome help hauling their belongings. Although carrying her shopping bags may be a broad-stroke example, choose another gesture that shows you are there for her, such as helping her into the house with the groceries or offering to move something heavy for her.

Have good table manners. Few things are a bigger turnoff than poor table manners. On the contrary, knowing how to behave at the table is very impressive to a woman and makes her feel she is with a man who knows what he's doing. If you were never taught proper table manners, glance at an etiquette book in a bookstore.

SECRET FROM LOU'S ARCHIVES

If the woman in your life likes strong fragrances, try tuberose, Casablanca, or Rubrum lilies. If these powerful flowers need a bit of toning down, add a spray of freesia, which is soft and gentle.

Razzle-Dazzle Her

Beyond incorporating good manners into your courtly behavior, there are romantic ways to get her undivided attention. These suggestions are designed to take you one step closer to the intimacy of the bedroom.

Be the chef. More men are capturing a woman's heart with

their culinary prowess. It happened to my identical twin sister. She felt airlifted when she first realized that among his many talents, her Greek husband is a wizard in the kitchen. Men who can cook are a huge turn-on. In the same way that a man feels loved and cared for when a woman cooks for him, a woman feels taken care of and oh so appreciated when a man cooks for her.

Serve her breakfast in bed. If you prefer sex in the morning, breakfast in bed is a sure way to start the day smiling. And you will be her Prince Charming for a day—or at least the morning. You may want to avoid crunchy cereals such as granola. In this delicate position, it's better to err on the side of soft food, easily eaten with your fingers. Try pieces of fruit and soft Danishes or croissants that can be pulled apart easily. Prepare her coffee or tea just as she likes it—in front of her. This entails putting a small creamer and sugar or artificial-sweetener container on the tray. Let me suggest another tip: There are more interesting resting spots for that imported preserve than the English muffin she's nibbling on.

Master the art of flowers. Throughout the ages, gentlemen have presented flowers to their ladyloves as a sign of their feelings. Flowers are always a true gentleman's move, which make even more of an impact when you know her preferences. In other words, red roses are lovely and may be the first to come to mind, but often there is another flower that touches her heart more. One woman from a seminar shared this: "When my current boyfriend discovered I loved lavender, he checked out all the flower stands on the Upper West Side [of Manhattan] to find exactly what I liked. I didn't find out until his sister told me that he had hunted for two hours for them. You have to love a man who'll do that!" A man told me, "If a guy sends a woman a dozen red roses after the first date, he either had a world-class date or he is not aware of the message he is sending. Red roses are not the casual thank-you flower."

> ### SECRET FROM LOU'S ARCHIVES
>
> *Assuming you want the memory of you to last long, please send fresh-cut flowers. Preset arrangements and roses have the shortest life span of flowers. And check the sepals of roses. These are the green "petals" at the base of the rosebud. If they are tight to the bud, it is a fresh rose. Otherwise you are getting old flowers that droop and will die in a day or two. Fresh roses should last five to seven days.*

Relaxation Is Key

There is no getting around one simple fact: A typical woman will not get turned on if she isn't relaxed. That said, as a partner to this activity, you are being challenged to get her in the mood. How can you help her relax? You'll be happy (and perhaps relieved) to know that there are some tried-and-true ways to help your partner loosen up so that she not only responds to you better but also enjoys herself more completely. As a forty-something physician told me, "I know I have to get my wife relaxed enough to get her turned on. If she can't relax, I know nothing is going to happen. And that's why I am king of foot massages." Another seminar attendee, an architect from Madison, Wisconsin, said that he draws his partner a hot bath, "with her favorite lavender salts. If she gets one whiff as she walks through the door, I know she's all mine."

But most women will agree that though the physical effects of your method are important, the key to relaxing her is *your* attitude. Quite simply, if she feels like you have gone out of your way to treat her as special, she will respond.

HISTORICAL AND HYSTERICAL FACTS	According to a report in the *New England Journal of Medicine*, women are 30 percent more sexually active during a full moon.

And why is relaxing so important for women? Because women's brains can juggle ten things at a time, and usually, out of necessity, they are doing just that. Unless the majority of those juggled items are put to rest, she won't be able to shift enough of her focus to the matters at hand. This is related to another one of those sex/gender differences: Women tend to experience their world in terms of relationships. Men tend to compartmentalize; this means you can go into the bedroom and turn off whatever happened that day. Yet when your partner lies down, a steady stream of to-do lists can still be crossing the billboard of her mind. Therefore, gentlemen, you need to help her decompress and become still if you want to arouse her later. The connection is very concrete and very clear: Unless a woman is relaxed in her mind, her body will not follow suit. And if her body isn't relaxed, it won't get excited.

It's Elementary

There are four essential elements to help a woman relax. Consider these in no particular order:

➤ Make her *comfortable*, mentally and physically.
➤ Minimize *interruptions*.
➤ Make the *space and time*, even if it is only ten minutes.
➤ Let her know you like *her body*.

1. Making her comfortable mentally and physically is about providing a good, safe, and enjoyable environment for a sexual encounter. For instance, if you are not married and do not live together, try to make your bedroom a place that is inviting for her. Does she have a corner of the room, perhaps a drawer or a dresser where she can leave her toiletries or some clothes? One woman in a seminar shared this story: "I had just begun dating a man and we were getting serious. We'd already slept together, but never at his home. He was a very successful investment banker, who was always well-groomed and wore nice clothes. But when I went to his apartment for the first time, I

nearly died. It was filthy. The drapes were dirty, the shower curtain was moldy. I was disgusted and felt totally turned off. I made up some excuse that night and went home. A few days later I told him, in a nice way, that he needed to do something about his apartment. He had the money, after all. I think he just didn't know any better." Cleanliness is next to godliness in most women's eyes. If you are married or live together, make sure that you pay attention to the state of the bedroom as well, participating in keeping it tidy, putting away your clothes, or simply making sure the bed is made.

2. By minimizing interruptions, you keep the environment a haven for intimacy. This is why there are answering machines, locks on the doors, and for those of you who are parents, baby monitors. One woman explained, "We have a four-year-old and a nine-month-old. We both work and typically are exhausted at the end of the day. We plan an escape day away every month. We hire an overnight sitter and take off to a corporate suite or a friend's place. This way we get to reconnect alone and rekindle what our romancing days were like when we were single. Then the problem was our crazy travel schedules, and we had to coordinate months in advance to see one another. When we got married and the kids came, I initially felt guilty about leaving the kids. But the effect on our marriage has been miraculous! Two months ago our nine-month-old was sick and colicky, the four-year-old had just clogged the washing machine by pouring cat litter into it, and the gardener

had flooded the storage area in the garage. We looked at one another amidst this chaos and both said at the same time, 'In two sleeps it will be Saturday,' which was our escape day. We both cracked up."

3. Make the space and time by planning. Just as you set aside time for your workout at the gym, a golf game, or a car tune-up, you need to set aside time for romance and relaxation. A woman from a seminar said that "the one thing that keeps me falling in love with my husband again and again is his ability to romance me. It can be something as simple as taking me into another room away from the kids and giving me my favorite ice cream bar. He can somehow create a quiet, just-for-the-two-of-us space and do something sweet. Often we have to wait until later, but when he has already lit my pilot light, we have had quickies in the bathroom, running the shower, with the kids on the other side, and he's doing me from behind and we're watching in the mirror." You never know when those opportunities may present themselves to give her your undivided attention, which is so key to relaxing her and getting her in the mood for sex.

4. Let her know you like her body. A woman will not relax and let herself be open to getting turned on if she feels self-conscious or bad about her body. Women blossom under attention and positive body comments. Most women, even those with model figures, question their attractiveness and often have negative feelings around their body image. I'm assuming since you're with her that you find her attractive and want to be with her. Let her know what

you like about her and what you'd like to do to her. She wants and needs to hear that you are attracted to her. A few chosen words from her man have been known to get one woman ". . . so wet. Sometimes he does it to me when I am at the office over the phone. He's so bad!" Another woman says she goes absolutely wild when her partner says, "I want my mouth where it was last Friday night."

SECRET FROM LOU'S ARCHIVES

The two biggest robbers of intimacy are being tired and having no time. Early in relationships, you make intimacy a priority, but later, you may let it slide—especially if there are children in the picture. Plainly and simply, you and your partner need to make attending to your intimate relationship a priority.

Have you recently told her about the part of her body you find the biggest turn-on? In a couples seminar a couple who had been married five years with two children shocked each other with their responses. "I love the way the hair curls at the back of her neck and the little dimples above her buttocks." His wife could only say, "You're kidding . . . I hate those," and he said, "I know, I love 'em." And then she jerked back and said, "No wonder you like doggy style so much!" In full-throated, blushing laughter he said, "Busted!" For her, his hands were her major turn-on—"'cause you're big and strong and I love to look at them and remember how they feel on my body." Once she knows how you feel about a part of her beautiful anatomy, remind her, often and regularly.

Tips to Help Her Relax

➤ Create a space that makes her relax. A woman responds keenly to her environment. Create an oasis for her—whether it's the bedroom, the living room, the outside porch, or the bathroom. Use lighting, scent, or other sensory stimulation to declare that the workday has ended, and now it's time to relax.

➤ Before she walks in the door, draw her a bath. Light candles or incense, help her undress, and sit beside her on the throne (obviously not using it) so you can share this wind-down time with her. Help bathe her or rub her back with a loofah. Perhaps you want to give her a glass of wine or a cool glass of water. One woman, a children's book illustrator from New Jersey, recalled, "I knew I was marrying my husband the first time he drew a bath for me and bathed me. I wasn't gonna let that one get away. And to this day he loves to wash my hair." The seduction you are offering here is in the fact that you have been thinking of her even before she arrives home. Every woman in the world wants to know in her heart of hearts that her man can and will take care of her physically and emotionally; and every woman wants to feel special and appreciated.

➤ Once out of the bath, ask her if she'd like you to give her a pedicure, or towel her off, or offer to rub moisturizing lotion on her. Analogous to the real estate mantra "location, location, location," women want "attention, attention, attention"—in whatever form you can imagine.

Engage Her Five Senses

By enticing her five senses—sight, smell, taste, hearing, and touch—you bring her one step closer to the second element of foreplay, awakening her body. Consider engaging her senses to be the crucial link or bridge that connects her mind to her body. Now that you have romanced her and relaxed her mind, it's time to begin awakening her body. As a CPA from Chicago said, "I want to touch as many of her senses as I can—all of them." Elicit and engage her senses, and she will become putty in your delighted hands.

Sight

Humans are essentially visual creatures. As such, sight is one of our most powerful senses because it is the one we rely on most. Men have shared again and again that they like and respond to the way a woman creates a home or an environment that is inviting. So why not capitalize on what you know works and do the same for her? By creating a special, intimate space, you are sure to score points with her.

The visual appeal of your love nest can have a wondrous effect on her, so it's to your advantage if you keep your room, apartment, or house neat and tidy. Please do not ask a lady to sleep in an unmade or already slept-in bed. And clothes strewn about on the floor, bed, or lampshade are not going to be considered art—believe me. Yuck! She'll think of you as stuck in college. In order to make a woman feel special, invite her into a place that shows you care about yourself.

➤ Dim lighting is flattering—to both of you.

➤ If you really want to seduce her, put a discreet bud vase holding one flower either by the bed or in a place that's visible from the bed. This can be one of your "tonight" signals.

➤ For single men, if you have any photos in your room, make sure they are not of exes—this could be a turnoff.

Smell

When it comes to eliciting her "scentual" responses, your use of smell either can engage her or repel her. So be sure you pay attention here. Smell is one of our most primitive senses, said by some to have the longest recall power. Chances are you have been with a woman who wore a particular scent that to this day makes you experience a rush of emotion when you smell it. You may have forgotten her face or name, but remember her perfume. Keep in mind, gentlemen, that your own body chemistry may be your greatest asset. You have your own particular scent, and for some ladies, how you smell is the ultimate pheromone. One woman said, "Oh God, I loved how he smelled. It wasn't his cologne; it was what emanated from his neck. One whiff and I wanted him all over me."

SECRET FROM LOU'S ARCHIVES

A woman's sense of smell is much more sensitive than a man's, and you may not be aware of what scent may be lingering around. A solution is to bathe regularly and use soap in important spots.

On the other hand, men sweat more than women, and as such, they need to be very aware of their hygiene. The apocrine glands, which are the specialized sweat glands in the armpit and groin, secrete a more viscous and pungent sweat. When this sweat comes into contact with normal body bacteria, the result is body odor. The best way to avoid offending your partner is to shower frequently and use deodorant. Some women will be turned on by your natural body scent, but don't confuse this with BO.

SECRET FROM LOU'S ARCHIVES

There are some men who by virtue of their smell alone are irresistible to the women they attract. One woman put it this way: "I loved what my pillows smelled like after he'd slept over. And when he wasn't there I'd have to sleep with one of his old sweaters. It was a major turn-on and soothing."

Since most women respond strongly to scent, a powerful way to engage her is through the practice of aromatherapy. For more on how these powerful scents can relax her and heighten her pleasure, see chapter 12.

TIPS

➤ Check in with her about your aftershave or cologne. Women either will be turned on or turned off by certain scents.

➤ Are your linens clean? You may not be aware of your own scent, and though she may like it, it's best always to use fresh sheets.

➤ Check your laundry detergent. Some of the name
   brands carry a very distinctive, not altogether pleasant
   odor. You may want to consider using a scent-free
   detergent.
➤ Check your deodorant. Does it work? Is its scent too
   overpowering or just right?

Taste

Arousing the taste buds literally can whet the appetite of
desire. Have you ever tried feeding her? In bed? Or had her
feed you? Grapes can be tons of fun, and if you drop them, it's
no big deal. The following foods are widely considered to be
some of the best (i.e., most seductive).

Strawberries—whole, dipped in chocolate or dipped in a
   mixture of sour cream and brown sugar—they're
   amazing!
Figs—Select fresh, plump figs, whose soft, downy
   surface may remind her of your testicles. Who knows,
   you may want to start showing up for dates with some
   figs instead of a bottle of wine.
Grapes—These delicate little fruits are truly a fun
   food. Hold one in your mouth and ask her to bite
   it out.
Plums—They taste best during summer, and these
   luscious sweet fruits cleanse any palate.
Chocolate—dark, milk, white, in whatever combination
   you desire. This bit of sweetness can be used as a
   transitional item, moving you from before sex to sex,
   as it contains phenylethylamine, the same chemical
   the brain produces when people fall in love.

Olives—If it's stuffed with pimiento or an almond, consider having her suck the filling out while you hold the olive in your mouth.

Oysters—in the raw, of course, as they are quite erotic and resemble female genitalia. They also contain a lot of zinc, an important mineral that increases male potency.

Nuts—almonds, Brazil nuts, cashews.

Cheese—some prefer a hard cheese like Jarlsberg, others a smooth-bodied Brie or Camembert.

Beverages—wine (FYI, red wine goes very well with chocolate), champagne, juice, cool water (flat or bubbly).

SECRET FROM LOU'S ARCHIVES

In Chaucerian England, the word "mussel" was a naughty synonym for vulva.

TIPS

➤ Cleanliness of the mouth and body is a given for all involved.

➤ Don't introduce *too* many tastes; otherwise you will overwhelm your taste buds. A sampling of a few items works best—remember, this is an appeteaser.

➤ Remember the basic rule when choosing a beverage: Don't let it overpower or mask the food.

Hearing

Forgive me for repeating myself, but I feel I need to remind you that women can and do get seduced through their ears. Yes, it can be the words you say, but you can also reach her in more subtle ways. Did you know that certain women's clothing stores play low, melodious music in the background, hoping to relax women while they shop? Do you remember the studies that led to Muzak? Both instances point to the powerful, soothing effect of music on the human brain, but especially on women.

When planning a romantic evening or preparing to relax your partner, you may want to consider playing music. Perhaps neither of you wants to listen to music, but rather hear it, gracefully, in the background. Any kind of instrumental music has a calming or soothing effect—even Beethoven's Fifth. Music without words allows the brain to move, wander, and let go of the outside world.

SECRET FROM LOU'S ARCHIVES

If your answering machine is in hearing distance of the bedroom, turn off the volume, and if you have a phone by your bed, turn off the ringer. There is no greater mood-shatterer than a ringing phone or the sound of your mother's voice.

If you're not familiar with instrumental music, try surfing through the classical or jazz section at your local music store. And of course, there is always Barry White, the Master of Seduction, and Marvin Gaye when you already know one another. But be forewarned about listening to Barry or Marvin unless you intend to take action. For those of you who want to begin more slowly, consider these suggestions:

Phillip Aaberg, *Out of the Frame* (New Age)
Enya, *Watermark* (contemporary vocals)

Kenny Rankin, *The Kenny Rankin Album* (contemporary vocals)

Keith Jarrett, *Arbour Zena* (New Age jazz)

John Barry, *Moviola* (contemporary composers)

Windham Hill Retrospective (New Age)

Verve Jazz Round Midnight series, featuring Chet Baker, Billie Holiday, and Ben Webster (jazz)

Another way to help relax her through her ears is to try a decorative fountain. Now, I don't mean putting a Trevi-size fountain in the middle of your living room. These decorative fountains are small, and fit easily on top of a stereo speaker, a table, or a bookshelf. Some men and women have remarked that the sound of trickling water in the background helps to decrease their tension as well as increase their sexual appetite.

TIPS

➤ Ask her if she has any favorite recordings.

➤ Suggest selecting music together.

➤ Play music low.

➤ Choose music that has a slow beat or rhythm, until you want to switch to the driving beat of "flesh-slapping" music.

Touch

By awakening her four other senses, you are now ready to begin to touch her. As such, the fifth sense is the ultimate bridge from her mind to her body. You may have noticed that women often act like cats when they are being stroked and will curve into your arms and around your body. Any kind of inter-body contact will help her relax, which in turn will enable her to become aroused. Not only is touching often the best way to relax a woman, which, again, is absolutely key to both a woman's involvement and her arousal, it is the simplest way for the two of you to connect. "I am that hard-driving successful woman, yet all my husband has to do is touch me in public on the arm or back, as he's walking up from behind. There is something about his touch that is so calming for me. And he has this invisible signal of 'Let's go' or 'Can we be alone?' He gently squeezes my hand. It works wonders at dinner parties."

In the next chapter, we shift focus from her mind to her body. As you begin to travel her body, look for signs of her relaxing: Has her breathing changed? Become deeper? Slower? Gentlemen, keep in mind one simple fact: Once she is relaxed, she's much more likely to unravel in your arms.

CHAPTER FIVE

Chart Her Erogenous Zones

Physical Seduction

Kiss Her, Touch Her, Tease Her

While romancing and relaxing get her in the mood by putting her mind in a receptive state for sex, this second stage of foreplay harnesses and catapults that energy into the stratosphere. Now it's time to take her body and charge it, subtly building the momentum of her sexual stimulation. One woman claims her husband is a magician when it comes to foreplay. "He has this knack for starting foreplay 24 hours ahead. He leaves little hints about what he might like to do, what parts of my body he wants to taste, where he wants to do things, and he leaves these on Post-its in my Dayrunner."

In the same way that getting her in the mood requires making her feel special, turning her on physically requires giving her your full attention. If she feels that you are completely engaged in the moment, focused on her, on being with her and

81

pleasing her, she is bound to open like a flower in the midday sun. And the moment she releases all her inhibitions and lets go—isn't that what really turns *you* on? In order to let go, however, she needs to feel safe with you. One investment banker from New York remembered this: "The first time my girlfriend really let go and let me reach her sexually was so awesome. I experienced her body and its reactions to me on a completely different level. I had never had that connection with any other woman and that's why we're still together. It was both awesome and something that at the same time stopped my heart."

SECRET FROM LOU'S ARCHIVES

You don't have to be in the same room or day to begin foreplay.

A woman, a photographer from Washington, D.C., told me this: "My old boyfriend had a way of stopping the world when we made love. He'd get this little smile on his face and lock the front door. There was something about how intense his attention was—that was a major, major turn-on. And everything else on my mind would disappear. It didn't matter that I had to leave for work in thirty minutes. I'd fix my hair in the car."

Unless she feels relaxed and comfortable, nothing you can do will rev her engine. That's why in the previous chapter I provided you with ways to romance and relax her. Now it's time to begin to please her body, and that means kissing her, touching her, and teasing her.

Often women have said they feel that their partners only touch them when they want sex. And although this may indeed be your goal, gentlemen, you will get much further if every touch or contact doesn't lead to sex. Honest. I am sorry to sound like a broken record on this subject, but it is a common comment I hear from women in the seminars. As one woman said, "I love him and want to be with him, but why does every touch have to be about sex? Sometimes when he just kisses the top of my head or hugs me when he walks by, I feel so loved. It makes me feel *more* open to sex." A man put it this way: "It doesn't take a genius to know that by touching all of her body, you get a sense of how she likes to be touched."

SECRET FROM LOU'S ARCHIVES

The more a man stays in contact with a woman in a nonsexual way, the more receptive she will be to him.

Kiss Her

There is nothing more appealing to most women than the sensuous power of a kiss. Whether that kiss is wet, cool, brief, or lingering, alone it can have the power to bring your lady to her knees. From my observations in women's seminars, I would say that kissing well is the number-one indicator of your general prowess as a lover. As one graphic designer from Florida said, "It is the thing that gets my motor running. All the touching in the world cannot take the place of how intensely his kissing turns me on." Another woman remembered an old boyfriend this way: "He loved me and I loved him, but our sexual chemistry never jelled because I hated the way he kissed, and he never would listen to the way I wanted to be kissed." Men also remark on the power of kissing. One seminar attendee said, "I find kissing intensely during foreplay very sexy and arousing."

On the other hand, the majority of us have memories of those great kissing episodes when we were younger. Well, let's get serious here. The reason they were such great kissing sessions is that they did what kissing is supposed to do—get everything going. In long-term relationships, it's natural to forget about how wonderful kissing can be. We tend to overlook the skillful kissing that used to really make things happen. If you knew it then, be reminded of that bicycle analogy and know you've still got it.

If you kiss a woman well, and kiss her the way she wants to be kissed, you are halfway to your destination of having her fall into your arms and melt in your mouth. How you kiss her and how she likes to be kissed are important; but more important, I think, is to kiss with feeling and intention. In short, this is where you communicate your love and intimacy. An architect from Coral Gables, Florida, said, "I had always heard about those 'wow,' totally-melt-you kissers and figured, yeah, they're like multiple orgasms. Until I met Stuart. All I can say is this: Kissing him made me leave my body. I can't honestly remember what he even did that sent me through the roof. Well, I can remember one thing: He did this lip-sucking move that to this day makes me wet when I think about it."

SECRET FROM LOU'S ARCHIVES

Some women love to have their tongues gently sucked into your mouth while kissing; others do not. It's always good policy for you to ask her what she likes and what it does for her, and to pay attention to her signals. Note: No human Hoovers please.

The next most important thing to remember is we all have our unique brand of kissing. Sometimes our styles change with our mood; others change with the weather. Regardless, variation is the key. You may want to ask her to "kiss me the way you want me to kiss you." So if she nibbles around the side of your mouth or sucks on your lower lip, definitely ask, "Do you want me to do that to you?"

Here are some helpful tips to keep in mind.

➤ A woman with a pouty, full lower lip probably likes having it sucked slowly and sweetly into your mouth.

➤ Try running the curved tip of your tongue along the inside of her upper lip. The underside of your tongue will be against her teeth, with your taste-bud side against the inner part of her upper lip. Again, not all women like this, so ask her.

➤ Suck on one another's tongues. "He had a way of sucking on my tongue. He'd do it slowly, then kiss me, then again, then suck me right in, then just the tip . . ."

➤ Please don't push your entire tongue into a woman's mouth—unless you know she wants you to. Chances are your tongue is bigger than hers. One woman said it felt like "he was shoving his tongue down my throat."

➤ Be aware of how loose your lips are. If they are too loose, they will feel sloppy to her.

➤ Avoid the Woody Woodpecker kissing technique, which entails a pointy-tongued devil who darts his stiff tongue in and out in an awkward semblance of French kissing.

➤ Best to adopt the tortoise's strategy, not that of the hare—slow and steady kissing will win the race.

Kisses

The Hand Kiss. One of the more gracious forms of courtly behavior. When she extends her hand as if to have you shake it, grasp it lightly, just as you would if you were going to shake it. Then turn it clockwise and kiss the back of her hand in the middle, making sure your lips are dry. Hold the kiss for two seconds, then release her hand. One woman recounted this story: "On our second date, we had just ordered the wine. When the sommelier had left, my boyfriend turned to me and said, 'I have wanted to do this all night.' Then, ever so gently, he picked up my left hand and, raising it to his lips, softly and very slowly kissed the back of my hand. Omigod, he couldn't have done anything more seductive and understated."

The French Kiss. This kiss, also known as soul kissing, gets its name from British and American soldiers during World War II who attributed anything sexually liberated to the French. This is by far the most widely known kind of kiss. A good French kiss can last for hours. Here, rhythm is everything. You need to alternate your rhythm, suck on her tongue, and move your tongue around. Be careful to avoid sucking on her tongue too hard or making your tongue too pointy (known as the Woody Woodpecker).

The Swoon. I've heard from my sources (the seminars) that one of the most seductive ways to kiss a woman is to cradle her head and neck with your hands so her head relaxes into them.

The Up-Against-the-Wall Kiss. Sometimes this is one of the hottest types of kisses because it is the most urgent and ardent. You can lean your body against hers with your arms on the wall on either side of her, or she can lean into you.

SECRET FROM LOU'S ARCHIVES

The Kiss-Anytime Card. *Use this homemade card, similar to Monopoly's Get-out-of-Jail-Free card, to spice up your love life. Since it never expires, you can leave it somewhere, send it, or deliver it personally.*

The Stair Kiss. This position is for those times when you want to be eye-to-eye, especially if there is a height difference. She may also respond to this position if she wants to see how it feels to tower over you. One man said that "on our first date when we were kissing goodnight, my girlfriend looked up at me and said, 'I want to try something.' Holding my shoulders, she walked to the stairs and stood so we were at eye level and said, 'Good. I just wanted to level the playing field.' She then proceeded to kiss me. Her being in charge really turned her on."

The Not-on-the-Mouth Kiss. Use your lips to their best advantage by kissing all over her entire body. As you know, her body is an enchanted forest you want to get lost in, with plenty of unexplored territory. You may want to try the insides of her arms, upper shoulders, buttocks, backs of her knees, armpits, and everywhere else.

The Picasso. Many women also like a form of genital kissing. As one gentleman from my seminar said, "I love to kiss a woman 'down there,' her nipples, or anywhere, and then go back to her mouth." For some women, your tasting her and being that open about it is a special act of acceptance—one of the most powerful aphrodisiacs, and akin to a lady tasting and/or swallowing you.

Touch Her

Here we return to the fifth sense. When you are touching all areas of her body, overlook no surface. One man has said after giving his partner a massage, "I know I've done a good job when she's almost asleep or she gets mad when I finish."

Of course, every woman is different and you may want to adhere to the cardinal rule of "ask first." It's also just as important for you to enjoy her whole body. As one woman warned, "I felt like I was a machine with operating parts. He'd touch A, then B, then C and I was supposed to be ready for sex. My God—enough already. I'm not on remote control." The key to amazing foreplay is in your willingness to travel her body, caressing it while at the same time staying away from the so-called action spots (i.e., her genitals).

You may also want to keep in mind that the majority of us will touch someone the way we like to be touched. But very often there is a difference between the pressure a man likes and what a woman likes. Men tend to prefer deeper, stronger pressure, while women respond more to gentler, softer pressure. Why? Because as a function of the male hormone testosterone, a man's skin is thicker and denser. As a result, the touch that works for you may be too firm for her and may make her feel uncomfortable or actually hurt her.

SECRET FROM LOU'S ARCHIVES

The fascination with a woman's erogenous zones is not new. During the eighteenth century, a miniature painting appeared in India, showing the erogenous spots on the female body. At the time it was believed that these spots changed each day during the lunar month.

Gentlemen, I know you may not be comfortable with asking or receiving directions, so I have provided you with a topographical guide, so to speak, of a woman's body. What I have heard again and again from men in my seminars is that you truly respond to maps and guides, liking to peruse them at your leisure, in order to familiarize yourselves with various routes or the logistics of a trip. I am going to be systematic here and start at the top of her body and move down, giving you hints and pointers about how to enliven each particular area. Consider this your road map to ecstasy.

Head

The majority of women like to have their head massaged and their hair touched, played with, and enjoyed. Remember the feeling of a good scalp massage? You need to employ that same kind of motion to your lover's head. You may want to do this on a night when you are not going out and she doesn't mind having her hair mussed up.

You may also want to try running your fingertips or a hairbrush through her hair gently and steadily. If you have a daughter or a sister whose hair you have brushed, you may be at an advantage in this area. Although the stroke can be a straight, downward motion, you can give yourself some varying moves by doing a J-shaped stroke, which is a long stroke through her hair with a little up tail at the end. Remember to brush her entire head, not just the back. You might also ask her to brush yours to show you how she likes her own hair brushed. This way, you can study how she varies the stroke, its location, and its strength.

TIPS

➤ Gently play with her hair at the base of her neck, lift it, and kiss underneath.
➤ Hold her against you and let her feel your warm breath on her scalp; this will be subtle but deeply felt.
➤ If your arm is around her shoulders, play with her hair as you walk.

SECRET FROM LOU'S ARCHIVES

According to a hairstylist who could have been the model for Warren Beatty's character in Shampoo, *the more hair on the nape of a woman's neck, the more abundant her pubic hair— some men love lots of pubic hair, and some men just don't. It's all individual.*

Face

Face touching is a very gentle, intimate gesture, and the key to making it as sensual as possible is the intensity of eye-to-eye contact. But be aware of whether or not she is wearing makeup. If she is, ask her to remove it, then use the back of your hand or finger to lightly trace the side of her jawline, down her cheekbone, and then down her neck. Believe me, women remember how you touch them.

TIPS

- ➤ Use the tips of your fingers to outline her lips. Close both your eyes and do the same to each other.
- ➤ Ask her to suck on your finger once it is close to her mouth. She may show you on your finger what else her tongue can do, and you can use this as a prelude to using your tongue elsewhere.
- ➤ Play a game in which each of you, eyes closed, kisses the other *just* on the side of the mouth. If your nose touches, you lose.

Ears

Remember how we spoke of being able to tell how your lover likes being touched by how she touches you? Well, the way in which a woman responds to touching of her ear is a perfect example of how men and women differ. As one male seminar attendee said, "A woman who puts her tongue in my ear is a straight-line boner for me." This makes sense, as men's ears are an androgenic receptor site; in other words, those cells receive signals from the male hormones, which is the reason men have hair in their ears.

For the majority of women, however, a tongue in the ear is like having their head in a washing machine. (There are, however, women who love this sensation, but they are definitely in the minority.) The action I am referring to here is glomming onto her ear with suction and pushing your tongue into the ear. It's best to use your full wet mouth on other parts of her body, not at this tender conical opening. If you can't resist her ear, best to try tracing along the outside rim and behind the back of her earlobe with your tongue, or sucking on her earlobes. Be sure to use a full open mouth for a less direct, warm breath.

TIPS

➤ Breathe lightly. She wants to know you are there, but you don't want to risk sounding like a hurricane.

➤ Be careful not to blow too forcefully into her ear; if too harsh, this move, while tempting in a romantic kind of way, will not arouse her.

➤ Lick, then lightly blow. This technique causes the opposing sensations of heat/moisture and then cooling. You may also want to try this on her nipples, the side of her neck, or the curve of her back.

Neck and Shoulders

This erogenous zone is invariably a doozy for women. Touching her neck and shoulders can create goose bumps and shivers all over her body if done in the right way. It's best to use a circular, wavy motion rather than a straight up-and-down motion. Your tongue, lips, fingers, and chin will work well for you here. She is more than likely going to respond like a cat and nuzzle into you. Her skin here is very sensitive and thin, so you don't need to use a lot of pressure. As one woman said, "When he starts down my neck, I can feel my crotch heat up. I can't believe such a small area can cause my whole body to react. I shiver all over."

The adage that variety is the spice of life is very true here. Don't always use the same motion. Make your fingers and hands continue down to her shoulders. Balance your touch on both sides—don't overlook what massage therapists have known for years!

TIPS

➤ The area from the base of a woman's earlobes to the top of her neck is one of the more sensitive areas on her body.

➤ Start softly with fingertips, mix in lips and tongue, and be sure to touch both sides.

➤ Lift up her hair and kiss down the back of her neck, and continue across her shoulders. This is a perfect move when she's wearing anything strapless.

SECRET FROM LOU'S ARCHIVES

Ladies have asked that you please don't go directly to action spots. Instead, delay arrival. They prefer a slow buildup. Paying attention to the minor areas first is critical.

Belly Button

Some women love to have a tongue, finger, or nose in their belly button. For others this is decidedly not the case. "I love it when he plays with my belly button ring, because his mouth is hot. He says he likes that side of me—I'm an executive by day and a club girl by night." Another woman, a mother of three, said, "No way. Poking anything in it makes me want to pee."

TIPS

> All points from the top of the pubic hair to the point between the breasts can be massaged in a gentle, circular (clockwise) motion with fingers or thumbs.
> Consider her belly button the perfect repository for champagne or other beverages. As it is just north of a highly enervated area, any attention to her navel will spread there.

Back

The area across her back right above the curve of her buttocks, which is called the sacral curve, is often a very sensitive pressure zone. By gently applying pressure with your entire hand, you may excite her in a way mysterious to you both. Stroking the whole of her back or lightly tracing the area with your fingers is another inventive move. As one lady said, "This is why you have hot breath and why we women wear backless gowns."

TIPS

> Some women may feel self-conscious when you pay attention to this area because of its proximity to her derriere, so be considerate and aware. Either tell her how much you enjoy touching this area, or, if she's too sensitive, concentrate on the front of her body.

➤ Moving from her back down to her buttocks brings sensation from her groin into her genital area.

➤ One way to build lubrication is to focus on the small dimples on her back. Tell her what you're going to do and then put your tongue there.

Buttocks

Dare we overlook one of men's more admired areas of a woman's body? As I mentioned, many women are sensitive or uncomfortable about not only exposing but having their derrieres be the center of attention. It's up to you to show and tell her that you love her buttocks. One woman from a seminar said, "When my boyfriend told me that part of me is the one part he loves to watch, touch, and taste, I was astounded. Now that I'm more comfortable, we read the Sunday paper and he rests his head in the curve of my back with his cheek on the curve of my butt."

TIPS

➤ If you position your lady on all fours, you can lean your chest against her buttocks and caress her breasts at the same time.

➤ If she enjoys anal play, you can begin to heighten her sensation by gently spreading her cheeks; this will stimulate her anus, reminding her of things to come.

Limbs

Think of all the room you have here! Legs, arms, wrists, hands! As with any touching, be sure to touch both sides of her, as balancing sensation is important. When it comes to touching her limbs, you can use more pressure because the skin is thicker. Recently on a plane, I watched a couple as the woman leaned into him, half asleep. Her partner was gently circling her hand and wrist with his fingertips, and judging from the serene smile on her face, she was in bliss. It was sweet to watch him watching her. He was making her feel so good.

TIPS

➤ Touching her limbs is a great way to enliven her nerve endings, radiating pleasure to the outer reaches of her body.

➤ The other benefit to touching limbs is they are external—you can have as much fun as you want in public! Limbs are also a great place to do the Swirl (see page 100).

Feet

In this area of the body, I have borrowed from the Chinese, who have used the feet as the entryway to the rest of the body. When rubbing or massaging a woman's feet, there are a couple of important things to remember. You both need to be in a comfortable position in which you can access both feet easily. Try sitting between her legs on the floor in front of her, or with her leg draped over yours as you face her toes. Use a body lotion to give you greater ease of stroking motion and drape a towel over your knee so no lotion lands where it shouldn't.

The main aim in a foot massage is to release the tension of the tiny muscles and ligaments holding the little bones in place. Your thumbs will be your best digits for foot massages.

Use small circular strokes from the heel up to the toes with both thumbs, the way a masseur would move up your spine. Don't use a two-handed squeeze from the instep up to the toes. Any compacting, squishing motion pushes all the little bones in the foot together, and that hurts. If she is close to getting her period, the outer side below her ankle may be very tender. Be gentle. Release toe pressure by gently pulling each toe in an upward motion. Start with your thumbs together at the center of the bottom of the foot and, using an outward stroking motion with both thumbs, firmly stroke across the ball of the foot. Use that same stroke all the way down the foot, top and bottom. Next, use the heel of your hand on her heel in a circular motion and then switch to your thumb or your index and middle fingers, bent like little knees, for more intense pressure. And of course you can add toe-sucking and/or any other oral play.

According to Valerie Ann Worwood, author of *Scents and Scentuality*, the foot contains a number of erotic trigger points, which, when pressed, will create sensation in a woman's genitals.

➤ Massage the big toes with thumb and fingers.
➤ Massage three inches along either side of the bone running from the back of the heel up toward the calf of the leg.
➤ Use a circular massage technique to connect the three points that run in a line from the end of the heel to the sole of the foot to the crease by the middle toe. You can also connect the fourth point on the sole, just inside the bridge.

Massaging these points, based loosely on reflexology (see foot diagram), will:

1. Increase relief.
2. Reduce anxiety.
3. Clear the mind.
4. Reduce neck tension.
5. Reduce eye stress.
6. Improve mood.
7. Reduce stress.
8. Regulate breathing.
9. Reduce tension.
10. Reduce nervousness.

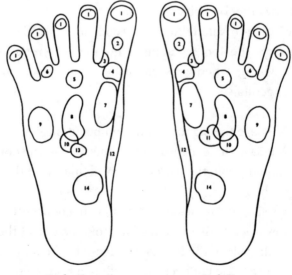

Right Foot   *Left Foot*

Reflexology Chart

11. Increase circulation.
12. Loosen stomach muscles.
13. Reduce anxiety.
14. Reduce nervousness.

Breasts

Some women love to be touched here and others don't. One woman in my seminar really doesn't like having her breasts massaged. "I'd rather take a cold bath," she says. For her, it's just not pleasurable. But other women love it! They love to have their breasts cradled, sucked, and played with. One male surgeon who attended a seminar said the woman he dated wanted her nipples bitten, and while doing her bidding, he thought he was going to bite them off. Someone's *ouch* may be another's *mmmmm*.

It is best to start from underneath and gently move toward the nipples. Like just about everything else, women need you to build toward the center of interest, and that includes nipples. The straight-to-the-nipples approach doesn't allow a woman time to relax into the sensation. And FYI, the majority of women *do not* enjoy intense pinching of their nipples. It is "like rubbing a cat the wrong way—and you are likely to get the same result—pissing her off." Also, the grab and squeeze technique is best left in the greengrocer's. Breasts may be shaped like oranges, but they rarely appreciate the squeeze test.

Again, it's up to you to experiment and discover how she likes to be touched. You may want to ask her to guide your hands by putting hers over the top of yours and showing you how she wants you to do things. You may also consider watching her masturbate, assuming she is comfortable with that. Does she flick her own nipple with a finger or hold the entire breast? Does she pull them up toward her face or cup them together?

If she enjoys intense nipple pressure once she is stimulated, you might try using nipple clips with adjustable tension. If none are available, bobby pins and clothespins are excellent substitutes.

The Swirl and Sensual Massage

Now that you have been introduced to a woman's erogenous zones, here are two ways to put all that information together. The first method is called the Swirl, which is a light touch enveloping her entire body. The second method is what I call the Sensual Massage, which is the same movement with more pressure and using both your hands at the same time.

THE SWIRL

A woman's skin is her largest sexual organ—despite what you may have heard to the contrary. As a result, anywhere that she has skin can become an erogenous zone, depending on how you touch, caress, and pamper her. Think of it this way: If you're in a boardroom sitting next to a woman you find attractive, and your elbows happen to touch, chances are you remember it, right? In my seminars, I suggest that men first see how this move feels on themselves. So, using the front of your thigh as the practice field (you can do this with or without clothing), scratch in a straight line from your knee to the groin. Do the stroke first with nails, and then with just your fingertips, to see the difference. Then do it again, varying the pressure. Immediately cover the same field using a wavy, undulating stroke. See the difference? The reason it feels so different is that the little nerves "know" they are getting sensation with the straight line, whereas with the wavy stroke, the little nerves anticipate, hoping they're next. As many men and women have noted, you can do this anywhere on the body with just a simple hand motion.

You can also use the Swirl as a transitional move to the action spots. Let your fingers make her moan for you. Another important feature of the Swirl is that it can be done in many public places without embarrassing either of you by getting you overly excited.

SENSUAL MASSAGE

There is an entire world of sensual massage and many books devoted strictly to the subject. I'm going to provide you with some of the highlights. These techniques do not require much preparation or learning, and they all rely on one simple premise: that you get into it.

Using both hands, gently but steadily apply pressure to the different parts of her body. I think it's always best to start at the top (her head) and work down (to her feet). Don't include her breasts or her groin area—the so-called action spots. These are too sensitive and may create an uncomfortable amount of sexual tension, thereby undermining the point of the massage.

Depending on how sensitive she is, vary and gauge the degree of pressure. Here are some important tips:

> Always balance what you do on one side by repeating the move on the other side.
> Use lotion or massage oil so that your hands move easily over her skin. Reapply as often as needed.
> Pour the lotion or oil into your hands and rub them together. This is a way to avoid touching her with cold hands.
> Use a towel or sheet to cover the parts of her body that you are not touching, and make sure the room is warm.
> Choose soothing music.

Tease Her

Kiss her, touch her, and now you're ready to push her over the edge. When teasing is subtle, with a precise purpose and direction (i.e., to make her swoon), then, gentlemen, it is totally legal. So for those of you who want to perfect the art of the tease, I have gathered some information taken from the hundreds of women with whom I have spoken in the course of writing my books and leading my seminars. After all, isn't our goal here to derive absolute pleasure for both of you?! The power of teasing is in the mysterious interplay of her mind and body. Here are some reported teasing delights.

1. Compose a fantasy scenario together. You write one line/paragraph and she writes the next one.
2. Share one of your fantasies in which she is featured. If you're afraid you may shock her with the frankness of your fantasy, you might edit it lightly, while you feel her out and see how she reacts.
3. Call her on the phone from work and tell her what you want to do to her that night.
4. Leave her a voice mail describing what you want to do to her, or read her a piece of erotica and leave it on voice mail.
5. Send her a postcard and write down what part of her body most excites you.
6. Use the lovely ritual of dining to build up the tension between you. One woman shared her and her husband's style of public foreplay: "It started because I had recently had surgery on my wrist. We went out for dinner and I was rather helpless, something I never am. My husband all of a sudden got 'that' look in his eyes over the menu and said, 'Let me order for you and feed you.' So when the waiter returned, my husband concocted a story about my situation, ordered, and then scooted up beside me on the U-shaped banquette. The next two hours were so sensual and so sexual. It was such a turn-on having him pay that much attention to me, and it was so sweet when he cut up my food and made it into little-girl size." If you're uncomfortable with a too-public display, just eat and drink slowly, savoring each bite or sip. Believe me: If you pay attention, so will she.

Checklist for Fantastic Foreplay

➤ Orgasm is not the only road to satisfaction; how you make one another feel is.

➤ Use lubricant and keep it nearby—on the bedside table or other appropriate place.

➤ Make sure your breath and mouth are clean. I know that's obvious, but just to be sure.

➤ Slowly, slowly, slowly.

➤ Involve her entire body. Put your mouth and hands everywhere and use the Swirl.

➤ Using that most powerful of your sex organs, your brain, consider approaching her body as if it or some part of it is new for you. Anyone can say, "Yeah, been there, done that," and what shows up is a "been there, done that" attitude. If, on the other hand, you have a fresh, new attitude, she will be able to tell. Add that to the comfort of already knowing one another and you have a whole new world to play in. Mentally treat her as new.

➤ Check ideas on yourself first.

➤ Check in with her regularly about pressure and speed, as her preferences can change throughout a given session.

➤ Check stubble. Men with beards can make their beards softer and more user-friendly with hair conditioner.

➤ If one of you is eating spicy or heavily seasoned food prior to being intimate, share a taste with the other. This tip was from an elegant European woman, who said in her thick Hungarian accent, "You both need to so your chemistries will blend better." So be sure to share that Caesar salad.

Foreplay, Some Final Words

Fabulous foreplay is all about enticing and exciting both her mind and her body. I think it's about time, though, that we came up with another term for foreplay. This term implies that foreplay is only a lead-in to something else, that it isn't enough in and of itself. On the contrary, for women, the kissing, touching, and teasing are necessary and often very satisfying parts of lovemaking on their own. As one woman, a magazine writer from Philadelphia, said, "When we have the time during lovemaking to really play, it is sex on a different plane."

PART II

Capturing
the
O

CHAPTER SIX

Debunking the Orgasm Myths

There's No Right or Wrong in Sex

The Myths

Literally hundreds of myths still exist about sex and orgasm, getting in the way of men's and women's enjoyment of sex. Consider this sampling:

➤ The best health is enjoyed by those who abstain from sex.
➤ Only certain types of orgasms "really count."
➤ Simultaneous orgasms are more satisfactory than those experienced separately.
➤ Simultaneous orgasms are necessary for sexual compatibility in marriage.
➤ All women can orgasm during vaginal intercourse.
➤ Women who are multiorgasmic are of lower moral virtue.

These statements are all patently false, and in that way, misleading. Some are based on outdated scientific information that was later disproven, and others derive from religious belief that has a didactic if not repressive purpose.

Another myth: Only men ejaculate. As I noted in chapter 2, nothing could be further from the truth! Many women, when they are aroused, will discharge fluid. This fluid is not urine; its source is the paraurethral glands on either side of the urethra. Hence the common assumption that it is urine.

According to Dr. Beverly Whipple, who along with researchers Alice Kahn Ladas and John D. Perry named the G-spot, another assumption associated with female ejaculation is that it occurs only with G-spot stimulation. Again not true. Some women ejaculate fluid when they get aroused, while others say they have never experienced ejaculation. Still other women realize that in fact they have ejaculated only after they hear confirmation that such a thing exists.

One woman in a seminar reported such a story about female ejaculation. She explained that she and her boyfriend were away on vacation staying in a "fancy hotel in London." One time, during sex, she was on top of him while he was giving her oral sex. She was getting more and more aroused, and getting closer and closer to climaxing, when her boyfriend gently pushed her away, claiming that she had just peed on him. Mortified, she ran to the bathroom. Needless to say, that ended their romantic moment.

Later, after they'd returned to New York, she'd wondered about the episode, not believing that she had actually urinated. When she came to one of my seminars and learned about female ejaculation, she had a "eureka!" moment. "Oh my God," she exclaimed. "That's what happened in London!" She had been so aroused and stimulated that her glands released the fluid. Relieved and no longer ashamed, she couldn't wait to go home and tell her boyfriend.

> ### SECRET FROM LOU'S ARCHIVES
>
> *Freud was one of the first scientists to bring female orgasms public attention. Unfortunately, he claimed that only a vaginal orgasm is a "mature" orgasm.*

This woman is not alone in such misconceptions about orgasms. How many of the statements from the list at the start of this chapter have you heard before and perhaps taken as truth? Is it obvious that they are outdated, half true, or completely false? How does one learn to distinguish?

Let's look at some other myths more closely:

➤ A man has to have an erection in order to orgasm. False. Men can have what is called a "softgasm," which is an orgasm and ejaculation without an erection.

➤ Men are always ready for sex. False. Just as women need foreplay to get relaxed and aroused, men need foreplay and can't be expected to perform as if on cue.

> One stops being sexual after a certain age. False. According to Drs. Milsten and Slowinski, a review of the data from Masters and Johnson Institute suggests that senior citizens have a very strong interest in sex. The oldest couple treated was a 93-year-old man and his 88-year-old wife. Age is only a number.

> Masturbation causes impotence. False. This myth was perhaps dreamed up in Rome, to try to control the urges of some frisky members of the flock. There is no physiological, emotional, or spiritual link between masturbation and impotence.

> Sexual frustration causes "blue balls." False. The blood engorgement of the scrotal testicle area may make it sore and tender, but certainly not blue. As one man pointed out, "I mean, let's get serious. Most men have a pretty good idea of how to take care of the problem themselves, and the balls don't actually turn blue anyway." Hard and hot, yes; blue, no.

SECRET FROM LOU'S ARCHIVES

According to Melanesian natives who preferred the position of the man kneeling between the woman's outspread legs, the missionary position only resulted in the man pressing downward, making the woman unable to respond.

HISTORICAL AND HYSTERICAL FACTS | The term "blue balls" is at least four centuries old and first appeared in England as "blue bollocks."

The Not-So-Subtle Power of the Media

In contemporary times myths continue to have power, sometimes in dangerous ways. Essentially, the media put pressure on women and men to perform sexually in bed and look a certain way (i.e., for women, tall, thin, and sexy; for men, musclebound, tall, and athletic). Many women and men can't live up to these standards. Furthermore, by not being able to duplicate the false ideals, they feel they have failed, and end up feeling badly about themselves.

Though myths may be based on certain nuggets of truth or fact, they often evolve into overgeneralizations and partial truths. Obviously, this information can quickly become misleading. For instance, when it was first discovered that some women were multiorgasmic, this information was immediately disseminated into the larger cultural arena as not only fact but a mandate. Instead of presenting this information as an opportunity to explore more pleasure, the media treated it as a tool to pressure women and their partners.

HISTORICAL AND HYSTERICAL FACTS	The know-it-alls of ancient times actually believed that every time you had an ejaculation, you lost a small amount of your brain. They called semen *cerebri stillicidium*, which roughly translates as "distillate of brain."

The same information backlash can negatively impact men. When a man hears that he should learn to be multiorgasmic in order to satisfy his woman, it can trigger performance anxiety. Sure, some men may be able to learn this technique (which essentially involves a very well-trained PC muscle that helps you refrain from ejaculating), but it is certainly not a skill required for being a wonderful, satisfying lover.

The most oft-asked question by readers of the women's magazine *Cosmopolitan* is how to have an orgasm during intercourse. These young women are feeling pressured by their male partners, who are often older or more experienced, to have an orgasm in a way and manner that doesn't typically work well for women. That is, a vaginal orgasm when the man is on top during intercourse. This difficulty is further increased in this position by the man's thrusting, which creates a motion against the clitoris that doesn't work for most women. Talk about a no-win situation! The men are trying to pleasure their partners based on information they learned from adult films, and chances are good that this is bad or inaccurate information. They may also be trying to satisfy their own goal of "giving her an orgasm." This just creates performance pressure for both women and men—which further erodes the ability to access the most pleasure possible.

HISTORICAL AND HYSTERICAL FACTS	Elephants are only able to have erections during mating season, and they have motile penises, meaning their organs can move by themselves. This is a good thing, as they weigh a ton!

Another negative aspect of the power of the media is their tendency to offer prescriptions or definitions for what is sexy.

This is dangerous because if we are inundated with images or advice on how to look or act sexy, we may begin to question ourselves. If the images or advice are different from how we naturally dress or act, then we might end up feeling insecure, inadequate, or unattractive. My policy has always been if you feel sexy, you are sexy.

In my sexuality seminars, the men and women who were most confident about their sexiness-factor were those people who were at home in their own bodies. There wasn't a single look for women or for men. The range of women included Rubenesque women, short women, tall women—in every possible combination of characteristics, from curvy to boyish to angular to lean and lithe. The women who felt sexy shared an attitude about how they felt about themselves. Rather than putting on an act of bravado that screamed, "I am so hot, baby," these women seemed quietly comfortable in their own skins.

The same goes for you, gentlemen. The outwardly gorgeous guy is not necessarily the most sexy. Rather, the sexiest man alive usually is the one who sincerely likes women, wants to please women, and loves paying attention to women. Why might a woman go for a funny man? Because usually that humor is a conscious effort to amuse and delight her.

HISTORICAL AND HYSTERICAL FACTS | A superstition among some Caribbean peoples held that the husband and wife should not have intercourse at night. This was because it was believed if a child were created at night, it would surely be born blind.

Sexiness is not about looks so much as it is about knowing yourself sexually and feeling comfortable and confident in your desire to be sexual. Letting your partner know how she excites or attracts you is always a good idea. This kind of feedback is not about an empty gesture; it's about being honest with yourself and your partner and letting her know what you like and what turns you on.

Read Between the Lines

I'd like to explain some things that have contributed to the fuzziness of the information that's out there about sex. Relative to women's orgasms, there have been regular bouts of controversy within the professional fields. According to such early scientists as the psychoanalyst Sigmund Freud, orgasms resulting from stimulation of the clitoris were in some way less "mature" than orgasms originating in the vagina. Later, the research conducted by Masters and Johnson indicated that all female orgasms resulted from clitoral stimulation and refuted Freud's belief in the vaginal orgasm. Then information started to emerge about the G-spot and it became clear that there is at least one area within the vagina where an orgasm can be triggered. The original Masters and Johnson research did not acknowledge the existence of female ejaculation. When validation of female ejaculation first hit the airwaves and magazine stands, it spread like wildfire.

I am all for disseminating the latest sex research to mainstream publications, but I am very wary of information being presented incompletely. Again, the idea that *all* women ejaculate during sex still holds a lot of sway, is often referred to in mainstream publications, and is often cited by doctors. However, much of this research is now considered outdated by doctors and experts. Yet, as you have seen above, inaccuracies continue to circulate and be believed.

Other examples of controversy include Masters and Johnson's report that there is only one reflex pathway in sexual response. They maintain that since the clitoris is the major source of sensory input in women, the pudendal nerve serves as the "orgasmic platform." However, other researchers, including Dr. Beverly Whipple, have demonstrated that there are at least two nerve pathways leading women to orgasm. These include those nerves tied to the G-spot, the vagina, and the urethra.

All these researchers have made important contributions to our knowledge and understanding of sex and orgasms. However, it's important to be careful of what is reported in a sensational or incomplete manner. Read between the lines and let your own experience be your best guide.

HISTORICAL AND HYSTERICAL FACTS

"Victoria Woodhull, prostitute, spiritualist, Wall Street broker, publisher of a national newspaper, ran for President of the United States against Ulysses S. Grant and Horace Greeley in 1872," notes Irving Wallace. "Her platform supported free love, short skirts, abolition of the death penalty, vegetarianism, excess-profit taxes, birth control, better public housing, easier divorce laws, world government, and female orgasm." Truly a woman ahead of her time.

Getting Beyond the Sin/Pleasure Tango

Myths also reinforce the cultural or personal barriers that prevent men and women from fulfilling their sexual potential. In his study of the history of sexuality, Dr. Mitchell Tepper, founder of Sexualhealth.com, points out that cultural or religious beliefs that said sex was bad, pleasure was a sin, and an orgasm might as well damn you and send you straight to hell have existed throughout history. These attitudes began with the Greeks, were adopted and further developed by the Roman Catholic Church, and then were transformed and assumed by the Puritans who came to America and very much influenced our national cultural attitudes toward sex.

Take for example the sexual impulse over which Adam and Eve had no control, which was referred to as concupiscence or lust by Saint Augustine. By naming it such, lust converted procreation into something shameful, which then led to the belief that Christians should have sex without passion and only for the purpose of procreation. This dictum essentially made it sinful for people to find enjoyment in sex. As Dr. Tepper points out, "Americans, whether or not they are Christians, are heirs to this tradition, and understanding this background might help us to come to terms with our own ambiguous feelings about sex."

SECRET FROM LOU'S ARCHIVES

Saint Augustine felt that woman was man's greatest obstacle to salvation. This, of course, is the same man who prayed, "God, please make me chaste—but not yet."

It has only been since modern psychology started developing at the turn of the twentieth century that sexual attitudes began to shift from a sex-as-sin attitude and men and women began to think about sex in a more open way. In this country, however, it wasn't really until the women's movement that people realized that sex was actually for enjoyment, and that it was good for you!

HISTORICAL AND HYSTERICAL FACTS	Back in the Middle Ages, straight pubic hair was a sign of too much masturbation, which presumably accounts for the wide popularity of miniature pubic hair curlers at the time.

The premise that sex is a sin has affected the way we think about sex, specifically orgasms, in a number of ways. One consequence is that in trying to control our urges, we cut off our natural sexual spontaneity. How can we feel lust and sexual pleasure if we are afraid—in some unconscious way—to let go? Without permission to play and enjoy, we automatically cut off access to the different levels or degrees of sexual pleasure.

Our Notions of Pleasure

Before we look at exactly how to increase the number of ways you can learn to orgasm and the degree of pleasure you experience while doing so, I agree with Dr. Mitchell Tepper that it's important to consider the nature (and notion) of pleasure itself. It's my experience that if you have a narrow view of pleasure, one restricted by either attitude or experience, then you will necessarily limit the degree to which you can feel pleasure. That said, the more open you are to pleasure—in all its forms—the freer you are to discover or deepen pleasure, especially in the sexual realm. So what is pleasure?

In his provocative discussion of the nature and notion of pleasure, Dr. Tepper cites *The Oxford English Dictionary*'s definition of pleasure as "the condition of consciousness or sensation induced by the environment or anticipation of what is felt or viewed as good or desirable; enjoyment, delight, gratification. The opposite of pain." One sexologist places pleasure in four specific categories: physiopleasure (based in the body), sociopleasure (experienced with other people), psychopleasure (emotional pleasure experienced from initiating or doing something—anything—for yourself), and ideopleasure (pleasure received from experiencing or creating something based on a theoretical idea, such as writing a book, making a movie, creating music, or constructing a building).

This use of categories suggests that we experience pleasure on different levels, which is also true of sexual pleasure. However, sexual pleasure is mostly thought of as something experienced solely in the body. In the past twenty or so years, the idea that sexual pleasure was restricted to the body began to be questioned. Specifically, in 1974, Masters and Johnson presented their findings that sexual pleasure involved the brain as much as the body, calling sexual pleasure psychophysiological and for the first time in scientific circles pointing out that sexual pleasure is experienced both in the body and in the brain. Now this may seem like common sense to most of us, but put yourself in your grandparents' generation and imagine what it would feel like to think it was either wrong or unnatural to get sexually excited in your head?!

The Masters and Johnson discovery was important because if you understand that sex happens both in the mind and the body, then you realize why negative or restrictive attitudes toward sex, absorbed from religion or basic cultural attitudes, can have such an enormous impact on us as people. If you believe that sex is dirty, that orgasms and sexual pleasure in general are unnecessary and an indication of a less-than-good character, then you will take that attitude into the bedroom with you.

These attitudes are both prevalent and buried deep in our culture, and while many of us consciously include ourselves in the group of the sexually liberated, it's often surprising how entrenched certain voices may be in our heads, preventing us from truly enjoying ourselves. As we saw in chapter 3, sex is very much a mental game. And the first step is to know how you think and feel about it. And one thing is for certain. As Dr. Tepper says, sexual pleasure is as unique to each person as his history, past learning, attitudes, and beliefs.

Why Goal-Oriented Sex Backfires

By thinking of sex as a goal-oriented event, with orgasm as the chief end, you automatically and immediately limit your ability to feel pleasure along the way. As Dr. Beverly Whipple notes in her important article "Beyond the G-Spot: Recent Research on Female Sexuality," there are two commonly held views of sexual activity. The more common view is goal-directed, which, she says, is "analogous to climbing the stairs." "The first step is touch, the next step is kissing, the next steps are caressing, then vagina/penis contact, which leads to intercourse and the top step of orgasm. One or both partners have a goal in mind and that goal is orgasm." According to Dr. Whipple, this goal-oriented approach to sex and, by extension, orgasm is flawed and naturally limiting to most men and women, and especially to couples.

The other view of sexuality is "pleasure-directed, . . . which can be conceptualized as a circle—with each expression on the perimeter of the circle considered an end in itself. Whether the experience is kissing or oral sex, holding, etc., each is . . . satisfying to the couple. There is no need for any particular form of expression to lead to anything else."

Dr. Whipple further points out the danger of goal-oriented sex in general: "If one person in a couple is goal oriented (typically the male) and the other person is pleasure directed (typically, but not always, the female), problems may occur if the goals are not achieved or if the person does not communicate the goals to the partner."

Do you or your partner think of sex in this linear way? Can you see how such an attitude might prevent you from meandering along the avenue of pleasures? As universal as sex is, it is also very individual particularly when it comes to orgasms. Researchers Hartman, Fithian, and Campbell coined the phrase "orgasmic fingerprinting," to stress the uniqueness of women's orgasms. I believe in this uniqueness wholeheartedly and agree with Dr. Beverly Whipple in her strong belief that we all should have our individual, idiosyncratic sexual responses validated.

Just as we are unique human beings, so we are unique sexual creatures. Trust yourself, and your own experience—

especially when it comes to sex and orgasms. Keep in mind, as you begin to observe the body in its sexual splendor, that there is no right or wrong way to enjoy pleasure or achieve an orgasm.

Any sexual myth does a disservice to the people who hear it by further eroding sexual confidence, which is the key to letting go of inhibitions and exploring sexual pleasure. This is true in all areas of life: The more confidence you have, the more freedom you will feel to try new things, be it driving a car, investing in a new company, or pleasing your lover. There seems to be a direct correlation between someone's personal confidence about their sexuality and their ability to enjoy sex. Above all, I think it's important for men and women to honor and respect their own experience of sex. If something feels right and good, then do it. If something feels false, misleading, or forced, then acknowledge your feelings and back off. You are in charge; you are the ultimate authority.

CHAPTER SEVEN

Your Orgasm

Get the Most from the Tools You've Got

Make a Good Thing Even Better

As I'm sure you're well-aware, men usually experience an orgasm through stimulation of three areas: (1) the penis, (2) the prostate or anus, and—for a lucky few—(3) the nipples. However, this doesn't give the whole sense of *how* men have orgasms. The key to understanding how you can have a better orgasm (i.e., experience more pleasure and control) is awareness: awareness of your body, its muscles, and its nerve endings.

Wherever or however an orgasm occurs, men tend to experience orgasms in terms of physical intensity and/or emotional connection. Sometimes you and your partner may "just want to have fun," in which case you're more focused on physical intensity. If you are in a more romantic mood, feeling very close to each other, you may be making love in order to increase the feeling of emotional closeness. In this way, you're using sex as a vehicle for emotional connection.

125

As we saw in chapter 2, the four stages of arousal are a helpful way of getting the "big picture" of what is happening during sex. But as noted, men and women are often on different schedules, with women taking longer to become aroused but staying aroused longer. On the other hand, men have a quicker response to stimulation, but generally a shorter arousal period.

> **SECRET FROM LOU'S ARCHIVES**
>
> *More often than in any other position, the partner on top is going to have better control of the thrusting and therefore will have better control of the orgasm.*

What I've gathered below are the seven different ways men can orgasm. Try these singly or in combination and you might just discover a new path to pleasure. I recommend that you read this section with your partner so you can share what interests and excites you. In fact, you'll notice that many of the following suggestions are techniques designed for her to do to you.

> **SECRET FROM LOU'S ARCHIVES**
>
> *Above all, anything she does for you has to work for her too.*

The Types

There are essentially seven different types of stimulation through which a man can experience an orgasm:

1. Intercourse
2. Manual
3. Oral
4. Prostate and anal
5. Fantasy
6. Nipple/breast
7. Toys

Yes, most men (and women) think the penis is the lightning rod of male orgasm. Of course, for most of you it is the part of the anatomy through which masturbation first introduced you to the power and pleasure of your sexuality (albeit done quickly so Mom wouldn't catch you). It's my hope that once you cover the material that follows, you will see that you can indeed expand your horizons.

For some of you, this expanded horizon will be the discovery that the stimulation of another area of your body actually enhances penis-centered orgasms. Others of you will find yourself crossing into new territory, experiencing orgasms from stimulation of other places in your body—the nipples, for instance. You may find that when your lover rubs your feet, you become aroused . . . who knows?!

| **HISTORICAL AND HYSTERICAL FACTS** | Here are a few orgasms I hadn't heard of before: eyegasm (maintain eye contact during sexual orgasm) and Jellogasm (if your normal physical response is all-over body tension, try letting your entire body be like Jell-O). |

Intercourse Orgasm

Because there are so many intercourse variations through which you and your partner can reach orgasm, the subject warrants a chapter unto itself. Therefore, in chapter 11 I outline the main positions along with information that will give you a sense of how to access a certain feeling or increase intensity.

Manual Orgasm

Manual stimulation of the penis deserves its own category because having your lover use her hands to arouse and bring you to orgasm gives both of you enjoyment—double the fun! As one woman said, "I feel I have the ability to make him go out of his mind." Another woman said, "His comment was, 'When I regain consciousness, I need to know exactly what you just did to me.'"

SECRET FROM LOU'S ARCHIVES

The average length of a male orgasm during a single climax is about ten to fifteen seconds. The average length of a female orgasm during a single climax has been clocked from ten seconds to one minute, with an average length of nineteen to twenty-eight seconds per climax.

The first technique is the Ode to Bryan. Bryan was the friend who first taught me, demonstrating with a spoon from a tall cup of latte, what feels best to men. Bryan used a spoon simply because it was the only thing available at that time. In the seminar we use an "instructional product," my professional term for a Doc Johnson Realistic dildo with a suction cup at the base.

Share these instructions with your partner. They are based on the demonstrations I give to women in the sexuality seminars. However, for your purposes, you and your partner can practice on the "real thing" (i.e., your penis), or use a dildo or a cucumber. Some women have tried using bananas, but the results were disappointing—bananas are not nearly firm enough.

ODE TO BRYAN (A.K.A. PENIS SAMBA)

Step 1. She'll want to apply a lubricant generously to both hands. She can warm it slightly by rubbing her hands together.

Step 2. She should start with her hands out in front of her, palms facing away and thumbs down. With one hand (it doesn't matter which), she gently but firmly holds the base of your penis. Her view should be of the back of her hand and four fingers. Her wrist should be cocked forward toward your body. Your view will be of her thumb, nestled into your pubic hair. Her other hand is ready to move into position (it can be resting on your thigh or testicles) once the first hand's stroke is complete. Once she has completed one "cycle," both hands typically will be in constant motion, so she need not worry where they will rest. They won't.

Step 3. She should maintain placement of her hand while stroking up the shaft in a single continuous motion.

Step 4. When she gets to the head, she rotates her hand slightly as if she were carefully opening a jar—but not *until* she reaches the head. Bryan's comment was, "The twist is the most critical part. Don't do it until you get to the top."

Ode to Bryan, Step 3

Ode to Bryan, Step 4

Ode to Bryan, Step 5

Ode to Bryan, Step 6

Ode to Bryan, Step 7

Step 5. Maintaining as much contact as possible between the head of your penis and the palm of her hand, she rotates her hand over the top of the penis, as if sculpting the head with her entire palm.

Step 6. Because of the rotation (a.k.a. the twist), her thumb will now be facing her and the back of her hand will be facing you. Next, she brings her hand down the shaft again firmly to the starting position and immediately moves her second hand into starting position, on top of the first hand. She should get into a flow of motion very quickly and maintain continuous sensation.

Step 7. She should follow steps 2–6 immediately with her other hand, and alternate them repeatedly until. . . .

Penis Samba is Ode to Bryan done very quickly and *only* at the top/head. And, as you will no doubt discover, this move takes on a rhythm all its own. She will create a mini-lifesaver ring with the index finger and thumb of one hand just below the head of your penis. This enables her to concentrate all the sensation in the first 1½ inches of your penis—the most sensitive area. She moves her other hand on the head of your penis in a circular motion (as if she had ink in her palm and was trying to apply an even coat). Once she finishes the application, she repeats the motion with her other hand.

BASKET WEAVE

Basket Weave is another seminar favorite. Not only does it do wonders all on its own, it is the motion that makes giving you a Pearl Necklace (page 281) the "bomb."

Step 1. Again, she'll want to apply a lubricant generously to both hands.

Step 2. She should clasp her hands together, interlacing her fingers.

Step 3. In order to make a hole, she should keep her thumbs relaxed.

Step 4. Then, she lowers her clasped hands onto your penis. The fit should be snug—in essence she is creating an impostor vagina.

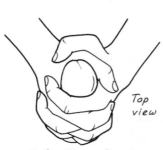

Basket Weave, Step 4

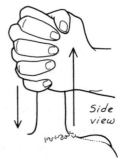

Basket Weave, Step 5

Basket Weave, Step 6

Step 5. She moves her clasped hands up and down the shaft, continuing the firm and gentle hold.

Step 6. She twists her clasped hands slowly as they go up and down the shaft, much like the motion inside a washing machine, only gentler.

Oral Orgasm

Gentlemen, I know you love to orgasm orally! So how do we bridge the gap between men's very real pleasure and some women's hesitation or disinclination to do this? In all the years I've been doing seminars and speaking to women about their sexual experiences, I've found that there is one obvious distinction between those women who *enjoy* performing oral sex on their lovers and those who don't. The difference is that the women who enjoy giving oral sex know they are giving something very special, and it is a huge turn-on for them to know "I can make him feel that amazing." The women who don't like to give oral sex often feel they "have to" or are "supposed to do it," and therefore resent it and find the concept unpleasant.

As with any experience in life, if the first encounter a woman has with oral sex (or any sex for that matter) is positive, she will likely maintain a positive attitude about it. However, as in life, there are many different ways of reacting to particular events, and sometimes women encounter partners who are less than understanding or gentle when they are learning or trying something new.

Until a woman experiences a supportive and sensitive partner, she won't know or have confidence in her skills as a lover, as her partners are her litmus test. And often men, and women as well, do not know how to guide their partners even when they ask. How can one not know? Easy. The analogy I use to explain it is this: When you are having a massage, your job is not to concentrate on what is being done to your body, but rather to relax and feel. So it is when you are with a partner—don't *analyze* what she is doing, just feel.

Women are like horses: you can lead them to water but do not expect them to drink—they will do so in their own time, if they so choose. I once heard of a hilarious Web site selling CDs with subliminal messages supposed to make women perform oral sex. How do you spell scam on the Net? Rather than a CD to manipulate her mind, why not be straight up and deliver the kind of attention that turns her head—that will give a man more access than any CD.

HISTORICAL AND HYSTERICAL FACTS	A recent survey of prostitutes revealed that the most frequently requested sex is fellatio.

However, there is a way for a woman to begin to enjoy this most intimate of sexual pleasures with her man. The secret to a woman's success and enjoyment is in taking *control*. As one man told me, "When she takes me into the back of her throat, first it is so hot just watching her do it and then when she swallows on the head of my cock it is like there are a hundred little fingers running all over it—as if there were three women in bed with me."

Some of the reasons I hear over and over again as to why women don't like giving oral sex is that they gag when the penis gets to the back of their mouths, they are asked to deep-throat, or they don't want to start what they don't want to swallow. Make no mistake: Performing oral sex is very much an acquired skill for most women.

About gagging: Mother Nature provided the gag reflex as a way of keeping our throats protected. So chances are women will gag when performing oral sex. Be patient and tell her not to worry if it doesn't come naturally or immediately.

Also the Ring and Seal technique will take care of how to handle the gag reflex. She can attach her index finger and thumb to her mouth like a little tube. They remain in a *ring, sealed* to her mouth so it doesn't have to do all the work. This technique also elongates the area of stimulation for you. And it lets her be in control of the speed and strength with which you enter her mouth.

The appeal of deep-throating is often a result of visual cues from the adult-film world, which is notorious for its high degree of fabrication. In other words, deep-throating is nearly impossible for most women. If she is controlling the pace and the placement of your penis in her mouth, and using the Ring and Seal, there's very little chance of gagging. She must decide how far your penis goes, and once she's reached her maximum level of comfort, she can simply pull it back out. As your penis begins to feel more comfortable in her mouth, she will gradually be able to take in more of it, should that be what she desires.

If you remember nothing else about receiving oral sex, let it be this: In order for it to be effective, *she* must be in charge. This is something she does for *you*, not something you do for yourself *through* her.

MOUTH MAGIC

It won't take long for her to discover that the secret to giving great oral sex is to find her "rhythm," and that rhythm depends on your specific likes and dislikes. What will ensure her success with every encounter is for her to remember the following four motions. When and how she uses them will depend on her rhythm, but the motions themselves stay the same.

Step 1. She *seals* her hand to her mouth in the *ring* shape. Or she can just use her mouth, but it will be more tiring.

Step 2. Her mouth (with teeth covered) moves up and down the shaft to increase length of the stimulation area.

Step 3. She keeps her tongue moving in a back-and-forth or circular motion across the frenulum area, which is the V-shaped notch at the back of the head of the penis. This allows you to feel the more textured taste-bud surface throughout the experience.

Step 4. Her free hand is stimulating another part of your body, such as the nipples, inner thighs, perineal area, testicles or anus, in order to broaden the area of sensual pleasure. She can also take time to lick your testicles. You can hold her hand on them to show her what you prefer. If she's worried about hair, she can gently stroke the area beforehand to remove any loose little hairs.

As long as she doesn't forget these four movements, oral sex experiences are always going to be pleasurable for both of you.

On the subject of swallowing, or allowing you to come in her mouth: her mouth, her choice. Should she choose to do

Mouth Magic, Step 1—Forming the Ring and Seal

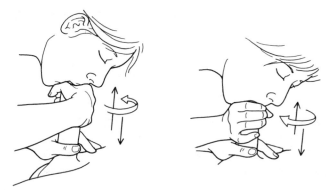

Mouth Magic, Step 2—Moving Up and Down the Shaft (while Twisting)

Mouth Magic, Step 3

Mouth Magic, Step 4

so, she can heighten the sensation you feel when ejaculating, in her mouth or not, by pulsing her now-still hands wrapped around your shaft in time with the ejaculations.

Prostate and Anal Orgasms

Analogous to a woman's G-spot, the prostate can be stimulated either externally or internally, and some men also enjoy being stimulated externally on the anus as well. The prostate can be stimulated with fingers (she should definitely use a lubricant without nonoxynol-9, which can be irritating) or with a toy, such as a dildo or butt plug, depending on how "full" you like to feel when penetrated. In any of these cases, it's also necessary to use lubricant so that no tissue irritation occurs. Remember, this isn't a self-lubricating area.

ROSE PETALS (A.K.A. ANILINGUS)

For this your partner will use her tongue like a soft sculpting tool on your anus. And again, I suggest she incorporate other complementary moves at the same time. A favorite among seminar attendees is for her to perform Rose Petals while giving a hand job at the same time—the intensity can make the orgasm sensational!

The best position for anilingus is for you to be on all fours facing away from her, or lying on your back with your hips on a pillow. This support allows your pelvis to tilt, which makes your anal area more available.

She uses a strong stroking motion with her tongue, as if she is creating sepals (the small green leaves at the bottom of a rose), and circles the rim of your anus (this is known as rimming). The off-the-charts move is for her to incorporate hand stimulation while her hot, moist mouth is on your anus. She can accomplish this in one of two ways: (1) by reaching her warm, well-lubricated hand around your thigh and using a gentle pulling stroke toward the head of your penis; (2) by reaching between your legs and, with one hand on your penis, doing a smooth, forward-stroking, gentle twisting motion toward your shoulders.

HISTORICAL AND HYSTERICAL FACTS	Anal intercourse is the most popular sexual practice depicted in pre-Columbian art.

Anal play definitely can add a new dimension to your sexual repertoire, but don't feel pressure to add it if you are uncomfortable. Talk with your partner and see if you are both interested in experimenting in this perfectly natural way.

Fantasy Orgasm

In all my years of doing seminars, I have met only one man who is capable of reaching orgasm without any physical stimulation at all. He says it is all about his willpower and mental control. Now, whether one can climax with fantasy alone or fantasy plus some stimulation, this is an area that has as much variation as people have imagination. Often fantasies have their roots in youthful experiences—be it the cool plastic apron worn by your mother or nanny who held you after the bath that lead to your enjoyment of latex, or the excitement you felt when you saw your next-door neighbor silhouetted through her bedroom window. Then there are fantasies that require others' participation. Often masturbation fantasies are best left for solo enjoyment, as the reality (or translation) never seems to match the mental experience.

Fantasy has a strange sexual power. There are ways to enhance your sexual experience through certain sources, such as erotic stories, magazines, videos, shared fantasies with your partner, or pure imagination. This is all a matter of taste and knowing what turns you both on. I generally caution against using erotic sources if one of you is uncomfortable.

Nipple/Breast Orgasm

I know of only one man who is able to come based on the stimulation of his nipples. But I figure if there is one man, there are others. The man I spoke with said that if a woman merely licks, sucks, and nibbles on his nipples the right way, he is sent into the stratosphere! "It is illegal how good this feels," he told me. So do not overlook this unheralded erogenous zone. She can stimulate your nipples with her tongue, teeth, hands, and fingers, or with toys such as nipple clips and suction cups. These are designed for the area, and come in vibrating versions as well. Of course, there are men, as there are women, who don't like this at all. As always, it's best to communicate with your partner.

Toys

As you no doubt know by now, toys are not just for children! I'm a big proponent of adding toys into your sexual repertoire because they add fun, spice, and variety.

Men who like anal play enjoy both butt plugs and anal

beads. Those who like to increase the intensity of their erection often play with cock rings. There are a number of toys that I describe in chapter 12, where I talk about enhancing your sexual experience. If you're interested, you might want to jump ahead now.

Enhancers

Though many women don't even want you to stay erect for hours (after all, sustained penetration can lead to soreness and irritation), there are ways you can improve your lasting power.

➤ The Squeeze Technique: While you're erect, squeeze your penis right below the head. This will help slow you down, enabling you to prolong sex. You can also have her do this for you.

➤ Cock rings not only can enhance her pleasure, by making you feel more full inside of her, but can increase the intensity of your feeling as well. Be sure to put the cock ring over both the shaft of your penis and the scrotum. Some men like to take it off just as they are about to come; other men prefer leaving the cock ring on. Men claim that the cock ring, which helps build up pressure, increases the sensation during intercourse. (For more on cock rings see page 281.)

➤ Desensitizing spray: I don't usually recommend these products, as they have a numbing active ingredient, benzocaine. However, men use these sprays to make them last longer when they want to have multiple sessions.

➤ Viagra: This pharmaceutical phenomenon is meant for men who suffer from clinical impotence or erectile dysfunction, and should only be used under a doctor's supervision. Though wide reports stress how Viagra is a "miracle" that lets men remain erect for hours, I have also heard reports of its misuse. After taking two Viagra, one young man in his early twenties had three orgasms and still remained erect. Remaining erect for too long can lead to permanent damage of the penile tissue, which is known as priapism.

SECRET FROM LOU'S ARCHIVES

Don't equate how hard you are with how aroused you are. You can have a terrific erection but not be anywhere close to the point of orgasm. Think of erection as a measure of the blood-flow to your penis, and arousal as the degree of sexual excitement.

Other Male Orgasm Facts

➤ Some men have full orgasms when soft.
➤ Some men enjoy a blended orgasm—the simultaneous stimulation of penis and G-spot/prostate.
➤ Some men have dry orgasms, in which they have the full sensation of coming, without releasing any

ejaculate. This occurs for one of two reasons: (1) they have controlled, or suppressed, their ejaculation or (2) they have already ejaculated a number of times and there's "nothing left in the tanks."

Sex for One

Although men are generally more comfortable than women with the notion and practice of masturbation, there still exist shameful or secretive associations with a man's desire, need, or preference to pleasure himself. Some men report that even though they have wonderful sex lives with their partners, they still like to "do themselves." Their reasons vary: Some say they like the autonomy and not having to worry about anyone else's feelings; others say "it's like an urge . . . and I want to do it quickly."

Many of the men and women in my seminars say that one of the most effective ways to orgasm is to masturbate, which is often the way they first learned to orgasm. That nerve response pathway is already set, and your body knows what to expect. So one of the simpler ways to show your partner how you like to be touched or stimulated is to show her what you do. Now, I'm sure some of you may not be comfortable with the concept of masturbating. Please know that I maintain that we should never have to do anything we don't want to. These are our bodies, and our choices.

However, if you are comfortable with or curious about how masturbation techniques can lead to better self-knowledge and ultimately to a stronger, more intense, or more pleasurable orgasm, then without further ado, help yourself.

Dr. Bernie Zilbergeld points out in his book *The New Male Sexuality* three very positive reasons for masturbation:

> ➤ Self-pleasuring is an excellent way to learn how you like to be touched and stimulated, not only on your genitals, but elsewhere as well. This information can then be given to your partner, thus enhancing your sex life together.
> ➤ Even if you're committed to partner sex as the best way of satisfying your erotic needs, there may be times when you don't have a partner or the partner you do have isn't available because of illness, fatigue, or something else. Why deny yourself sexual pleasure at such times?
> ➤ Masturbating can also help to overcome sexual problems such as erection difficulties and rapid or premature ejaculation. (I go into this in more detail in chapter 14.)

Dr. Zilbergeld also points out that the only way masturbation might be bad is when a man regularly uses it as a substitute for sex with his partner. Obviously, this would not be good for his relationship, and I'm sure the woman would feel extraneous or not important.

Here are some techniques for increasing your pleasure while masturbating:

> ➤ Using a silk scarf, cup your testicles as you touch yourself. This will give you new and different tactile sensations, and can heighten your sensitivity to touch.

➤ If she's comfortable, invite your partner to partake by having her hold your testicles or shaft and having her nestle in close to you as you touch yourself.

➤ Use a lubricant that helps to maintain a smooth flow of motion when you are pleasuring yourself.

You should feel comfortable exploring your own range of orgasmic pleasure. The techniques and types described in this chapter are meant to prompt interest and curiosity, not pressure you into anything that may feel uncomfortable.

However, since you know your own "shortcuts" to orgasm, trying some alternatives may lead to even greater ecstasy. By all means, enjoy yourself!

CHAPTER EIGHT

Her Orgasm

Going for the Unexpected

The Magical O

This chapter is about her orgasm and its potential magic. Specifically, it's about what you, as her expert lover, need to understand in order to bring her to orgasm, increase the depth of her sensation, and discover new ways that she can come.

Orgasms can be wonderful, transporting, exhausting, and relieving. And they can also happen too quickly, take forever, feel elusive, and not occur at all. Orgasms are the most natural thing in the world and yet are one of the most anxiety-provoking when they don't happen as easily as we think they should. When it comes to orgasms, we are often held hostage to unnecessary and potentially debilitating pressure:

> ➤ To perform
> ➤ To have multiple orgasms

> To come in the right sequence
> To come the way others do
> To come together

In particular, many women feel pressure to respond. "My old boyfriend was always so concerned that I 'came' that I started faking. I felt so pressured, I couldn't enjoy myself. He felt he had to give me 'one,' and whenever we headed for the bedroom, I began to feel performance anxiety. He didn't believe me when I said I was fine not coming. His need for me to come broke us up."

Just take a look at certain women's magazines, where there are endless articles asking women to evaluate themselves with questions such as "Do you consider yourself highly orgasmic or regularly orgasmic? For clitoral, vaginal, or G-spot orgasms?" As one woman put it, "Good God, how would I know? All I know is what happens with me—not what everyone else is having happen."

In a study published in *The New York Times*, when asked whether they had ever experienced orgasm during any kind of sexual activity (oral or manual stimulation, or intercourse), 26 percent of women said they regularly did not have orgasms, 23 percent of women said sex was not pleasurable, and 33 percent of men said they had persistent problems climaxing early.

What do these statistics mean? First, they show the high level of sexual dissatisfaction among American women and men. Second, they are an indirect reflection of how much pressure many women and men feel about orgasms. Indeed, an August 1999 study in the *Journal of the American Medical Association* stated that sexual dysfunction is "highly associated with negative experiences in sexual relationships and overall well-being." Both studies confirm and reinforce the psychological and emotional dimension of sexuality, which is especially strong for women. Specifically, there is a direct correlation between how nervous or uptight a woman feels and how easy or controllable an orgasm is. However, by looking at how women orgasm, from both a biological perspective and an emotional one, you will greatly increase your ability to help your partner to a satisfying, even thrilling, orgasm.

You do her and yourself a disservice by placing so much importance on the act itself, taking away the fun, the pleasure, and the potential thrill. I agree with Dr. Beverly Whipple who says that whatever we do in this arena should be "a pleasure-oriented sexual experience, not a goal-oriented experience." She also believes, and I agree, that no one has the right to tell another that his or her sexual experiences aren't valid or adequate. We all deserve to experience our own particular orgasms—however and whenever they occur.

A New Approach

So how can you approach the almighty female orgasm, take away its mythic proportions, and bring it down to its natural size and place? First, you have to become aware of the feeling of pressure and then commit to reducing it. I think the best way to do this is to take a less goal-oriented approach to making love. The direct result will be that her "Big O" will lose some of its power. Then—surprise! Often it happens in an even more intense way! A less goal-oriented approach means being open and spontaneous and resisting the focus on or expectation of orgasm. A real estate developer from Houston pointed to his frustration about too much emphasis on orgasm in this way: "With little kids running around our house, it seems like we never have enough time to take our time. We have to resort to mercy [sex] when one of us needs something now. But when we have our Saturday night or Sunday morning sex and can play, it is so different, the feel, the connection, and the orgasms."

Again, if you have already helped your partner relax, in her mind and body, then she is in a much better place to experience an orgasm. A lawyer from Pittsburgh told this story: "I had never had an orgasm with a man until my boyfriend at the time, who was this sweet, younger man, went down on me. While he was 'down there,' I thought, 'Well, nothing is going to happen.' Then he said, 'I just want to do this—I love eating you.' So I figured, well, let him go ahead if he's enjoying himself. Ten minutes later—*boom!* Out of left field I had my first orgasm. Now I realize it was because I had just totally relaxed and not been tied to what was supposed to happen. I knew the feel from my hand and vibrator but it was like I needed that to get the nerve pathways opened up to know what to feel and expect. After that I had them regularly from oral sex."

Another woman related this experience: "My lover and I were spending a stolen afternoon together, and I just sort of drifted mentally as he played with me clitorally. It was a lazy, quiet day and I was so relaxed by what he was doing, and all of a sudden, the orgasm snuck up on me. It was the first time I'd ever had one honestly with a man." In both cases, these women let go of any expectation or plan and were pleasantly surprised by their orgasms.

Another key that will enable you to help her orgasm is to remember how and why foreplay is so essential to women. Most women orgasm through manual and oral stimulation. Men generally prefer to "wait" until intercourse to come. If you approach the whole idea of foreplay as a vital component of sex, not a mere stage before intercourse, then you may feel more engaged in getting her where she wants to go instead of focusing on where you want to go next. A bartender from New York said, "Yeah, I love it when she comes—like no kidding, I'm a guy, I love results. But the even bigger turn-on for me is getting her there and knowing I can make my wife feel *that* good. It is the ride that does it for me, not just the finish line." Since most men reach orgasm more quickly than women, it's up to you to concentrate on her first. Though of course she wants you to come, you may need to put her pleasure before yours. If you incorporate this more altruistic attitude into your approach to sex, I guarantee she will return the favor in triplicate.

SECRET FROM LOU'S ARCHIVES

According to noted sex therapists and authors Dr. Michael Riskin and Anita Baker-Riskin, most men orgasm in the first three minutes of intercourse, but can learn to control their climax for up to seven minutes. A woman, if she's going to orgasm, typically takes more time to come. However, some women can orgasm within three to seven minutes of stimulation.

Getting her to that place of no return is 95 percent determination and dedication—and just 5 percent talent. The talent portion is very straightforward and simply requires that you know the topography of the area and your partner's likes and dislikes.

Timing

As I said, since most women can have or are used to having orgasms through oral or manual stimulation, they tend to come before intercourse. This is not a rule, it's merely a standard operating procedure that most men and women use when it comes to sex. However, you may want to consider shaking up this sex formula by asking, "Who wants to go first?" You may be pleasantly surprised by what you discover. For example, a number of women in my seminars put off coming until they are penetrated. An architect from Dallas said, "The more aroused I get, the more I want him inside of me." Another seminar attendee stated, "There are times when I absolutely crave having him inside of me. I may have already had an orgasm from being eaten, but I don't feel complete until he's inside me." Another woman said it more succinctly. "Oh God, sometimes I just grab him and say, 'Now, I want you in me now!'" My point here is twofold. First, although the exact trigger for the orgasm may be your fingers or your lips on her, the feeling or experience of the orgasm *extends* beyond that time. Second, for many women it's your penetration of her that *completes* the feeling of the orgasm.

Another aspect of timing that you might want to keep in mind is the very consistent biological fact that women cycle. Sometimes her cycle asserts itself as a wonderful feat of nature, making her want you unexpectedly and intensely. Other times you may want to curse Mother Nature, as your partner seems distant, irritable, or just plain uninterested in sex. By now, I'm sure you all have heard of PMS (premenstrual syndrome), during which some women suffer drastic mood swings, while others experience no real symptoms. But, gentlemen, you need to understand that these swings of temperament (and sexual readiness) are very much part of her biology. Sometimes not being in the mood simply may be about being tired and grumpy, but sometimes it may have an even closer relationship to where she is in her cycle.

The obvious sign of a woman's cycle is her monthly period. Between puberty and menopause, healthy women menstruate on a cyclic basis, every twenty-four to thirty-two days. Although most people are aware only of the days of a woman's menstrual flow (her period), these days are only the most obvious stage in the complete reproductive cycle. Essentially, the first phase of a woman's cycle, called the follicular phase, lasts up to twelve days, beginning with the first day of her period. During this time she sheds the lining of her uterus, causing bleeding. Most women bleed for three to five days and some experience cramping—in differing degrees. This is usually a good time for sex for two reasons: (1) If she has an orgasm, it may alleviate some cramping of the uterus, and (2) there is a very reduced chance of her getting pregnant. At the end of this phase, endorphins peak and increased estrogen gives her ample vaginal lubrication. Her endorphins are highest in the morning.

Some women and men experience uneasiness about having sex during the woman's period. In some cases, this reluctance is related to a taboo that goes back at least to the Old Testament, when a woman's blood was considered "unclean" and it was therefore "bad" to have sex at this time. Even today, many women prefer to avoid sex during their period because they find it messy or uncomfortable. Women also worry that men will be turned off by the sight, feel, or smell of blood. Some of the messiness is unavoidable, as condoms and blood, in particular, don't mix well, creating vaginal dryness and possibly causing a tear in the condom. A possible solution is to use Instead, a vaginal cup that acts as a diaphragm and holds blood-flow in check until it is removed.

Men have also voiced their worries about it being "all right" or safe to have sex at this time. My advice to you, gentlemen, is this: If you don't mind, you should encourage her to be open and receptive to sex. You may want to tell her that you don't mind her bleeding. Such an attitude can create a wonderful feeling of acceptance.

The next phase is the ovulatory phase, which lasts for three days, between days 13 and 15. This is when she's in full baby-making mode. An indicator for most women is seeing the egg-white-like mucus in their secretions. An egg moves into one (or two) of her fallopian tubes, and her cervical mucus thins, making it easier for sperm to reach the egg. Some experts say women produce more testosterone in this phase, creating a stronger sex drive in these three days.

The luteal phase takes place in days 16 to 30. If she gets pregnant in the ovulatory phase, this is the time for the fertilized egg to respond and grow. She produces progesterone, a hormone that thickens the uterine lining and inhibits endorphins that would throw off proper fertilization. As you may be aware, at this time of the month she may feel irritable because of the cryptic yet real PMS, which usually ends with the onset of bleeding.

Now, gentlemen, when it comes to your timing and how it affects her, I have heard, again and again, cries of frustration. Most of you first learn to orgasm by masturbating, which, of course, is perfectly natural. However, because masturbation is all about you, and you know just what to do in order to bring yourself to climax, you tend to come quickly. Consequently, if you're used to coming quickly, then it's hard to break the habit when you're aroused with a woman. The nerve pathways have already been established, and you have to consciously learn how to control your timing. Unfortunately, "quick" has become too often confused with "premature," further offending you guys. That's why, in chapter 7, I discussed how men can learn to control timing issues.

> ### Secret from Lou's Archives
> *The definition of premature ejaculation is when a man ejaculates before he wants to.*

It's on the Chromosome

I feel it's necessary to say yet again that men and women are different, and this difference is very clear in the arena of the orgasm. Both men and women have two separate nerve pathways for orgasms, the pudendal and the pelvic. It is because there are these two pathways that men and women can experience climax differently.

Specifically, as Dr. Lonnie Barbach says in her book *For Each Other*, "The pudendal nerve supplies the clitoris, PC muscle, inner lips, skin of the perineum, and skin surrounding the anus. The pelvic nerve goes to the vagina and the uterus. The fact that the pudendal nerve has considerably more sensory fibers than the pelvic nerve and contains the kind of nerve endings [that] are very sensitive to touch may be responsible for the higher percentage of women being more responsive to clitoral stimulation. The two-nerve theory may account for more than differences between vaginally induced and clitorally induced orgasms. Because these two nerves partially overlap in the spinal cord, it may also account for blended orgasms which are both clitorally and vaginally induced."

In women, clitoral orgasms go along the pudendal nerve pathway; vaginal and G-spot orgasms go along the pelvic nerve pathway. With clitoral orgasms there is a pulling-up sensation, and with vaginal and G-spot there is a pushing-down sensation. For men, the stimulation of the penis is along the pudendal pathway, and the male G-spot/prostate stimulation is along the pelvic pathway. Now, isn't it nice to get that straightened out?

SECRET FROM LOU'S ARCHIVES

Blended orgasms are when both sexual nerve pathways are stimulated at the same time: for women the clitoris and the G-spot, and for men the penis and the prostate.

Types of Female Orgasms

Did you know that women can orgasm in at least ten different ways? In general, most women experience an orgasm in three areas: the clitoris, vagina, and G-spot. But an orgasm can originate anywhere from the clitoris to the nipples—sometimes even a head massage can create an orgasm. Women are so connected to their minds that with the proper arousal techniques, anything may then stimulate the area of orgasm.

I always like to encourage variety in all forms of sexual intimacy. My purpose in sharing this information with you is to let you know what is possible and, if you are interested, encourage you and others to push back the boundaries of self-imposed limitations to pleasure. I am *not* suggesting you do anything you don't want to do—I want you to do only what makes you comfortable. As with any buffet of ideas, sometimes we want merely hors d'oeuvres or dessert. Sometimes we long for the comfort-food entrée and sometimes we want the whole-meal deal. The following outlines what women have experienced and shared, and I share it here with you.

There are ten ways or places in which women have experienced orgasm:

1. Clitoral
2. G-spot and the AFE (anterior fornix erotic) zone
3. Vaginal/cervical
4. U-spot/Urethral
5. Breast/nipple
6. Mouth
7. Anal

8. Blended/Fusion
9. Zone
10. Fantasy

Clitoral Orgasm

The clitoral orgasm is the most common, and often the strongest, orgasm in women. Indeed, the majority of women need some form of clitoral stimulation to reach orgasm. This stimulation can occur manually, orally, with a dildo or vibrator, or during intercourse. Some women like light, soft touches to become aroused, followed by more intense or fast pressure. Other women prefer to be touched only with soft or only with hard pressure. As always, ask what she likes or watch her touch herself.

Keep in mind that the majority of women come through manual or oral stimulation of the clitoris, not penetration. If a woman prefers vaginal penetration while being stimulated clitorally, the female-superior position provides the most direct control. (See chapter 11 for more information regarding specific positions.)

Secret from Lou's Archives

The clitoris is the only feature of the human body whose function is solely for pleasure.

G-Spot and the
AFE (Anterior Fornix Erotic) Zone Orgasm

Female orgasms during intercourse without direct clitoral stimulation are often associated with what is commonly known as the G-spot. I'm assuming, gentlemen, that you remember the guide I provided you earlier and can now locate her G-spot. For those of you who need a quick refresher, the G-spot (named in honor of German physician Ernst Grafenberg, who first noted the tissue distinction) is an area approximately the size of a dime, located about two-thirds the length of your middle finger inside the vaginal entrance, above the pubic bone, felt through the front wall (tummy side). When stimulated, the G-spot can enlarge to the size of a quarter. For some women, continuous stimulation can lead to a powerful orgasm. For others, G-spot stimulation is unpleasant. And just so you know, there are still other women for whom the much sought after G-spot simply doesn't exist at all.

Ever since the G-spot was brought to public light in 1982 with the publishing of *The G-Spot* by Alice Kahn Ladas, Dr. Beverly Whipple, and John D. Perry, it has been controversial. Does it exist or not? Well, for some it does, and is exceedingly pleasurable when stimulated, and for others, there is little or no sensation. This makes sense since this area above the anterior (tummy side) of the vaginal wall is considered to be vestigial tissue from genital evolution. Yet the G-spot is hardly new. It has been known to other cultures in the past since the first century A.D. The Chinese called this erotically sensitive area "the black pearl," and the Japanese referred to it as "the skin of the earthworm." It's also been called the female prostate.

Not surprisingly, there are a number of misconceptions surrounding the G-spot. Dr. Beverly Whipple points out that the G-spot is not in the vaginal wall, but felt through it, and therefore requires more direct and firm pressure to stimulate it. Because of its position, many women have trouble finding their G-spot.

It's easiest to find when the woman is aroused enough that the area is engorged with blood and so can be felt more readily. Then, as Dr. Whipple suggests, she can squat and reach up inside herself to locate it. Lying down isn't the easiest way for her to find it, and often women's fingers are not long enough to reach the area. Another misconception involves female ejaculation. G-spot stimulation does not necessarily lead to ejaculation, though it can and has. But it's not required.

Stimulate it using your finger in a "come here" motion, with a specifically shaped dildo/vibrator, or during penetration. The best intercourse positions for G-spot stimulation are:

1. Rear entry
2. Woman superior—either facing toward you or, often better, facing your feet
3. Male superior—with the woman putting her legs over your arms or shoulders. In this position a man with a prow-shaped penis actually has a better chance of stimulating the G-spot because of his curvature. Some men with straighter erections use a strong arching-back position to attain that same angle.

The AFE zone is an area so named by Malaysian sexologist Dr. Chua Chee Ann. It is a spongy area of the vagina and, like the G-spot, is located on the tummy side, but farther up the vaginal canal, closer to the cervix. Whereas the G-spot is a defined area, the AFE is a longer, less defined area. However, the AFE responds to very gentle, light strokes, not the firm strokes used in G-spot stimulation. In his study of 193 women in Malaysia, Chua states that all but eleven "reported vaginal lubrication and increased erotic pleasure, and often orgasms, from stimulation of this zone." However, as Dr. Herbert Otto notes, this may be proportional to the number of women who can orgasm from G-spot stimulation, as Dr. Chua's population was very specific.

Vaginal/Cervical Orgasm

This form of orgasm uses the same nerve pathways as the G-spot: the hypogastric and pelvic. Now that you are aware that the clitoris is much larger than it appears, its legs extending alongside the vaginal walls, you probably understand that women can experience an orgasm vaginally.

The essential truth about vaginal/cervical orgasms is that they are not as precise as the other locations. The vaginal orgasm involves the barrel of the vagina as well as the cervix (the mouth of the uterus), and may involve even the uterus itself. There is a major physiological difference between clitoral stimulation and vaginal/cervical stimulation. With clitoral stimulation, there is an expanding and ballooning of the vaginal barrel and a lifting of the uterus back into the body, which prepares the vagina for the penis's entry. With vaginal stimulation, the uterus does not elevate. It pushes down into the vagina. As Dr. Herbert Otto says, "This orgasm takes place at the peak of stimulation of the vagina and cervix and expands from there. Sexologists Whipple and Perry call this process the A-frame effect."

With the approach of this orgasm there is a bearing-down effect and the vaginal opening becomes more relaxed. At the point of orgasm, the penis (or any object used for stimulation) sometimes is pushed out by the strength of these contractions. Also, it's the pelvic and hypogastric nerve systems that power the vaginal orgasm. Since the pudendal nerve system is the pathway for clitoral orgasms, it makes sense that the two would feel different!

One woman described the vaginal orgasm in this way: "When my boyfriend gives me head, the orgasm has the sensation of pulling up and into myself. But when we do it doggy style, the orgasm has a much broader feeling. It seems to flow outside my body. It makes me want to arch and bear down."

For some women a deep and constant pressure on the cervix can lead to orgasm. Some women who enjoy fisting say they enjoy having the cervix held.

SECRETS FROM LOU'S ARCHIVES

Also known as CAT, the Coital Alignment Technique requires the alignment of two parts of the genitals: her clitoris and the pubic bone region at the base of your penis. Your pubic area is cushioned by fat tissue, so it isn't just hard bone. If you're deep enough inside, and maintain constant contact between her clitoris and your pubic bone, she can achieve an orgasm when you use a gentle rocking motion. In this way, you maintain contact with her clitoris with the added stimulation of penetration.

U-Spot/Urethral Orgasm

Like the clitoris, stimulating the urethra is also very pleasurable for some women, which makes sense since the urethra (and its paraurethral glands) is surrounded on three sides by the clitoris and is located between the clitoral glans and the vaginal opening (introitus). So the urethra, where urine exits a woman's body, is just below the clitoris and above the vaginal entry.

SECRET FROM LOU'S ARCHIVES

The majority of women report the most regular orgasms with oral sex or manual stimulation.

Breast/Nipple Orgasm

This is not a Ripley's Believe It or Not—I promise. Some women have reported that the licking and manual stimulation of their breasts and nipples can get them so excited that they come. I think it's a testament to the sensitivity of our skin and our minds!

Dr. Herbert Otto describes the breast orgasm as happening at the peak of stimulation when the sensation seems to radiate from the breasts. He claims (and supports) that it is the second most common form of orgasm among women, which seems especially true of women from our grandmothers' and mothers' generations. Women of an earlier time were much more likely to be afraid to "go all the way" because of the moral restrictions of their day or a fear of getting pregnant. Instead, they enjoyed a lot of heavy "petting" and "necking" sessions, in which they had breast or nipple orgasms.

One man told me, "I had one girlfriend who had extremely sensitive breasts. Until I heard about a breast orgasm, I just thought she was making it up. I couldn't touch them enough." Statistics support the evidence of breast orgasms, although the frequency is in dispute: Masters and Johnson report a 1 percent occurrence; the Kinsey report gives the same 1 percent; and in Dr. Herbert Otto's study group, 29 percent of the women had experienced a breast orgasm at one time or another.

Also, many women state there is a direct connection between stimulation of their breasts and nipples and feelings of arousal in their genitals. For other women, there is no direct connection, but the stimulation does add to their overall orgasmic build. For others, it is bothersome to have their breasts played with. Nursing mothers have often experienced orgasms when breast-feeding. These are referred to as suckling orgasms, and in all but one case, Dr. Otto cites that this kind of stimulation during nursing was accompanied by uterine, vaginal, or cervical contractions.

Mouth Orgasm

If we understand that as babies we experience our entire universe through our mouths, then maybe it's not as hard for us to imagine actually experiencing an orgasm through our mouths. Women have reported experiencing these starting in the lips and spreading out, and they would often be triggered by stimulation of lips, tongue, roof of the mouth, and the throat—*without any genital stimulation.* Some women experience a mouth orgasm through kissing, or while giving oral sex to a man. Other women describe the sensation as a whole-body orgasm accompanied by uterine and vaginal contractions.

When I first asked a seminar group if they had ever been with someone who had had a mouth orgasm, one man looked at me like I had five eyes, and another man looked taken aback and said softly, "Yeah, yeah I did." According to Dr. Herbert Otto's research, of his 205-member research group, 20 percent had experienced a mouth orgasm. They do exist.

The best technique is great, long kissing. Use more lip play, sucking on the lips. Dr. Mantak Chia suggests taking your partner's upper lip into your mouth and running your tongue along the inside of the upper lip.

One woman reported, "I don't know what he did, but he did this tongue thing and my knees buckled. I then asked him to do it again. Same result. I think it was all in the lip sucking."

Anal Orgasm

I like to think of anal play as the new frontier—similar to how oral sex used to be treated before it too became "normal" instead of associated with things "dirty." One thing I've noticed in the past few years of giving seminars is that more and more women and men are asking questions about anal sex. Now you can take this as a gentle suggestion to try or not—your body, your choice. However, the men and women who have added this option to their sexual repertoire say it can create more fun, spice, and, often, a lot of sexual pleasure.

Women have to be comfortable being penetrated, so I suggest first using a clean, well-lubricated finger to test the waters. Once she is relaxed and begins to respond to the stimulation, you can experiment with other playthings.

There is a physiological reason anal penetration can be difficult: There are actually two anal sphincters—one under voluntary control, so you can consciously relax it, and another under involuntary control, which requires dilation with a finger or toy to be relaxed.

Blended/Fusion Orgasm

The blended orgasm, as named by Whipple and Perry in 1982, is when more than one area of the body is stimulated at the same time, increasing the overall intensity and expanding the orgasmic sensation. As an example, stimulation of the clitoris becomes greater when combined with breast or G-spot stimulation. This is understandable since we know from research that the two areas are enervated by the two separate nerve systems—the pudendal for the clitoris, and the pelvic for the G-spot. With more nerves involved, there is broader sensation.

Zone Orgasm

Zone orgasms vary among individuals because they occur in parts of people's bodies that are rarely associated with stimulation and orgasm. For example, people—both men and women—have experienced orgasms from having their necks licked or their fingers sucked, or their thigh/groin area stroked.

Fantasy Orgasm

A fantasy orgasm is described as the ability to orgasm by fantasy alone—with no genital stimulation. Suffice it to say that this is likely the one type of orgasm that most people would like to be able to create at will, and there are probably only a chosen few who can. It differs from fantasy aiding and abetting orgasms, which is a common practice. Fantasy orgasm was documented in the lab in 1992 by Whipple, Ogden, and Komisaruk, and showed that the body's physiological response to an imagery-induced orgasm was no different from one induced by physical stimulation. The same increase in blood pressure, heart rate, pupil diameter, and pain threshold were reported.

SECRET FROM LOU'S ARCHIVES

Some women report that all-over body stimulation can lead to an orgasm. Now, they may feel the actual orgasm in the pelvis, but it is your roving hands, fingers, and tongue that build the sensation.

Female Ejaculation

As I noted in chapter 6, when some women orgasm, they will also feel a gush of fluid. This is not urine. This is an expression of fluid from the paraurethral glands. There are approximately 150 Skene's glands ducts (also called paraurethral glands) that lead into the urethra—"para" meaning that these glands are on the sides of the urethra. In studies performed by Francisco Cabello Santamaria, a Spanish sex researcher, urine samples were collected from women before and after stimulation without a male partner, and he found that there was PSA—prostate specific antigen—in the urine post-stimulation. This is another reason to refer to the G-spot area as the female prostate.

Some women ejaculate regularly, some occasionally, and some never—although because the amount of ejaculate is usually so small (2 to 3 ccs), it might just seem like normal vaginal secretions and therefore not be obvious.

> ### SECRET FROM LOU'S ARCHIVES
>
> *Both men and women have love muscles—PC muscles—that if toned, can enhance orgasm. And like any muscle, these can be exercised, and one need not go to the gym. When you tighten your PC muscle, your penis will jump up and down. Or try placing a washcloth on your erect penis and doing penis lift-ups. A woman can tighten her PC muscles by stopping the flow of her urine.*

One man from my seminar recalled how when he began stimulating his partner's nipples, she became "phenomenally wet." "She just started flowing, soaking through not only the sheets but the mattress pad as well," he explained, "and then when I went down on her, there was this squishing sound— made more obvious because there wasn't all that much to listen to down there." This story goes to show you that some women respond to the slightest touch.

Creating an orgasm is just one test of a man's lovemaking skill, though it is often used as a barometer to measure whether or not the sex was "good." Some people even claim they really haven't made love if one or both of them don't come. Instead of judging your lovemaking, enjoy it. An orgasm is meant to delight both of you, not be a barometer of your pleasure. Your ability to *share* pleasure with your partner is a truer test of your lovemaking skill.

CHAPTER NINE

Manual Finesse

Let Your Hands Delight Her

Her Action Spots

I call this chapter and the next the finesse chapters—where the men who want to be expert lovers learn to stand out from the crowd. Although we've discussed orgasms and the power of touching her erogenous zones in arousing her, we haven't yet focused on her specific action spots. Referring to some of these techniques, one woman asked, "Couldn't you please tell me where you are having the men's seminar so I can wait outside the door and drop my hanky?" It's not the picking up of the hanky that she was after, though that would have been a nice opener. What this woman was really looking for was a man who knew his stuff and was confident enough to know there is always more to know.

There's no doubt about it: Most women love to be touched genitally. In the same way that you enjoy being stroked, coddled, and sometimes even squeezed, women become gloriously aroused when your fingers and hands pay attention to them.

Your typical woman enjoys, and sometimes relies on, genital touching to get her wet, and ready for penetration or orgasm. You will learn techniques and approaches that will make a lady more comfortable, especially in asking her what she wants when she's not sure what that is. We women are thankful when you ask what we like, but sometimes, gentlemen, even *we* don't know. A seminar attendee from San Diego, who is now in her mid-thirties, said that it was her husband, whom she'd met when she was just out of college, who taught her about her own body. Growing up in a conservative Catholic family where it was not okay to talk about sex, never mind learn about her own body, she didn't even know what felt pleasurable until her husband touched her. The key here is that women need your participation and may welcome it more than you ever expected.

SECRET FROM LOU'S ARCHIVES

According to Science *magazine, a physical skill takes six hours to sink in. After learning a physical skill, such as a variation on your golf stroke or a variation of your cunnilingus stroke, it takes six hours for the info to be stored in permanent memory. But interrupt the storage process by learning another new skill and that first lesson could be erased.*

To some women, your hand or mouth on her genitals is more intimate than sexual intercourse. She is allowing you access to the most intimate and private part of herself, and she is doing so in a receiving position, which makes her feel vulnerable. Many women have been culturally programmed to be the giver, not the receiver. Men have told me that it is very important for them to realize that this most intimate of acts can take women some getting used to. However, if a woman isn't comfortable being touched genitally, you should respect her likes and dislikes.

In terms of what works best physically, there is truly a buffet of moves and ideas to consider when touching a woman's genitals. Some women prefer that you start out with a soft, barely-touching tapping on the clitoris. Other women don't want you to go near the "lovebud" until they are much more stimulated. On the other end of the continuum are the women who love very firm, direct, and fast touching directly on the clitoris and all around the area. Others prefer a very specific repetitive, subtle touch. Again, the best guide for you is her. If you already know the oral moves that work for her, try mimicking them as best you can with moistened fingers. Your fingers will create a different sensation, yet you will still have the memory to draw on. A musician from Seattle said, "Learning what a woman likes is like learning to play a completely new instrument. You have working knowledge of the chords for x, but this is y, and it takes practice, practice, practice to feel comfortable and get to where you know what you're doing."

SECRET FROM LOU'S ARCHIVES

Although watching a woman masturbate will definitely give you ideas, you will still not be touching her as she touches herself. Instead, the best directions will come from her guiding your hand.

Getting Started

The absolute key to perfecting your ability to arouse her to heights of pleasure with your hands and fingers is knowing how and where to touch her. Without a doubt, if you don't know where you're going, you won't know what to do once you've arrived. With that in mind, I have provided you with another guide so that you will not feel like you're lost in the wilderness.

Before letting your fingers do the talking, please wash your hands. There are two main reasons. First, the mucosal tissue of a woman's genital area is extremely delicate, and second, the natural salt in the sweat of your fingers can make that area feel like it's burning. And trust me, if that happens, she's not feeling good. The solution is to wash your hands and get all soap or cleanser off. Lick your fingers if there is no water around or use a diaper wipe.

Watch your nails. As one woman said, "Man, when he hits me with his nail, all I can think of is when he's going to hit me again. There is no way I can relax after that." This is a clear signal that at no time will a manicure be more appreciated. A manicure is, without a doubt, the sign of a well-groomed, confident man. Ladies do look at your hands, not just for the urban-legend reasons associated with genital dimension, but also to imagine what your hands would feel like on their bodies. If they see jagged, bit-off nails, your appeal factor may drop significantly. And no woman wants a man with dirty fingernails to touch her!

Use lotion if you have or tend to have rough hands. Remember, a woman's skin is not as thick as yours. Calluses may scratch her and will feel rough against her skin. One woman told me, "My husband works with his hands, and he used to scratch my skin when he touched me. Now he knows that a foot massage is the best thing to relax me and get me in the mood, so when I walk in the room with the lotion, he knows he's likely to 'get some.' I get my foot massage, he softens his big ol' rough hands, and things just happen from there. Brilliant, huh?"

SECRET FROM LOU'S ARCHIVES

To test if your nails are short enough and won't accidentally nick her, test their length by curving your finger downward like a fishhook and rub the gum area below your lower front teeth. If you can feel your nail, she will, too. You might consider trimming them. Remember, your fingers are gaining access into and onto the most sensitive areas of a woman's body. She won't be able to enjoy herself if your fingers cause her discomfort.

Her Genitalia

I am presuming you're familiar with the nuts and bolts of this region, but I thought you might welcome some extra information so you *really* understand what you're touching, where women want you to touch them, and in some cases, how you might want to touch them for her maximum benefit and your maximum results. Let me be frank here. It is not unusual for men to be found rooting around in the dark in this area. A woman's body is a bit mysterious—ofttimes as much for us as for you. Most noticeable of the physical differences between men and women is the fact that male genitals are in full view, front and center, while some of the most important parts of a woman's genitalia can be seen only if the woman spreads her legs. And this applies only to the external genitalia. She also has internal genitalia.

Secret from Lou's Archives

Men have a gazillion names for their genitals, some more privately known than others. Women typically have one: "down there."

Despite the differences, a woman's genitalia in many ways correspond to your own. In fact, up until six to eight weeks there is no difference between the XX (female) embryo and XY (male) embryo. We all start out female in utero. It is during the embryonic stage, at about eight weeks, that the production of the male hormone testosterone starts. The addition of testosterone turns the potential labia into a scrotum and the potential clitoris into the head of a penis.

Vulva

The entire area of the external female genital anatomy is called the vulva. The mons pubis is an area of fatty tissue that forms a soft mound over the pubic bone. The mons is covered by skin and pubic hair. The labia majora (often called the outer lips) extend down from the mons to below the vaginal opening. These consist of a fold of skin on each side filled with fatty tissue, sweat and oil glands, and nerve endings. The two outer lips usually meet and cover the urinary and vaginal opening

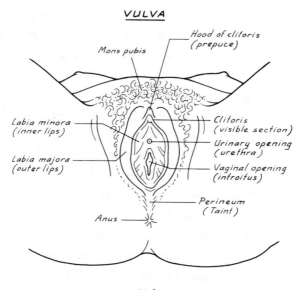

Vulva

when the woman is not aroused or has her legs together. The labia minora (the inner lips) are inside the outer lips and extend from just above the clitoris to below the vaginal opening. These two folds of skin are thinner and, while they do not have pubic hair or fatty tissue, they do have more nerve endings than the outer lips. Even though they are called "inner," it is not unusual for them to protrude beyond the outer lips.

SECRET FROM LOU'S ARCHIVES

In 50 percent of women the inner labia extend past the outer labia.

The color of the genitalia varies among women (pink, red, purple, and black are all normal) and may change during arousal. Just as men's genitalia differ in size, shape, and color, so do the labia minora and majora vary in size, shape, and degree of sensitivity. The head (or glans) of the clitoris is just below the point where the inner lips meet at the top, and is covered with a small fold of skin, the prepuce (equivalent to the foreskin/prepuce in an uncircumcised man). The clitoris is a small, sensitive organ at the upper end of the vulva, made up of tissue, blood vessels, and nerves. Hooded by skin, it looks like a tiny dot to the naked eye, but, in fact, most of the clitoris is internal, not external. According to research done by Dr. Helen O'Connell, Urological Surgeon at the Royal Melbourne Hospital in Australia, "the external tip of the clitoris, or glans, connects on the inside to a pyramid-shaped mass of erectile tissue, far larger than previously described. The 'body' of the clitoris, which connects to the glans, is about as big as the first joint of your thumb. It has two arms (or legs) up to nine centimeters long that flare backwards into the body, lying just a few millimeters from the ends of the muscles that run up the inside of the thigh. Also extending from the body of the clitoris, and filling the space between the arms, are two bulbs, one on each side of the vaginal cavity."

During sexual stimulation, the pelvic region fills with blood and the clitoral "tip" swells and becomes firm. This is why after you have stimulated the area, a woman's clitoris is harder to find and doesn't seem as prominent. Like the penis, it has engorged with blood, become erect, and lifted under the prepuce. Since the "clitoral legs" run underneath the labia, any stimulation to the urethral, vaginal, or anal areas will indirectly stimulate the clitoral body as well. This forking of the clitoral legs down and under either side of the labia explains why for some women the most pleasurable use of a vibrator isn't directly on the clitoral bud. They say it is too intense. Rather, holding it against the side of the labia, pressing on the fatty tissue of the outer labia, reaches a broader field of the clitoris with less intense vibration.

Just below the clitoral tip is the very small urinary opening, the urethra, and below that is the entrance to the vagina. When you see how close these two openings are, it is easier to understand why so many women experience urinary tract infection after having sex. The infection is a result of new and different bacteria being introduced into the urethra due to the rubbing and thrusting action of intercourse.

Below the vaginal opening and where the labia meet is a small area of smooth, usually hairless skin called the perineum. And below that is the anus. This entire perineal area can be very sensitive to stimulation (as it often is in men). Sometimes it's called the taint—"'tain't one, 'tain't the other." One seminar attendee called it the Veranda, and suggests sucking on it or massaging it with your fingers. Some women love the sensation!

Vagina

Let me start this way: You cannot see the vagina, as it is inside the woman's body. This can be confusing. As I've just described, the vulva and outer labia are visible with the naked eye, but the vagina is not. It's also true that the vagina changes in size and shape, according to the stage of a woman's arousal.

The vagina begins in a constricted state, and when a woman is stimulated mentally, visually, or physically, she will start lubricating within thirty seconds. Just because she is lubricated, however, does not mean that she is "ready" for penetration—whether with your fingers or your penis. Instead, the biggest indicator that a woman is relaxed is her breathing. The deeper it becomes, the more relaxed she is.

> ### SECRET FROM LOU'S ARCHIVES
>
> *The vagina lubricates and relaxes, allowing for deeper penetration and deposit of the sperm near the cervix. Mother Nature knew what she was doing in the design category. The penis and vagina make an amazingly great fit! Not that I had to tell you.*

In its unaroused state, the vagina is a tube about three to four inches long, which is why an average, five-inch erect penis feels like enough for most women. The vagina is made of muscle and textured on the inner surface with rugae, or little ridges, and is covered on the inside walls with a mucosal surface—similar to the lining of the mouth. This is the surface that produces the vaginal lubrication. Unless a woman is sexually aroused, the vaginal walls touch each other. Any woman who has inserted a tampon knows this—it feels much tighter than when she is aroused and a penis is inside of her. When a woman becomes aroused, the walls of the vagina produce a slippery liquid and balloon open so that a penis will fit inside. And, of course, they can stretch even further during childbirth.

The degree of a woman's tightness is related to the tightness of the pubococcygeal (PC) muscles at the opening of her vaginal barrel. (The rest of the vaginal barrel expands to accommodate the penis.) The appearance and texture of vaginal secretions vary throughout each monthly reproductive cycle, as conditions inside the vagina respond to changes in hormonal levels. This will account for changes in discharge and the woman's natural lubrication. Menopausal and postmenopausal women also have variances in their lubrication.

As I mentioned in chapter 2, other factors also affect a woman's ability to self-lubricate, including alcohol and medications, which can dehydrate the body. In general, a woman's vagina is one of the most self-maintaining and self-cleansing areas of the body. Semen naturally flows out of it, and with regular bathing and cleansing of the labial areas, it requires little else. Unless directed otherwise by a physician, there is no need for women to douche. Besides being unnecessary, douching can be harmful and is the number-one cause of bladder and vaginal infections in the United States. As an ob-gyn once said, "Women who douche pay my mortgage."

The G-Spot

The G-spot was first recognized by the gynecologist Ernst Grafenberg. But it was Dr. John D. Perry and Dr. Beverly Whipple who named it the G-spot, after Dr. Grafenberg. The G-spot is yet another non-visible part of a woman's anatomy. It is located in the tissue above the vaginal wall surrounding the urethra, the tummy side. An area of soft, often ridgy tissue, the G-spot is about the size of a dime when unstimulated and when stimulated swells to the size of a quarter.

Some women are capable of orgasm from direct stimulation of this area, which may result in ejaculation. As I said in the previous chapter, the source of the female ejaculation is the paraurethral glands, which are located on either side of the urethra, which is why some people think that the fluid is urine. The paraurethral glands act like a salivary gland, squirting or expressing fluid when stimulated. All women have this urethral sponge or G-spot, but not all respond in the same way to its stimulation. Some women find their G-spot feels no different from other parts of the vaginal barrel; for others, stimulating this dime-size area can send them through the rafters. Again, the difficulty can be in locating it. I know a sex therapist who even had difficulty locating her own G-spot, despite being very comfortable with her body and aware of all her parts. She had to have her partner show her where it was. Truly, in some cases, it's like trying to find the Holy Grail, but if you are patient and sensitive, between the two of you, I trust you will be able to find her G-spot.

Positions

There are five main positions for manual play, and each position has moves best suited to that position. As with any new idea or technique, use the suggestions below, adding to or incorporating them into what you already do. You may want to refer to the diagrams to get the full benefit. Like dance steps, however, it's hard to know how to move until you actually see how it's done. In all of these positions, you can maintain good body contact, which is key.

> ### Secret from Lou's Archives
>
> *For all moves, start with a big motion, go to a smaller, more concentrated motion, and build from slow to quick tempo. Moving too quickly and firmly may numb or hurt her. Most women are not ready for that kind of instant intensity. Let the intensity build.*

The Classics—Positions 1 and 5

These are probably the easiest and simplest positions in which to initiate manual stimulation and yet they are also the ones that foster the most bad habits. One woman in a seminar said, "If he did that 'staying in one spot right on top of my clit' for a second longer, I thought I would have to kill him." Another woman added, "Where are the directions that call for 'find it and rub furiously'?"

One of the reasons these popular positions have garnered bad habits comes from the fact that you've been fed a bill of goods by the adult porn industry through its videos and magazines. Their goal is to sell. They are not thinking of your personal pleasure, and they are certainly not thinking about what pleases women. They are focusing on action, whether or not the action works. In real life, intense rubbing too soon or at all

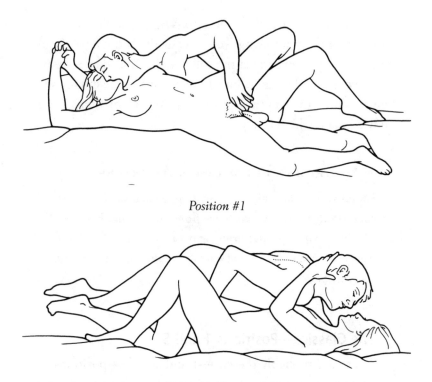

Position #1

Position #5

is often a sure way to cause your partner discomfort, not pleasure.

Gentlemen, the good news is that you can easily learn how to please your partner by simply adjusting the motion of your fingers and hand, your tempo, and your degree of pressure. After applying lubricant or moistening with saliva, you can use your fingers or the entire palm of your hand in a circular motion to (1) evenly spread the lubricant and (2) use a broader overall motion to warm things up in this area. It's best to start with the broad strokes and reduce the area of stimulation as sensation builds.

In both of these positions, it's a good idea to rest the heel of your hand (and the wrist) on her mons pubis, the area where the pubic hair starts, and gently apply pressure. You should feel the pubic bone underneath the base of your wrist. This will also help stabilize your wrist and arm. In other words, keeping your arm and hand in the air will tire you out more quickly and affect the overall fine-motion mobility of your fingers. With your wrist anchored, you can deliver more of the gentle circles and back-and-forth motions that women prefer.

These are also the manual positions that lend themselves best to kissing and snuggling. You can also use the index and middle fingers in a straight up-and-down and/or circular motion with the clitoral ridge and tip between the two of them. Often a woman uses this technique to stimulate herself. You can also use the palm of your hand.

If your penis is inside of her while you are touching her, try pulsing your PC muscle to make your penis pump. One woman remarked, "He does this penis-lifting thing when he is in me from behind that feels so good. It makes me all stretched and full of him." A male seminar attendee noted that "most women respond to this move by tightening inside, while the man moves his fingers back and forth."

IT TAKES 3

This move will work best if you are behind or on top of her. To start, use three fingers held together to curve over the inner and outer lips. Keep your index and fourth fingers on the outer

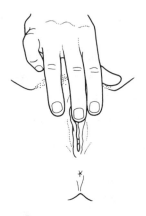

It Takes 3, Step 1

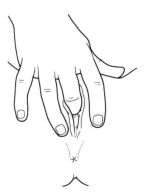

It Takes 3, Step 2

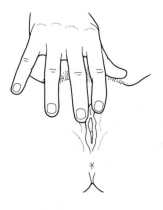

It Takes 3, Step 3

edges of her outer labia, with your middle finger positioned on top of the entire clitoral ridge and bud. The benefit of starting with all three fingers is you don't shock the clitoris by going straight to it. Rather, you build sensation around it. And because your hand shields her from airflow, your partner feels the heat from your hand more directly and stays wetter.

Now maintain a slow up-and-down or circular motion (consider outlining the alphabet if you need some inspiration for how to move your fingers). Then subtly slip the middle finger inside the vagina. Finally, with your index and middle fingers together, do a short range of motion over the clitoral ridge, moving from front to back, with a gentle squeeze, or a pulse up and down.

Position #2

This is a position chosen by men who love their lady's derriere. One man, a marketing executive from Portland, Oregon, said, "I love the roundness and feel of her ass and being able to play with her and smell her sex at the same time." This position also allows good access to her breasts. In this position, the man can use his thumb most effectively by inserting it into the vagina and doing a circular motion. Because the thumb is so much stronger than the fingers, it is the natural choice for long-term stimulation. This is also a great position for exploring G-spot sensation. Try using a curving pressure-stroke with your middle and index finger on the front wall of her vagina. The G-spot will be felt more clearly, the more aroused she becomes. And if your partner likes anal play, this is a good way to initiate it.

Position #2

Even before you get to the smaller action zone, you can build sensation over the back of her thighs, back of her knees, and the small of her back. Consider starting with a flat hand and finger so you can massage the greatest area. Then you can shrink down the area of stimulation by shifting the motions to your fingertips. And if she likes, you can shrink the motion even more by concentrating on the clitoral ridge and bud. Most men have said that bent index and middle fingers held together work best here, with the clitoral ridge cradled length-wise between the two fingers. And remember to use your free hand to its greatest advantage by letting it roam around!

Position #3

The beauty of this position is that the woman can remain in very close contact with you and "melt" into your body. This is a favorite of those who like to watch and talk. On the next several pages I offer you a number of technique options; however, it should go without saying, feel free to incorporate any of you and your partner's favorite moves.

Position #3

JR. DREIDEL (A.K.A. MINI-FIRE STARTER)

This is a move in which she will truly appreciate your finesse. You imitate the spinning motion that generations of Jewish children have done with Hanukkah dreidels—only this version is for the sole delight of your partner. Apply a touch of lubricant on your thumb and forefinger and use a gentle rotating motion. Be sure to use gentle pressure to start. This move will be easier for women with a larger clitoris. As with any move, make sure you ask her if she'd like to try this.

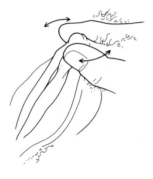

Jr. Dreidel

DOUBLE DUTY

In this variation of the #3 position, your arms are on either side of your partner. Use a strong, upward stroke, starting with the inside of her thighs and working toward her genitals. The idea behind this move is to relax her so she can "melt" into your body. As one woman said, "I feel so safe when we do this, even though I am totally exposed." You can create more buildup and sensation through her entire genital and pelvic area.

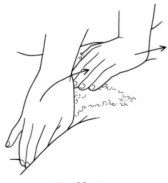

Double Duty

TOURING THE DANCE FLOOR

This move requires a very light circular touch around the clitoris and labia. Start with simply tracing the outline of her genitals and then do the same move while gently pulling the lips. Pulling heightens tension and builds sensation because stretched skin tends to have greater feeling. Sometimes couples incorporate an ice cube here. It's best to use it sparingly at first and just on the outside for ten to twenty seconds. One woman said, "My husband did it once and I almost went through the ceiling. The cold was cold, but when he went down on me after with his mouth, he never felt so hot. The difference in temperature is what made it so awesome." A man noted that this move was "very successful. It encourages taking your time." Some women, however, will not like this cold sensation, so don't surprise her.

Touring the Dance Floor

Y-KNOT

Spread the labia with two fingers of one hand, and with your other hand on top, position the middle finger, or two together, to massage the clitoris in a circular and/or up-and-down motion. This move is great in that it doesn't tire your hands. She also has a nice "big" feeling when your hands are covering her, instead of just a finger. You can also cover a greater area. You may want to try coming down on top: insert one or two fingers inside and curve them in and out of the vagina.

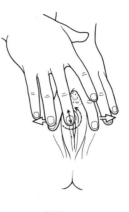

Y-Knot

Position #4

This position is ideal for those times when a lady needs to feel she is "on her own." Some couples prefer the leg over the shoulder as a way to stay in contact while she concentrates on

Position #4

what you're doing. This provides a better view and it is easier on your back when you are at a lower level—consider stairs covered with pillows as an option. Your partner can cover her tummy with sheets, should she get chilled.

THE WORLD IS YOUR OYSTER

This technique is best in the #4 position for two reasons: (1) There is more range of motion for you, and (2) you can concentrate on her while she concentrates on what you're doing.

The World Is Your Oyster

You will literally be touching her whole genital area as if it is soft, delicate clay and you are in the stages of final shaping and molding. Have lubricant handy, since this position and move require her to be quite spread open. (This is another place to watch those nails.) It's a slow buildup of sensation that will unravel her.

VENUS BUTTERFLY

This move is best done when you are sitting up beside your partner. Cradle your lower hand under her hips, resting it on the surface of her body. Stroke up and down the clitoral area with the middle finger of your upper hand as if you were spreading butter on bread. Use a light touch as if your middle finger is a delicate butterfly wing. Be sure to use enough lubricant so she doesn't dry out and that your hands are smooth and your nails trimmed.

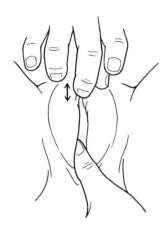

Venus Butterfly

THE SCULPTOR

This move alternates between two placements—static, in which you stay in one place, and dynamic, in which you change the hand orientation. The women in the seminars refer to both as the "take-me-home" moves.

Static Position: Curve your hand in the shape of a big "C." Imagine a clock over your partner's vulva; your thumb enters toward six o'clock and curves up toward the twelve. There are a few critical things to remember as you do this: (1) With the web of your hand between thumb and forefinger

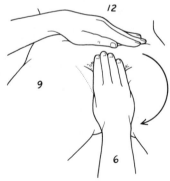

The Sculptor

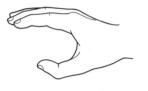

Sculptor, Static Position—
The Big "C"

and the inside knuckle area of your index finger, you will be creating sensation while you use the circular, rocking "C" motion; (2) the inside edge of your thumb can be putting pressure on the G-spot by maintaining an upward pressure, toward her belly button, on the upper vaginal wall; this sensation can be further heightened by (3) using your other hand to press on her abdomen, in the pubic hair. You should be able to feel the slight pressure of the side of your thumb

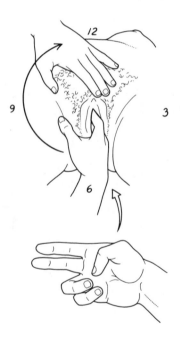

through her abdomen. Also while using the rocking "C" motion, try spreading your "C" fingers and put the pressure on the mons pubis area. Many women enjoy pressure there while being stimulated.

Dynamic Position: In the dynamic position, your thumb moves from the twelve o'clock position and, using a continuous motion, moves to each position of her internal clock (twelve to six). When you reach six o'clock, change and insert your index and middle fingers to complete the cycle back up to the twelve position.

Sculptor, Dynamic Position—
After Six O'Clock

Use your free hand to apply a stretching pressure to the skin on her abdomen, and upward toward her belly button, to heighten sensation.

G-MAN

The G-Man also has two hand-placement variations, positions A and B.

"Come Here" Motion

Position A: Insert your index and middle fingers and use a "come here" motion against her G-spot region. Since the G-spot is above the vaginal wall, you can press on her abdomen to heighten the sensation for her.

Position B: It's important to remember that your top hand is not just supplying pressure. Remember these points: Use your middle finger or thumb of your top hand to

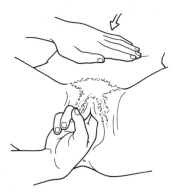

G-Man Position A

G-Man Position B

stimulate her clitoral area while using the fingers of your other to caress her G-spot. Maintain pressure and stimulation on her lower pelvis with the heel of your top hand.

FROG PRINCE

Remember those swim lessons? You will be doing a frog kick stroke inside of her using your index and middle fingers. Your hand can be in either a vertical or a horizontal orientation. The idea behind this move is women's differing sensitivities in vaginal walls. The Shimmy can be done in combination with the Frog Prince. In this submove, you shimmy your two fingers in and out of her, so you can feel both sides of the vaginal walls.

Tips to Keep in Mind When Touching Her Genitals

➤ Avoid homing-pigeon fingers. Chances are, if she shifts her hips ever so slightly, that is *exactly* where she wants you to stay, so please do not go back to the spot she has just moved your fingers from.

➤ Cease and desist from the Dip-Test, which looks like this: kiss, kiss, kiss (the lips); tweak, tweak, tweak (the nipples); dip, dip, dip (between her legs). This is not considered relaxing or stimulating to most women.

➤ The poke between the legs and "Oh goodie, she's ready" makes women feel like they are operating parts. Solution: Pay attention to her breathing. The more relaxed she is, the deeper and more relaxed her breathing becomes. The change in her breathing will let you know the other mental "stuff" is melting away.

➤ A woman will start lubricating intravaginally within thirty seconds of being stimulated either mentally or physically. Some women naturally have lots of lubrication; it is very individual and also subject to the influence of how well hydrated she is, if she is on medication, and where she is in her cycle—and that includes menopausal women as well.

➤ Avoid always going immediately to the action spots, such as her breasts and genitals. Her skin really is her largest sexual organ, so take full advantage of that. Linger all over her body and use your Swirl techniques.

Manual stimulation can lead anywhere, but many women love for it to be followed by a man's most intimate gesture: kissing her "down there" with your tongue. With that in mind, the next chapter will help illuminate the wondrous delights your tongue can deliver.

CHAPTER TEN

Oral Finesse

Tricks of Your Tongue

Rising Humidity

Your mouth can create many more sensations than any other part of your body. Ask most women and, if they're being honest, they will admit that what makes them hottest and come hardest is when a man can use his tongue well. If there is one story that women gratefully and ofttimes wistfully share in the seminars, it is about the man who can give her great oral sex. One woman said, "I love having him between my legs. There isn't anything that feels better." Another woman said, "I can't describe what he did, but it was phenomenal! I knew he loved women. He didn't care how much time it took. If there is one word to describe him, I would say perseverance. I must admit, his technique was legendary."

Another testament to the alluring power of your tongue comes from an advertising executive from Seattle, who said, "What makes [oral sex] so good is that it doesn't leave me feeling sore. When he goes down on me, his tongue and mouth are so hot and soft, it's both soothing and exciting."

Need I say more? Women respond to oral sex.

As you know by now, I am a firm believer that anything worth doing is worth doing well. Therefore, this chapter contains information that will not only make you a competent purveyor of oral treats but an expert who will bring a woman to her knees when she sees you licking your lips.

Now, I know some of you are uncomfortable with this whole subject. Indeed, some of you may actually avoid it altogether. And while you have every right in the world to refrain from doing what makes you uncomfortable, I will point out some of the reasons either you or your partner may feel hesitant to let go and enjoy the pleasures of oral sex. But if, after you've gone through this entire chapter, you still feel reluctant to give her oral sex, then you should be honest about it. In a gentle, kind way explain your feelings. Keep in mind, however, that your partner is especially vulnerable to the slightest rejection in this area. Women will take it personally if you don't handle it with kid gloves. Also remember that women know or sense when a man is not enjoying himself, and the last thing a woman wants is for you to do something you're not enjoying.

Part of the reason that some women feel uncomfortable about oral sex is that they carry around with them the feeling that their genitals are unclean or that men find oral sex distasteful. We can thank Madison Avenue and their clients for that charming legacy. It was the advertisers who developed the "need" for douching and reinforced negative or shameful feelings about female genitalia. To the contrary, as I've already stated, a healthy woman's genital area is one of the most self-cleansing and self-maintaining aspects of her body. But I have talked to women who say that they're afraid they smell and/or will taste bad.

Ironically, sexual intercourse is the number-one reason behind most genital problems in women. Specifically, yeast and bladder infections and STDs can result from having a foreign substance (semen) introduced into a woman's body. Women can also suffer from problems in reaction to the spermicide nonoxynol-9. As one of the top specialists in this area said, "Women who do not have sex have the most pristine vaginal canals."

Secret from Lou's Archives

It is possible for women to be unaware of the symptoms of vaginal infections. Bacterial vaginosis (BV) is a condition in which the natural balance of organisms in the vagina is changed. The exact cause of bacterial vaginosis is unknown. Among women who are aware of BV symptoms, the most common complaint is a foul or "fishy" odor. This odor often becomes stronger after sexual intercourse. (Yeast infections generally have no odor.) If left untreated, BV may cause complications, including abnormal Pap smears and increased risk of pelvis inflammatory disease (PID), and in pregnancy it has been associated with premature birth and low-birth-weight infants. A variety of antibacterial medications are used to treat bacterial vaginosis.

If a woman is clean and doesn't have infection, she should not smell or taste bad. Then again, there are individual preferences—she may just not smell good to you. However, if you pay attention to her scent, you may find it stimulating—this is, after all, the idea behind pheromones. Just as she is at-tracted to your male scent, so you are to hers.

Factors that will change your lover's taste:

> Vitamins
> Medication
> Diet
> Where she is in her cycle
> Infection
> Degree of hydration
> Spicy or heavily seasoned foods
> Alcohol, drugs, or tobacco

SECRET FROM LOU'S ARCHIVES

A pheromone is a substance produced by the body that pro-vides chemical means of communication between animals and certain insects, detected by smell. It may affect development, reproduction, and behavior.

It's important for you and the women in your life to partic-ipate in tearing down some of the old myths having to do with oral sex being dirty or unnatural. Some men and women still believe this, and I feel they are missing out on one of the most pleasurable experiences two people can share and give one an-other. If it's so "unnatural," why do male animals invariably ap-proach a female's genitals with their nose and mouth? It's up to you to release her inhibitions and your own. Chances are you both will find boundless pleasure in this activity.

In my countless seminars, women have shared with me that they often feel safer and more enthusiastic about oral sex if you refer to it in a nicer way. Sadly, many of our cultural references having to do with the female body are derisive or unpleasant. Here are some options that women report preferring: "eaten out," "going down on me," "cunnilingus," "giving me head," "dining out, "going south of the border." Phrases that are not liked include: "box lunch," "eating pussy," "bush burgers," and "muff diving."

Secret from Lou's Archives

Not all women are able to orgasm with cunnilingus, just as not all men are able to orgasm with fellatio.

The majority of men who are great at this have learned from women—not from adult material or friends. Why? Because, as I've said before, the porn industry insists on depicting cunnilingus as a long tongue pointed in the general direction of a woman's anatomy. Invariably, the tongue is not even close to the clitoris. Another problem some men have shared with me is they don't know their way around a woman's anatomy and feel they are "rooting around in the dark." This is perfectly understandable, and another reason why I included the guide to genitalia in the previous chapter. If you know that the clitoris is under a hood, for instance, then you'll know where to focus and why when it is stimulated it becomes engorged, lifting under the hood.

Herein lies a great faux pas of oral sex: the "flicking" problem. Flicking directly on the clitoris, especially in the initial stage, is not stimulating for most women. Now, some women enjoy flicking, but not until they are already stimulated. It's better to start with a full, warm mouth on her, and then some flicking, and then back to full, warm mouth. One male seminar attendee suggests "leading up to her clitoris by stroking your tongue on her inner thighs, and working your way up to the pubic bone, where you put on a bit of pressure."

Three things are bound to happen with flicking: (1) Your tongue dries out; (2) she dries out; and (3) your dry tongue pulls on her clitoris—not pleasurable. As one woman aptly put it, "What is it with those flickers? Why do they stay so far away? Are they afraid to come close? Tell them to suck on us the way they want us to suck on them," she said, muttering as she walked out of the room.

The clitoris does like to have isolated touch (with tongue), but the whole area responds to gentle sucking and pressure. The key is in knowing (which may require asking) what your lover enjoys. And, gentlemen, she may not know her own body. Again, as a compassionate lover, it's partly your role to help her understand her own body.

SECRET FROM LOU'S ARCHIVES

Amazingly, there are 23 states in which oral sex is still illegal, plus the District of Columbia and our military bases.

Maintenance and Hygiene

The best and most effective way for a woman to maintain herself in "dining condition" is regular bathing and cleaning of the genital area. If you are concerned that she is not fresh as a daisy, perhaps you can suggest taking a shower together. One woman from a seminar told me that her boyfriend lays her on the bed, inches up her dress, and slowly washes her with a warm, wet washcloth. When he's finished, she is completely aroused and he is, too. As she explains, "I feel like he is completely embracing of me, which just gets me so hot."

If you try the washcloth method, remember not to use soap. The pH in soap is incompatible with the natural pH of a woman's body. The soap will upset the natural acid balance that keeps the vaginal environment stable and braced to fight off foreign, infecting substances. The lemony tartness of a woman's natural lubrication is from the more acidic lubrication, the lactic acid. Vitamins will also change her taste (usually for the worse). While we are on this subject, if you are concerned about how to let her know her smell or taste is strong, try telling your partner about the last time she tasted *good*, after eating such foods as fruit.

Secret from Lou's Archives

If your partner shaves her pubic hair, be careful of regrowth during oral sex and intercourse. Stubble could be abrasive for you.

The Triangle Debate

Some men love a lot of pubic hair. The wife of a major television star said, "He'd love it if I never shaved my legs, armpits, or bush. I'm the one who prefers it off." For other men, less hair is definitely more. You may want to know that the current fashion trends do favor some pretty close manicuring of women's pubic hair: (1) naked lips, (2) clean thong (area between buttock cheeks), and (3) a small triangle or "runway" of hair. Some women will have special-event waxings done—hearts for Valentine's Day and shamrocks for St. Patrick's Day are two rather vivid examples. However, these designs do require skilled estheticians. One woman from a seminar told me about having her pubic hair dusted with gold powder (to match her lingerie) for a special occasion. After a night of complete enjoyment, her boyfriend left the next morning to play his regular basketball game. As he walked on the court, his teammates looked at him and asked, "What the f— is all over your face?" You guessed—her gold dust. Just check yourself in the mirror before going out in public.

SECRET FROM LOU'S ARCHIVES

If you are worried about stray hairs in your mouth, do a stroking move with your hand through her pubic hair. She will take it as a caressing move, when actually you are grooming her and removing loose hairs.

While we are on the subject of her hair, I'd like to address *your* facial hair. Make sure that after shaving, you are smooth enough to approach her. Rub the inside of your wrist on your beard, particularly just below your lower lip. If you feel anything scratchy, so will she. One woman, who has particularly sensitive skin, told me of being left with a rash on the inside of her thigh—ouch! Short mustaches and goatees can be the most abrasive, so longer hair (beards) is generally better.

The significance of your hair is best captured by this anecdote from one of my seminars. In a group of thirty-five men, I asked the three men with facial hair if they ever used their beards as a tool in oral foreplay. (Please note that these men did not know each other.) The three men shyly looked at each other and then smiled. In unison, all three nodded yes. Then one of them, a big trucker, announced as he stroked his very full beard, "Hell, I even use hair conditioner on mine so it's nice and soft."

But as a standard policy, ask her what *she* prefers.

Lifting the Clitoral Hood

For those ladies who enjoy and prefer direct clitoral stimulation, you will need to lift the prepuce, or clitoral hood (akin to the foreskin in a man). Here are some tips.

Option #1: Using the index and middle fingers of both hands, put upward pressure on the inside of the outer labia and lift the entire area. The best positions for this are the Classic, Sit on My Face, and Chair Therapy.

Option #2: The woman's legs must be in a "V" with her feet on a flat surface. You are between her legs and have one arm under and around her thigh. With a flat hand on her pubic hair, use a firm, upward pressure toward her head. Again, this will move everything up and create a more taut, open area for your mouth.

Option #3: If she is comfortable doing so, ask her to hold herself open. She might get a better hold on the slippery surface of the skin if she wears those little white cotton gloves—the type women wore in the 1950s. Of course, she may feel silly doing this, so it's up to both of you to decide.

Positions

A quick note before I describe the best positions for oral sex. I'd like to share what some men recommend as great ways to practice tongue technique.

1. Eat an ice cream cone. The upward, elongating tongue strokes are quite similar to what you would use on her. For more subtle moves, try eating Jell-O or pudding straight out of the container with no spoon.
2. To perfect your tongue finesse (and as Whoopi Goldberg suggested in her comedy routine), hold a Life Saver at the front of your mouth in the flat position either between your lips and gum or just inside your teeth. Using tiny tongue motions, "eat" or dissolve the Life Saver from inside out. Like great oral sex, this takes time, patience, and a strong, nimble tongue.

That said, we're ready to move on to the positions. Essentially, there are seven positions, with each position containing subpositions or variations on the main theme.

The Classics

The following seven subpositions use the standard technique of the man between the woman's legs, with his mouth against her genitals. Although these all belong to the same "family," each has its own variation on the theme. As a rule, it's best to have pillows under her hips and under your chest. This allows for a better range of motion for you and positions her hips so she can be spread more openly. It also saves you from abrading the underside of your tongue on your teeth.

STRAIGHT ON: *POSITIONS A AND B*

These positions allow for good upward stroking, lifting the clitoral hood. The woman can adjust how open she is by holding her thighs open. She can also use her hands to pull up on the outer labia. You can easily incorporate the "hand assist" (see page 225), using the thumb to stroke the anus or putting pressure on the bottom of the vaginal opening with one or two fingers. Use slow motion and circular movements.

T-CROSS

This is good for women who are more sensitive on one side of their clitoris than the other. Alternate between a broad stroke and a pointy one, circling the clitoral bud.

LEGS TOGETHER

This is a good starting point and often the best for a woman with a hypersensitive clitoris, who cannot tolerate strong direct contact.

Straight On, Position A

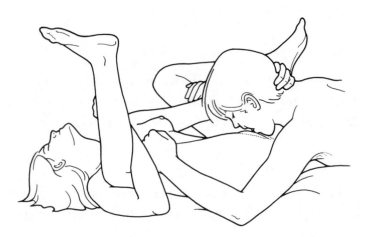

Straight On, Position B

T-Cross

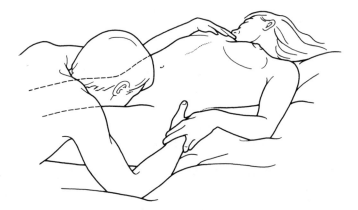

Legs Together

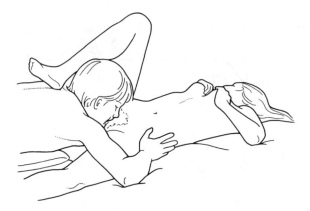

Her Leg over His Shoulder

Loving the Prize

HER LEG OVER HIS SHOULDER

Have her place one leg over your shoulder, and with a slight twist of her hips, you will be able to reach the right spot. Women have said they feel more connected in this position. Again, use an upward-stroking motion.

LOVING THE PRIZE

This is an ideal position for staying more connected to each other. Using a downward stroke, you're able to relax the angle of your head, relieving your neck muscles.

DOWNWARD DOG

This is a play on the downward-facing-dog yoga position— she does a shoulder stand, resting her buttocks on your chest and wrapping her legs around your neck. For most couples, this is more of a novelty position, but it does allow for a good view of your partner. And some women enjoy feeling their partner holding them tightly around the middle and playing with their breasts. Again, use an upward stroking motion and be sure not to put too much weight on her.

> ### SECRET FROM LOU'S ARCHIVES
>
> *When some women orgasm via oral sex, there is a change in consistency of lubrication. One man said, "She got thicker and there was more of it."*

Side by Side and the 69

The Side by Side and the 69 are good transition positions for oral sex, but require tremendous concentration. One woman reported, "I couldn't give head and receive it at the same time. It was too much like that tummy-rubbing, head-patting move. I like to warm up in this position and then switch positions."

Make sure there is a lot of saliva so she won't dry out.

Side by Side

69

While you're busy, she can be sucking on your penis or testicles. It's a relaxing position for your neck, too.

On your side, you can cushion your head on her thigh. As one man put it, "My tongue stays more moist, saliva pools in my mouth, so I can taste her more." You can also reach around and play with her buttocks and anus.

With her over the top of you, you can relax every part of your body—except your tongue. Use a downward-stroking motion. This is ideal for partners who enjoy oral/manual anal play.

The Arch

This is another novelty position that requires the man sitting up, with his partner on top. She then stays in place by locking her ankles behind his head while her thighs rest on his shoulders. Some women enjoy the blood rush to the head when they go horizontal again.

Sit on My Face (SOMF) and Hovering Butterfly

These positions are two of the easiest for the lady to control the motion. In both the forward-facing Hovering Butterfly and the away-facing SOMF, she can adjust the pressure and speed as she chooses.

In SOMF, your head and neck should be supported by a

The Arch *Sit on My Face*

Hovering Butterfly

pillow—not only for comfort but so you have some vertical give in the stroking area. You can easily play with her breasts and use your hands to open her more. Use both downward- and upward-stroking motions and lots of suction. This way she is able to concentrate on her own pleasure, as she can't do anything to you.

Hovering Butterfly is a ladies' favorite for a number of reasons. She can rest on something and feel very much in control while you concentrate on her. Use a good upward-stroking motion. An optional move is to cover yourself from the waist down while she faces your feet.

Kivin Method

In the Kivin method, you lie perpendicular to your partner. Her only responsibility is to receive sensation as she lies back. Use your tongue to stimulate her in a back-and-forth motion

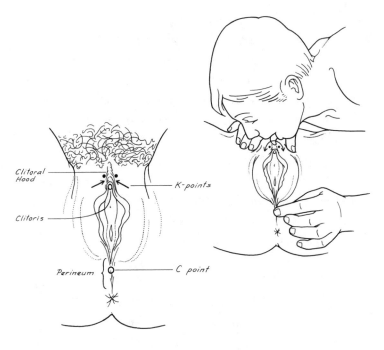

Clitoral Hood

Clitoris

Perineum

K-points

C point

Kivin Method

across the "K" points located on either side of the top and back of the clitoral hood. At the same time, maintain contact on her "C" point (the perineum) with your fingertip so you can feel her preorgasmic contractions. (Those contractions are a guidepost that you are in the right place and making the right moves.) In a real-time video of this technique, where the demonstrations have not been edited, it is quite clear that women experience rapid and intense orgasms in a short period of time.

Rear Approach

This position is a favorite of men who love a woman's buttocks. It requires a shallower stroking motion, however, and if you decide to go into any anal play, remember not to go back to her vulvar area, as you don't want to transfer fluids or organisms from one area to the other. Since the naturally occurring organisms of the anal (both yours and hers) and vaginal areas differ, you risk upsetting her natural vaginal environment, which may then cause her to get vaginal or bladder infections.

You have limited access to everything here, but it is a good starting position. You may have to crook your neck quite severely. One woman's comment was, "I love when my husband does this. It's so animal—it turns me on." In this position, with her shoulders dropped, she can help pull herself open with her hands and open up the entire area.

SECRET FROM LOU'S ARCHIVES

Don't go anywhere with your tongue or finger after you've gone near the anus; you risk introducing foreign organisms that can then cause infection.

Chair Therapy and Stand and Deliver

These two positions lend themselves to activity outside of the bedroom.

With Chair Therapy, whether she's perched on a countertop or a sofa, the lady has a great view and you have a position you can maintain for an extended period without getting a sore neck. She can stay connected by holding your head, though some men claim this feels like being "grabbed behind the ears and steered like a boat." If she sits or reclines on a table and you're on a chair, the benefits are obvious: You're to-

Rear Approach

Chair Therapy

Stand and Deliver

tally comfortable and can concentrate on the job at hand, so to speak, using "hand assist" moves to pleasure her more.

Stand and Deliver is another acrobatic position, often used in the shower or while getting dressed or undressed. Use an upward stroking here. This position is a terrific way to increase what I call the "fun factor" of great sex. Anytime you introduce a new position, new move, or new item, you increase the spirit of adventure, which will in turn make you both feel more spontaneous, playful, and excited. Unfortunately, the only downside is you sometimes get a bad crick in your neck.

Special Moves

Strumming the Frenulum. Technically, the frenulum is a skin attachment point. Men have one on the head of their penis, and women have it on the top of their vulvar/clitoral area. To please a woman here, use the undersurface of your tongue (it's much smoother) with a quick side-to-side stroke. Your tongue will be curved up close to your upper lip.

The Elevator. Use the top surface of your tongue in an upward stroke and use the undersurface on the downward stroke.

Doing Your ABCs. I believe it was the late Sam Kinison, a raunchy-style comedian, who brought this technique to fame. Alternate tongue moves that are easy to remember: Write the letters of your alphabet. To make it even more exciting, try enlarging the font and italicizing. You may want to ask her to hold herself more open for you.

Mr. Hoover. This technique is all about suction, which most women really enjoy. Have her suck on your fingers to show you exactly how she likes to be stimulated.

Cradle and Diamond Tip. Suck on the clitoral bud and use the tip of your tongue to stimulate it while you are creating suction pressure with your pursed lips.

Ice Cubes. Some women love this, but others don't like the cold sensation at all.

The Picasso. Use your tongue to create a line drawing all over her body, using her clitoris as a launching point. This is also where you can show her what she tastes like by surfacing and kissing her.

Some General Tips from the Field

➤ One woman finally found a way to tell her partner how she liked to be licked. "I told him to kiss my pussy the same way he kisses my lips—big, soft, wet, and warm. Then I told him that I wanted him to suck on my clit the same way he sucks on my tongue."

SECRET FROM LOU'S ARCHIVES

Blowing into a woman's vagina at any time is uncomfortable and not wise, but during and a few weeks after pregnancy, blowing can force air into the uterus, and if air enters a blood vessel (a condition called an air embolism), it can be deadly.

➤ When women say "That's great," or "There," men often speed up, or increase the pressure. This ends up rushing her, which will totally cut the legs out from under her "slow buildup." At the risk of repeating myself, you need to let her relax into the sensations—that's how things really build. On the other hand, when she says "more," by all means stay with that motion.

➤ Men who are best at this use their entire face, and say they resemble a glazed donut when they're through. If your tongue gets tired, use your nose and chin to execute your moves.

➤ Men have shared that some women like when you put pressure on their mons pubis with your nose.

➤ While you are using your tongue to stimulate her clitoris, consider using firm, steady pressure on the urethral area, just below the clitoris, with the front of your chin. Also, some women enjoy chin pressure on the base of the introitus.

➤ A woman who was extremely sensitive to touch directly on her clitoris wore silk panties when her husband went down on her. She would still be highly stimulated through the silk, but not too much. After all, silk isn't waterproof.

➤ The slower you go, the faster you'll get there—honest. "Sometimes he's at speed 4, and I haven't even gotten into gear." In order for a woman to orgasm, she needs to have a buildup of tension. The speed of movement should build slowly and gradually. Then, as she begins to approach orgasm, speed up and direct your tongue more intensely.

➤ During oral sex, women tend to feel that a man is far away. You may want to consider a more body-contacting position (see Loving the Prize in the Classic position, on page 212).

➤ Some women like you to move your tongue in small, repetitive motion, whereas other women want variety. She may want you to use your tongue in broad, general strokes in the beginning, and then as she becomes excited, she may want you to zero in on her clitoris and concentrate on that spot. Check in with her and ask if she would like you to change the motions of your tongue.

➤ Keep in mind that for most women, especially if oral sex is the first move of foreplay, it's going to take longer than you think to orgasm. Some women take fifteen minutes; others take up to a half hour. It depends on many variables, including how relaxed and comfortable she is.

➤ One of the best ways a man can tell if a woman is relaxing and getting more excited is through her breath: It will change, slow, and deepen. As she gets closer to orgasm, use her breathing as a guide to quicken, slow, or change the degree of movement of your tongue and mouth. Another indication of her arousal may be if she arches her back and goes up on her shoulders.

➤ Some women get overstimulated during oral sex. If that's the case, you need to either vary the intensity or range of your tongue's movement or orally caress another part of her body and give her genitals a rest. Often if you return your tongue to her clitoris or labia after a short rest, she will still be aroused, and able to have an orgasm.

➤ Some women who feel they are not going to orgasm during or from oral stimulation can experience anxiety. Try to help your partner, letting her know that it's perfectly okay not to orgasm.

SECRET FROM LOU'S ARCHIVES

Some women like the sensation of a man "humming" on them.

Troubleshooting

We all know, women included, that pleasing her orally requires some slight contortions of your head and body. Here are some solutions:

KNOTS IN THE NECK SOLUTIONS

1. Pillows, pillows, pillows. Use them under her hips and/or under your chest. (In Hovering Butterfly, use a pillow under your head.)
2. Use the wag. This is an action of wagging your head like you are signaling "no" while keeping your tongue extended and in contact with her.

YOUR TONGUE GETS TIRED

1. If your tongue gets tired, curve it up against the outside of your upper lip. This way, you can relax your tongue and not break the sensation of softness and heat she is enjoying.
2. There are two surfaces on your tongue—top and

bottom. If your tongue tires in a side-stroking motion, relax with a big upward stroke with the top surface. Then use the soft underside of your tongue on the downward stroke.

USE THE HAND ASSIST

1. The hands and mouth work in concert. While your mouth is on her, use your fingers, too. Specifically, try sliding your thumb around the perineal or anal area.
2. Pressure the bottom of the introitus area, inside the vagina. If a woman is on her back and you are looking at her genitals, the introitus is the vaginal opening. Using your thumb or chin, pressure the bottom of this entry within the first two inches. Some women become very aroused.
3. Keep a hand under your chin. This is a multitasking move. Not only can you support your chin in the crest of your thumb and forefinger, you can also use the second joint at the front of your index finger to continue the stroking motion while your tongue takes a break. By the time you need to do this, there should be enough lubrication from her to avoid any dryness.

FACIAL HAIR SNAFUS

1. Make sure you shave yourself as smooth as a baby's butt, especially around your mouth and right under your lower lip. Test on the inside of your wrist. If you feel it, so will she, and for her it will feel like sandpaper.

2. I have learned that a lot more men are enjoying the pleasures of trimming or shaving their partner's pubic hair. You may want to try it as a form of erotic foreplay. Men have also said it's neater and tidier, which they like.

Since so many women enjoy oral stimulation in order to orgasm, indulge her. Your tongue is a magical instrument, and your lover will be eternally grateful if you learn to use it as openly, generously, and playfully as you like. Remember, your tongue on her is a sign of your total acceptance of her.

CHAPTER ELEVEN

Nights of Ecstasy

Intercourse That Will Leave You Breathless

Deep Connection

You've gone to the place of ultimate relaxation and romance. You've explored the heights of arousal through oral and manual sex. Now it's time to push over the top with the most sensual, soulful intercourse imaginable. Ultimately, we all want to get to this place, where deep connection feels complete.

In order to be a master lover during intercourse, a few premises must be acknowledged. First, consider your attitude in general. A woman wants to know not only that you find her attractive and want her, but that you also respect her. Once this level of comfort and trust is established, then she wants you to take her with abandon.

Second, by this stage you need to have paid attention to her entire body before you begin to penetrate her. Finally, let go and see what happens. Let your bodies lead you without any preconceived ideas of exactly what will happen.

Most women realize that intercourse is strenuous and requires work and energy. With that in mind, I'd like to share a story with you. A friend of mine and I were hanging out one day discussing sex, and he mentioned how sex can be such hard work for men. When I laughed at this notion, he said, "Okay, Lou, I'm gonna prove something to you, you think I'm kidding." He stood up and walked to the center of the room and plunked down on the rug. He then said, "Okay, I'm the woman, you're the guy, lie on top of me." With a quizzical look on my face, I lay on top of him. He looked up at me and said, "Now, get your hips in the right position; they are not in the right position. Okay, now start thrusting."

I looked down at him and with a look of amazement said, "I didn't know your toes had to be in a certain position in order to push. This hurts the abs."

He nodded and said, "Keep thrusting and be careful not to put all your weight on me."

By now my arms were exhausted.

He said, "Now keep thrusting, maintain your erection, don't put all your weight on me, and then stare into my eyes and tell me you love me!"

Needless to say, while I collapsed, laughing, I got his message!

SECRET FROM LOU'S ARCHIVES

Some women say their best sex was not from those men who were the biggest or longest. On the contrary, it was with those men who were less well endowed, because they weren't relying on only one body part to carry the show. The better lovers were more involved, using more of their bodies and involving more of hers.

But for all this hard work, the beauty of sex remains in the fabulous friction created when bodies move together. The main movement of intercourse will always be the thrusting in and out. But there is a decided art to thrusting well. Here are some of the suggestions I've collected from the ladies' seminars:

1. Please start slowly, very slowly, and build the tempo.
2. Mix short strokes with long and deep.
3. Make different moves with your hips—try wiggles and circles. Often a lady has different areas of vaginal entry with specific pressure sensitivities. Your movement can uncover these hot spots.
4. While thrusting, stay close to her clitoral area. Banging on top of the clitoris does nothing. The motions that really work are pelvic rocking and slow circular movement. There is a reason why the pelvic grind works—you are stimulating her clitoris.
5. If you take too long, she will dry out. Sometimes women can enjoy sex for forty-five minutes and sometimes we prefer it in five. Even if she is totally turned on and fully lubricated in that area, her tissue is extremely delicate, and once exposed to air, as it is during sex, the friction of thrusting can dry it out, particularly when a condom is used. I can assure you, gentlemen, this does not feel good. Consider a couple of solutions: (1) use a lubricant; (2) after some time, ask her if she is comfortable or if you feel smooth enough.
6. Ask her to control the show and ask her to get on top—that way you can get an idea of what

she likes and duplicate it when it's your turn.

7. Please stay inside. Once you are in there, we really like you to stay there.

Does Your Size Really Matter?

Well, I won't lie to you. There are some real size queens out there. They may not measure you, but just as men can be "breast" men or "ass" men, women have their share of preferences. Some women like very small penises, in part because they have small vaginas. For other women, the larger the penis, the better. But for many women, it's what you do with your penis that really matters.

Most men are smaller erect than you think. Take, for example, the four sizes of instructional product (i.e., dildos) I use in the ladies' sex seminars. When I place them all in the center of the table and instruct the women to choose the size they are most comfortable with, most often they choose the five-inch executive model or the six-inch model because that's the size with which they are most familiar.

That said, women see your erections from completely different angles than you do. During oral sex for example, we see from below, where it looks bigger. In that way, you could say that we have the home-court advantage. It's all a matter of perception.

Secret from Lou's Archives

The smaller he is, the closer in he has to remain, which is a very good thing. And a smaller man can use deep-penetrating positions with a woman because he won't be ramming into her cervix.

Positions

Don't let those "1,001 Positions" books overwhelm or distract you or make you feel inadequate because there are some positions you haven't even heard of. Please remember that the biggest determining factor for choosing a position is the preference of you and your partner. Note that most of the positions in porn movies are not at all pleasurable for the ladies. One male friend of mine said he'd watch films in order to gauge his own performance. When I told him that these performances were scripted, acted, voiced-over, and edited, he seemed shocked. And this reaction came from a television producer!

Couples typically use two or three positions during one lovemaking session, moving from one position to another before completion, whether completion is orgasm or not. Nevertheless, I don't want you thinking that there is something wrong with you or your lover because you prefer your old standard of you on top and her beneath you. Above all, do what is comfortable and what works best for both of you in terms of pleasure. I encourage variety in all forms of sexual intimacy—the purpose is to push back the boundaries of self-imposed limitations and find your ultimate pleasure.

Secret from Lou's Archives

Once, when I told a friend that there were only six intercourse positions, he said, "No, there's not. There's only one—in!"

Essentially, there are only six positions, with everything else being a variation on a theme: man on top, woman on top, side by side, rear entry, standing, and sitting/kneeling.

Man Superior (Man on Top)

In the man-superior position, you are on top during intercourse. This is one of the most common positions and one women and men often enjoy the most. This preference is mostly because of the position's degree of closeness and the ability to watch each other's expressions and look into each other's eyes. You're also able to sense and feel your partner better and make her feel most connected to you.

The name of the so-called missionary position is ascribed to South Seas natives who saw the missionaries doing this. According to Kinsey, those of us who are of European descent seem to rely on the missionary position as an old standard. However, because the South Seas tribes favored the woman-on-top, sitting, and rear-entry positions, they considered the man-on-top position to be different.

In this position, the woman lies on her back with you lying over her or slightly to the side of her. Men say they like it because they can control the depth of penetration as well as the speed of the thrust, according to how close they are to orgasm. Women like the position because there is more body contact than in the other positions. While the other positions are perhaps more erotic, this one is the most romantic. Kissing and hugging are easily done in this position, and many women say it makes them feel safe and protected.

This position is also good for coital alignment technique (CAT). In Position A, observe a variation on the positioning of the feet that can add greatly to coital alignment technique, in which you brace your feet against hers. By keeping your hips together so your pubic area is in continuous contact with her clitoral and vulvar areas, there is no break in the stimulation or connection, and you can penetrate her most deeply. She can assist this by firmly holding your buttocks.

This is all fine and good as long as you can maintain motion, which is difficult because you are not using your knees and feet for leverage. Look at the feet in the drawing on the next page. See how her legs are fairly close together (about a foot apart) and she holds her feet out to the sides with her toes toward the outer edges of the bed? Once she has her feet and legs in this position, you can use the top of her flexed feet to brace yourself. This is perfect for those close, constant pelvic thrusts that make the CAT. It's also desirable for those women who need muscular tension to orgasm. If you are taller than she is, use a wall or bed footboard as the brace.

An athletic variation of Position A allows you to maintain full body contact while increasing pelvis pressure/tension, and allows a greater ability to create tight close-thrusting mo-

Man Superior

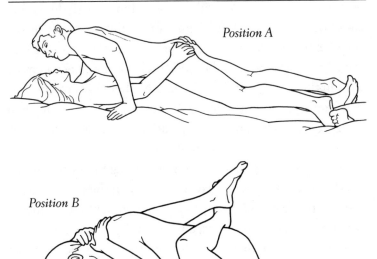

Position A

Position B

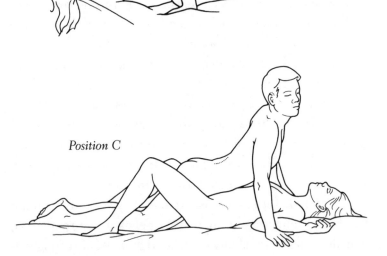

Position C

tions because you use both legs as a fulcrum. This is how it's done:

Step 1. After entering her you squeeze her legs together with yours on the outside.

Step 2. You then bend your knees and hook your ankles underneath the woman's legs.

Step 2. You lift your legs up, and in doing so gently lift up her legs, increasing pelvis/clitoral pressure while maintaining full, warm body contact.

In Position B the lady rests against a pillow. Think of this as a perfect sex toy under her hips to increase her vaginal entry angle. The pillow creates a comfortable spot for her back, and makes it easier for you to thrust vigorously and still remain inside. Fewer spills or "fall-outs" occur when pillows are used. With her legs wrapped over your hips, she can also control the motion and open herself to more penetration. Need I mention that this position also allows great access for kissing?

In Position C you are arching back, which is a great boon for women who enjoy front-vaginal-wall/G-spot stimulation and stroking, and who aren't comfortable with rear-entry sex. This is not a good position for a man with a bad back, but it enables the man with tight ab muscles to show off his ripples.

SECRET FROM LOU'S ARCHIVES

Any kind of exercise, including sex, can help abort an impending headache.

Woman Superior (Woman on Top)

Many women prefer woman superior because it allows her to control penetration and the speed, since she is the person doing the thrusting. It also works well if a woman happens to be taller/smaller than you. In Position A, the woman is doing the same to the gentleman that he was doing to her in man-superior Position A above. She uses his feet to brace herself for close clitoral and pelvic rocking, and because her legs are on the inside, she can create more pressure on the vulvar and clitoral areas by squeezing her legs.

In the woman-superior position, she is usually straddling you with the bulk of her weight distributed evenly between both knees. This can be done with her either facing you or facing away from you (Position C). Another variation on this position would be for her to lie down on you with her legs on either side (Position B).

The woman-superior position does require a lot more work on a woman's part, and some say it requires a "ski racer's quads." Men tend to enjoy this position a lot because it provides them with a good look at a woman's body; you can be the captain of the proverbial ship. They love to see a woman's breasts move up and down with each thrust and see her hair falling or hitting them in the chest or face. A magazine editor from San Francisco remembers: "I knew this would be my favorite position from the time I saw a porn film when I was fourteen when this woman in a big skirt lowered herself onto a man. When my wife lowers herself onto me, it takes all my power not to shoot off right then."

In general, women find the variations of this position exciting because they allow them to control movement and the depth of penetration. They feel like they are running the show,

Woman Superior

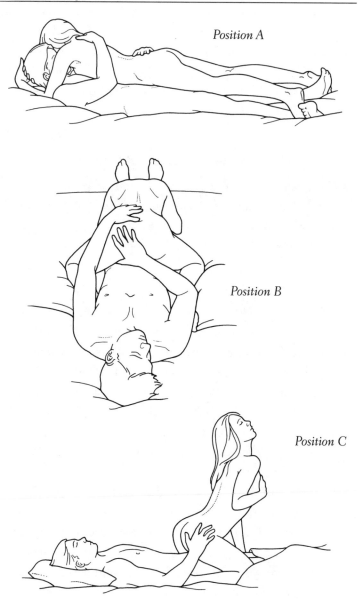

Position A

Position B

Position C

so to speak. On the other hand, the women who don't enjoy this position say that it's because they feel self-conscious about having their bodies exposed and in full view. If you think your partner may feel uncomfortable, reassure her that you love her body, or don't encourage her to put herself in a vulnerable position. She may be more comfortable in this position keeping a pretty bra or teddy on.

SECRET FROM LOU'S ARCHIVES

No matter how attractive you think a woman is, don't tell a woman you love her body before you've slept together. She will only hear it as a ploy to get her into bed. Save that comment for afterward. Then it will be believable.

TIPS

➤ To increase the odds of coming during intercourse or coming with her, stimulate her clitoris to the point where she is about to orgasm, then get her into the woman-superior position. If you thrust, there is a good chance she'll be able to reach orgasm with you inside of her (Position C, facing toward you).

➤ She can stimulate the G-spot area of her front vaginal wall, and if you love her butt, you can play with it.

➤ Position B is only good if your erection will flex this way. It's often not very good for younger, tight-to-the-tummy guys. But it is great for a couple that enjoys anal play. If she leans forward and has her chest on your legs, you can stroke her anus and perineal area and she can be in her own world.

Side by Side

For this position, the man and woman are on their sides with their legs entwined like scissors. You can be facing each other or you can be behind her. The beauty of side by side is that most men can thrust for a long time in this position without climaxing. It provides couples the opportunity to make their intimate encounter last. And because penetration is not as deep in this position, women who have lovers with exceptionally large penises say that intercourse is more comfortable. Much like in the man-superior position, kissing and hugging are almost inevitable here.

Position A shows the true scissors of the legs; now all you have to do is lift your upper leg and have her drop onto the bed. Now you have a totally new position, in which you will be able to manually play with her clitoral area or breasts. In this "X" position, you can keep your hands joined together and use them to create your thrusting pelvic motions.

Side by Side

Position A

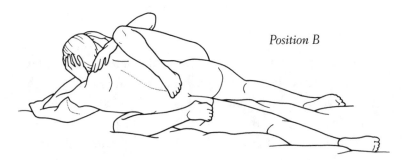

Position B

Position C

In Position B, she has wrapped her legs firmly around you and can keep you in as closely as she likes.

Position C is good for spooning, which allows you easy access to her entire body. Perhaps the best thing about making love side by side, however, is that it is the one position that lends itself to falling asleep in each other's arms afterward.

There is a variation on Position C, again for the more athletic. This is how it's done:

Step 1. You penetrate her from behind. She places her upper leg close to her chest or between her breasts.

Step 2. While maintaining penetration, you shift your position from behind her so that you're more on top of the woman's hip. Now all of your weight will be balanced between her hips and your knees. Because your hands are not supporting you, they are free to create more stimulation from behind.

Step 3. Assuming she is on her left side, you can insert the pinkie finger of your left hand into her anus (just a little, and it is best to start conservatively with this motion). While you gently insert your right thumb into her vagina to increase the width sensation for her, you can use the index finger of your right hand to stimulate the clitoral region.

TIPS

➤ When you are positioned behind her, you can also stimulate her clitoris.

➤ Rear entry in side-to-side position can be good for pregnant women, as she will be able to support her abdomen and you can play with her full breasts, assuming she likes this.

Man from Behind (a.k.a. Doggy Style)

Many women have said that the man-from-behind or doggy-style position makes for some of their most erotic sex. Men as well find this position highly charged. Women have said their reasons range from the intense depth of penetration to the feeling of being taken. Some women also enjoy the speed that a man can create by holding onto her hips and thrusting, creating momentum. Then again, a man can control the speed of his thrusting if a woman enjoys variation or slow thrusting.

Women who have given birth have an increased sensitivity to G-spot stimulation in this position. Since their vaginas are more elastic, the G-spot is more reachable for the penis.

This position can be done with the woman lying flat on her stomach, which allows for a tight entry with a feeling of being taken (C). Other options are: the woman on all fours (A), the woman standing up bent over at the waist, or the woman lying on her side with her back to you. You enter her vagina from behind her rather than in front of her. That's why it is often referred to as rear-entry sex. Men say this is the position in which they experience the most heat, created by the touching of her crotch and butt against his thighs. (FYI: Backdoor sex is anal sex.)

In Position A, you can kiss down her back. And again, pillows can come in very handy for under the chest. Position B gives you full access to her body and she can feel your heat and relax into the sensations. She can also extend her legs down to create more thrusting capability.

Man from Behind

Position A

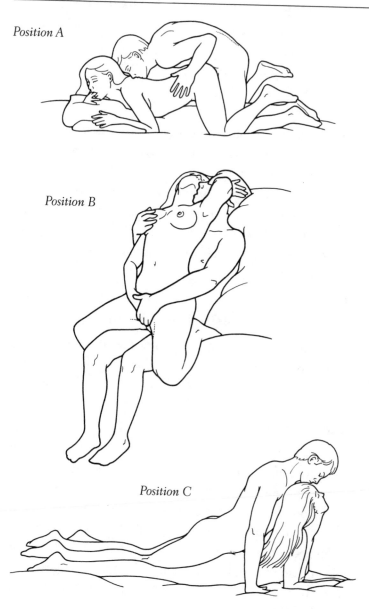

Position B

Position C

TIPS

➤ The only drawback to rear-entry sex is that because it is so highly erotic, you may climax more quickly than you would in other positions.

➤ This position can be painful if a woman has a tilted uterus or a very large partner, because he will likely hit the neck of her cervix.

➤ You can stimulate her with your hands as you penetrate her.

Standing Up

For the sake of balance, this position is best done with the woman standing against a wall and you standing in front of her. The shower or pool is often not as nifty as one would like—for one main reason: Water washes away any natural lubrication; therefore thrusting is made tougher, not easier. Standing positions work better when you have the lady in a recumbent (lying down) position. You can use the strongest muscles in your body, your glutes and thighs, to their greatest

Standing Up

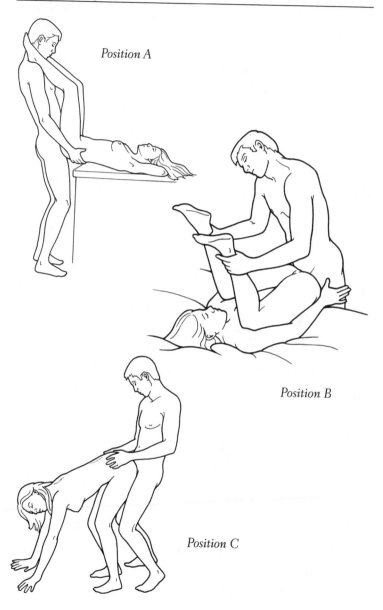

Position A

Position B

Position C

advantage. Though another position is probably best for a long romantic sexual encounter, this one is excellent for hot and urgent sex or athletic sex. In its simplest form, try both of you standing. This can be done without the complete removal of clothes (a plus when you're both in a hurry) and requires very little space to do it in.

Position A shows a variation on the woman-on-the-table theme. Once you have entered her, hold on to her hips and place the back of her heels on your shoulders, so her hips and open labia are flush against you. Men have stated that they get a great view and more scent, rather like the rear entry in reverse. Her back should be in a straight line. This is easiest if she locks her heels over your shoulders. Why does it work? Your penis is stroking very firmly over her G-spot area while she can be playing with her clitoris manually.

In Position B, you can see all of her sex and penetrate as deeply as possible. The woman can control your penetration by flexing her thighs. These are the biggest muscles in the body. The variation on this is to place her knees out to the side.

I call Position C the "take her from behind in the garden." Great for quickies! One man commented, "She has these great mirrored doors in her hallway and I love watching her breasts sway while I thrust. That's the ticket!"

TIPS

➤ If you are doing this standing up, be sure your knees are locked and you are comfortably leaning against a solid wall. I have heard of men falling over at inopportune moments.

➤ If the lady is going to wrap her legs around you, make sure she has removed her stilettos. It has been reported that these can cause serious damage to calf muscles.

Sitting/Kneeling

Sitting or kneeling positions are simply a variation of the side-by-side and face-to-face positions. Many couples enjoy sitting or kneeling because the positions feel novel and give them a break in their routine. However, even though some positions have a reduced range of motion, unless she is standing over you, this position generally does allow for great face-to-face and/or body contact.

Positions A and B suggest a whole new use for dining room chairs. In A the lady needs to hold on to the chair so she's balanced—or you could thrust her right off the chair. This allows her the greatest range of hip motion while you remain still.

In Position C, your thighs support the backs of her legs and she has a pillow under her hips to keep her at the right level for entry. Meanwhile, you hold her hips to keep her in as close as possible. Your thrusting will likely cause her breasts to jiggle, an enjoyable sight. A variation is to place the back of her knees in the crook of your elbow, like a barbell curl position. By doing "curls" with your entire arm, not only will she see your hard work from the gym, you'll experience internal glans stimulation and she'll have internal G-spot zone stimulation.

THE BETTER THAN SEX (BTS) POSITION

The BTS position allows you to remain kneeling or standing while you enter your partner at a 90-degree angle. She is lying face up on the bed and then places her heels on

Sitting and Kneeling

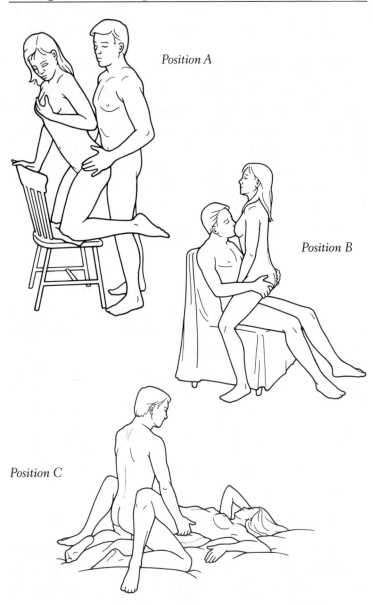

Position A

Position B

Position C

Better Than Sex

your shoulders, or her knees into the crook of your elbows. In either position she can easily adjust to her preferred angle. You can show off your gym work by flexing your arms. By further pulling up on your partner's hips, you greatly increase the pressure stroke along her G-spot area. One man said, "I could watch her all day when I do this. Her breasts jiggle, she arches her back, and gets that flush around her neck. I thought I would get off balance doing this, but I was surprised how easily I could maintain my hip and arm rhythm, the one helped the other build... it has become our new favorite."

A woman described the sensation this way: "The first time he did this I almost went out of my mind. There was a buildup of heat unlike I'd ever felt. But I need to be careful because, depending on my cycle, sometimes I am too sensitive and it becomes sensory overload. But when it works, girllllll!"

➤ Sitting, she can be straddling you, facing away while seated on your lap, or facing sideways in your lap.
➤ An easy position to move to from the woman-superior position; she pulls her legs forward and you can sit up.
➤ Sitting on a chair is good for couples that want a quickie or if the woman is pregnant.

General Tips for Intercourse

➤ If you experience a burning sensation during intercourse, check to see if you need more lubricant or if you mistakenly used a lubricant with nonoxynol-9. If neither of these is a possible explanation, you may want to visit your doctor and check for an infection or STD. Or she may be having an allergic reaction to your semen.
➤ If your partner complains of pain during intercourse, your penis may be hitting the neck of her cervix or uterus; try changing your position. You may also be irritating episiotomy scars or, again, it may be an STD-induced soreness.
➤ Regardless of how much you exercise and how many different techniques and positions you put into your sexual repertoire, just remember that the most important factors in determining your level of sexual fulfillment during intercourse will be the release of your inhibitions and wanting to be with her.

The Best Pregnancy Positions

Mother Nature never intended for us to stop having sex when women are pregnant. Some women report their best sex ever is during their pregnancies; some women can't take it at all. The lesson: Ask her how she feels. One woman said, "I'd love to go back to pregnant sex. I could come so easily. Now, ten months after the fact, it's much harder." On the other hand, there are those women who, because of terrible morning sickness or general physical discomfort, may not want you penetrating her. Again, in this case, it's very much up to her. In general, male and female superior are fine in the early months of a pregnancy, but as the woman's stomach enlarges, these positions become more and more difficult. In later stages of pregnancy, side by side (Positions A and C) and sitting and kneeling (Positions A and B) all work well. In this case, you are not on top, but still close. The classic spooning position side by side (C) works well because her tummy is supported and deep penetration is not possible. For very late-stage pregnancy, some prefer the sitting positions—either facing sideways or toward one another, depending on the size of her tummy.

SECRET FROM LOU'S ARCHIVES

As a physician said, there should be three sexes: women, pregnant women, and men. Pregnant women are as different from nonpregnant women as they are from men.

Anal Penetration

Some women love it, some women hate it. Like swallowing your semen, there tends to be no in-between when it comes to how women feel about and experience anal sex. Most women have tried anal sex at least once (usually because their partner has suggested it). Women who love being penetrated in this way claim that the sensation is intense.

Part of the reluctance of men and women regarding the very idea of anal sex is its negative associations. According to Tristan Taormino in her book *The Ultimate Guide to Anal Sex for Women*, there are ten pervasive yet inaccurate myths about anal sex:

1. It's unnatural and amoral.
2. Only sluts, perverts, and weirdos have anal sex.
3. The anus and rectum were not meant to be eroticized.
4. Anal sex is dirty and messy.
5. Only gay men have anal sex.
6. Straight men who like anal sex must be homosexual.
7. Anal sex is painful.
8. Women don't enjoy receiving anal sex; they do it just to please their partners.
9. Anal sex is the easiest way to get AIDS.
10. Anal sex is naughty.

These attitudes toward anal sex are tied to outdated and moralistic beliefs that sex is meant only for procreation, which also implies that sex shouldn't be enjoyed. As far as I am concerned, nothing could be further from the truth. Sex is not only meant to give two people a way to express their love and commitment through deep pleasure; it's also a manner of human expression that should never be judged outright. If it doesn't hurt, then it's perfectly natural and essentially good.

Some women like being anally penetrated while they are also being stimulated clitorally. For other women, the intensity of anal penetration is too overwhelming, making it impossible for them to climax. One reason it is difficult to enjoy anal play is the fact that there are actually two sphincters that need to be relaxed. As I pointed out earlier, one sphincter is under voluntary control and the other is under involuntary control, which, no matter how much you try, is impossible to consciously relax. A good way to try to relax the anus is to insert one finger for one minute, two fingers for two minutes. I also suggest lubricating generously, as this is not a self-lubricating area. Consider asking your partner to bear down, which will relax the sphincters and ease entry.

TIPS

➤ The best position for backdoor entry is shoulders down, pillow underneath. You can massage her anus with your thumb.

➤ Another good position is her on her back with her legs rolled forward, with a pillow under her hips. She can hook her forearms under her thighs to increase the curve and give you more access to her anus.

➤ Removing the finger/toy/penis should be done *very* slowly!

➤ Do not return to vaginal intercourse until you have washed your penis or changed your condom; otherwise you risk giving each other an infection.

PART III

Exploring Uncharted Territory

CHAPTER TWELVE

Expand Your Tool Chest

The Beauty of Enhancers

The Wide Angle on Sex

By this stage of the book, you could probably guess that in my opinion great, mind-blowing sex does not occur in only one position or manner, much less is it tied strictly to intercourse in the missionary position. I'm not only an advocate of bringing oral and manual techniques into the bedroom, but also of enhancing your sexual pleasure in any way possible, or at least, in any way with which you are comfortable.

Of course there are toys, and in doing my sexuality seminars I have noticed that more and more couples seem to be curious about, or have already begun experimenting with, some fabulous little (and not so little) gizmos. More on that later. But enhancing your sexual response is not limited to toys. There are many and varied ways to build more intense and broad sensation.

I'm also going to give you tips on aromatherapy stimulants, and more practical information on supposed aphrodisiacs. The skinny? Some work, some don't. I have also gathered some tips on lubricants so you can add lots of wet-and-wild fun to improve your orgasmic control and degree of pleasure.

HISTORICAL AND HYSTERICAL FACTS	The Marquesans were one of the few peoples whose women controlled the sexual relationship. At feasts, which generally turned into orgies, the males sucked the females' breasts and performed cunnilingus. When the women felt prepared, they demanded intercourse.

SECRET FROM LOU'S ARCHIVES

Scientists now know why touching is so therapeutic. Massage has been shown to trigger the release of oxytocin in the brain. The hormone produces feelings of sedation and relaxation, lowers blood pressure, and creates a metabolic environment that encourages the storage of nutrients and stimulates growth.

Aromatherapy

As I discussed in chapter 4, aromatherapy can be used not only to enhance moods, but also to induce moods—from relaxed, romantic, and sensual to heightened sexual states. For those of you interested in creating your own aromatherapy repertoire, you might consider the recipes for essential-oil combination that are said to induce some of the responses listed below, or see the chart on pages 260–61 for a thorough listing.

Mildly sedates—chamomile, sandalwood, lavender, vetiver
Heightens alertness—black pepper, rosemary, lemon, peppermint
Normalizes—bergamot and lavender
Predisposes mind and body to sexual ecstasy—vaporized oil of frankincense

During the course of writing my books, I had the unique opportunity to become my own aromatherapy guinea pig. I can certainly attest to the efficacy of the lemongrass-rosemary combination, which helped my mental clarity. I used a small water-style diffuser with a votive candle, which smelled delightful. When I started getting fuzzy, I'd refresh the scent, make a cup of herbal tea, and walk around my home for a few minutes while the scent spread throughout the rooms.

Scented candles or incense also work to create relaxation. You may want to try patchouli, ylang-ylang, and vanilla, which are popular scents, as well as clary sage, rose, and geranium.

The reason aromatherapy is so effective is that the scent detected by the olfactory nerve impacts the brain immediately, unlike other substances you may drink or eat, which have to pass through the blood before they fully impact the body.

Essential Aromatherapy Oils

FOR YOU	FOR HER
FOR IMPROVING MOOD	
Vanilla: unleashes deep emotion and hidden sexuality	Jasmine: enhances femininity
	Chamomile **(B)**: clears emotional debris
Orange **(A)**: helps sort out emotional tangles	Neroli: intensely female
	Grapefruit: for a liquid face-lift; brightens things
SEXUALLY REGULATING AND STIMULATING	
Cardamom: evokes the exotic nature	Bergamot **(B)**: enlivens sex life
Vetiver: sexually arousing and stimulating	Geranium **(B)**: balances; creates harmony between the sexes
APHRODISIACS	
Sandalwood: profoundly masculine; a sedative; seductive	Ylang-ylang: intense exotic (however, in large doses it has the opposite effect)
Clary Sage **(C)**: a sexual opiate	Jasmine: empress; 100 percent feminine
Patchouli: associated with ancient eroticism, earthy	Clary Sage **(C)**: like a seductive man
Cumin: a powerful stimulant for the flow of body juices	Rose: enlivens the heart
FOR AN INVIGORATING ENERGY BOOST	
Juniper: a sexy oil	Lemongrass: clean, lively
Ginger **(A, B)**: inviting and arousing	Rosemary **(B)**: increases creativity, lifts exhaustion

Essential Aromatherapy Oils

FOR YOU	FOR HER

FOR INCREASING MENTAL ACUITY AND STRENGTHENING MEMORY

FOR YOU	FOR HER
Black Pepper: promotes stamina and strength (use sparingly) Bay: stimulates imagination; not for the submissive!	Melissa: gentle, soft; good for when suffering from mental exhaustion Rosemary **(B)**: royal in stature; stimulates sensitivity

RELAXING, REGULATING, SOOTHING

FOR YOU	FOR HER
Frankincense: releases subconscious stress Cinnamon: sensually calming for nerves	Lavender: steadying influence Marjoram: for when she needs a cuddle, not sex

HOW TO USE

For all: through vaporizing, mixed with oil for massage, or in a bath. Or: as a mouthwash **(A)**; as a hot **(B)** or cold **(C)** compress.

FOR A FACIAL MASSAGE

Dilute 15 drops of chosen essential oil in 1 ounce almond oil. Use an oil appropriate for your skin type.

SKIN TYPE	OIL
Dry	Sandalwood, Rose
Sensitive	Chamomile, Lavender
Oily	Lavender, Ylang-Ylang
Normal	Geranium, Neroli

Caution: When using essential oils in any form, make sure never to apply them to her genitals or yours.

Aphrodisiacs

There are a number of myths about aphrodisiacs, and some of these age-old products work, while others are pure hooey. As I mention above, such products as essential oils (in the form of candles, incense, or bath foams) can and do increase libido, simply because they relax you and put you in the mood.

A definition of "aphrodisiac" according to Brenda Love, author of *Encyclopedia of Unusual Sex Practices*, is "a chemical that increases or enhances sexual desire and stamina. The term comes from Aphrodite, the Greek Goddess of Love and Beauty." She then categorizes aphrodisiacs into two groups—dietary and drug. Experts believe that the most successful aphrodisiac harmonies are those that are subliminally reminiscent of bodily secretions or excretions. Just about anything can be considered an aphrodisiac if it works on one of your five senses and creates a sexual response. Any image or substance that elicits a response from your sense of taste, smell, hearing, sight, or touch, or any combination made from all five, can be considered an aphrodisiac. As Cynthia Mervis

Watson, M.D., author of *Love Potions*, states, "[W]hen all are stimulated at once, look out!"

Aphrodisiacs have taken the shape of food or drink, herb or spice, charm or ritual, drug or homeopathic remedy, flower essence or aroma. Although they varied in form, aphrodisiacs were among ancient cultures' great common denominators— remedies promising similar results have been found in China, Egypt, Mesopotamia, India, Europe, Africa, South America, and Polynesia. The bottom line is, if you think they work, they will.

Certain aphrodisiacs, such as oysters, which contain zinc (a potent mineral for sexual functioning in men), have some science to back up their effectiveness. According to Dr. Watson, it's "really simple as high school chemistry." The body is able to manufacture hormones, neurotransmitters, and neuropeptides only when fed certain essential ingredients. Many traditional aphrodisiacs are high in amino acids and the required enzymes and vitamins, which is why they work. Watson mentions that such plant extracts as yohimbe, spikenard, suma, muira puama, guarana, damiana, saw palmetto, vanilla, wild yam, ginko, bee pollen, and kava kava have been understood to show some aphrodisiac effects.

Some aphrodisiacs, such as the recreational drug MDMA (known by its street name, Ecstasy), work by altering the levels of neurotransmitters and neuropeptides. Ecstasy causes a huge release of serotonin, which produces a feeling of euphoria, but at the same time, the drug also inhibits orgasm. Another way an aphrodisiac can work is to act as an MAO (monoamine oxidase) inhibitor. That means it inhibits the production of the substance that recycles neurotransmitters, so their concentration increases in the body.

Lubricants

Lubrication is one of mankind's greatest inventions, and you should use it to your heart's content. As one mortgage broker from Cleveland said, "I had no idea there was so much fun in one of those little bottles." Sometimes people shy away from using a lubricant, as if the very existence of this slippery, slidy, marvelous stuff were some kind of reflection on their lack of sexual prowess. After his girlfriend attended one of my seminars, a man called and asked me why his partner would need "that stuff." I knew that he was really asking, "What am I not doing to get her turned on enough?" I'll tell you what I told him: that there are many different factors that affect a woman's ability to lubricate, with sexual excitement being only one of them.

> ## SECRET FROM LOU'S ARCHIVES
>
> *Women lubricate when they are sleeping; it's a sign of REM sleep.*

The mucosal tissue of a woman's genitals is some of the most delicate tissue on her body, and even if she is totally wet and lubricated when you first start to stimulate her, once that area is exposed to air or condoms, it often dries out. So she can be totally turned on and still dry out. If the activity continues, she will start to feel a pulling and tearing and I can assure you *that* feels none too nifty. The fact remains that some women, even when they are most aroused, don't always lubricate on cue. This biological fact reinforces the beauty of lubricants. And as I mentioned above, as with almost every facet of their anatomy and biology, women lubricate to varying degrees.

TIPS FOR USING LUBRICANTS

➤ During manual sex especially, put on lubricant by letting it drip through your fingers, hand in a downward trident shape (use three fingers). This works well for two reasons: (1) It warms up as it passes through your hand, and (2) the change in sensation from warm fingers to smoother, slicker palm can feel great.

➤ If you use saliva for lubricating your fingers, and you've had a glass of wine or a beer or two, remember that alcohol is a natural desiccant for your system. It dries you up, so you may not have as much saliva as you normally would. You'll have dreaded desert mouth at the wrong time.

➤ Putting oil inside a woman can give her a vaginal infection.

One-Stop Shopping

From what I understand, gentlemen, you don't want to waste your time hanging out in the drugstore aisles or at an adult-novelty store choosing among the huge array of lubricants on the market. What I have assembled for you is a list of the best lubricants, keeping in mind not only her pleasure but your own as well. For indeed, though she will enjoy the use of lubrication, *you* will reap the rewards.

There are many products to choose from, including those that are water based, oil based, flavored, nonflavored, scented, unscented, colored, clear, liquid, and gels. It can be a bit overwhelming. I asked my field researchers to investigate which lubricants felt and tasted the best. The results of our efforts are listed below, though this is by no means an exhaustive study.

Secret from Lou's Archives

Many women I know prefer colorless lubricants, as they won't stain the sheets or other materials.

FAVORITE LUBRICANTS

Again, this is not an exhaustive list, but you can use it as a general guide. (* means the product is colorless.)

> **Very Private Intimate Moisturizer.** * One of the best new products I have found. The creator behind this product came up with it because she couldn't find a product on the market that met her own needs. She had spent years in the cosmetic business and has now created her own private line, working with dermatologists and gynecologists. This is an outstanding lubricant, especially for women. It

actually feels more like a moisturizer in that it doesn't just sit on the surface of the skin but is lightly absorbed. It's water based, colorless, and fragrance free. If it's not available in your area, you can order it from my Web site, www.loupaget.com.

➤ **Sensura/Sex Grease.** * This is the water-based lubricant of choice for many connoisseurs. It is a clear, thick liquid with a velvety texture that maintains a slick feel for a long time. The same product is marketed under two different names and packaged in two different ways. For the ladies it is called Sensura and bottled in pink. For the men it is called Sex Grease and bottled in black.

➤ **Midnite Fire.** * This lubricant comes in a small container with a snap-on lid. A woman from one of my seminars told me that whenever her husband wants her to come home "for a quickie," all he has to do is call her and snap open the lid of Midnite Fire over the phone. "It doesn't matter where I am—at my desk or in my car on the cell phone. When I hear that 'snap,' I am instantly wet!" Need I say more?

Midnite Fire is almost guaranteed to bring you lots of enjoyment. It not only comes in a variety of flavors, it also becomes very warm with gentle rubbing, and even warmer when you blow on it following the rub. Not to worry, though, because the heat only builds to a certain level, so there is no risk of getting burned. It is the CO_2 in your breath that causes it to heat when you blow on it. Midnite Fire is a water-based lubricant, so it is safe for application both internally and externally. Although billed as "The Hot Sensual

Massage Lotion," it's really too thick to be used for a straight massage without adding water or another clear water-based lubricant. It feels especially erotic when applied to the nipples or inner thighs. Be aware if your partner has a predisposition for infections, and test before going wild. It has also received rave reviews when used on the head of the penis and the testicles.

SECRET FROM LOU'S ARCHIVES

Beware of certain lubricants on the market that call themselves "body glides." Eros, Venus Millennium, and Platinum are newer products that are made of dimethicone (silicone) and carry no protective value and aren't water-soluble. Some even have a caution "flammable" or "for external use only" on the label. These are not only impractical, they also may be dangerous if the silicone is absorbed by the body.

➢ **Embrace.** Truly one of the nicer-tasting and -feeling, this lubricant has a thick, velvety consistency similar to Sensura yet with a taste some prefer. A favorite of those who want a lubricant to stay put when they apply it rather than having it run for lower elevations. It comes unflavored (which is slightly sweet) and in Strawberry and Lime Sherbet flavors.

➢ **Liquid Silk.** The name describes it all. This creamy water-based, British lubricant in a pump bottle contains no glycerin, so it doesn't get sticky, and has become a favorite of field researchers. It is great for manual techniques and intercourse. It does, however, have a slightly bitter taste, which detracts from its use during oral sex.

➤ **Maximus.** * This is the clear version of Liquid Silk. It comes in a clear plastic pump bottle and is also a big favorite.

SECRET FROM LOU'S ARCHIVES

Be aware of inserting massage oil or any sugar-based product, including fruit, into your partner. These products can cause vaginal infections by altering the normal pH balance of the vagina.

TIPS FOR CHOOSING LUBRICANTS

➤ Always remember that oil and latex don't mix. Oil in any form is the mortal enemy of latex condoms, often causing them to break. Check the label of anything you're using, such as hand or massage lotions. If it says "oil" anywhere, you shouldn't use it as a lubricant with latex condoms. (Remember to read the label in its entirety. The big print alone can be misleading. If you see the word "oil" listed anywhere in the ingredients, chances are the product is not water based.)

➤ Know how sensitive you and your partner are to new products. Some women are so sensitive they can get bladder and vaginal infections from merely changing toilet tissue or soap. Remember that your partner is much more at risk for irritation and infection than you are. She is the receptive partner and the products you choose typically remain inside her.

➤ Check to see if the product is okay for the genital area. Often the fine print on the package will say "for topical or cosmetic use" or "avoid contact with eyes."

➤ If you are sensitive or susceptible to irritation, watch out for the spermicide known as nonoxynol-9. It can be extremely irritating to both men and women. This is the *only* manufactured spermicidal in the United States, and it's the active ingredient in contraceptive foams/jellies, suppositories, film, and on condoms. It was introduced in the United States in 1920s as a cleaning solution for hospitals. Translation: It's a detergent. Can you imagine rubbing a detergent on her down there? This will give her pain, not pleasure.

It's about time we consumers hit the manufacturers of these products where it hurts—their bottom line. If you're reading this book, read *their* labels. If the bottle's back label in teensy-weensy print says "for topical cosmetic use only," what does that mean? And when they say "for external use only"? Hmmmm, I'll let you be the judge. Manufacturers assume they can get away with dangerous or hurtful products, such as nonoxynol-9 and silicone, which can cause an allergic reaction or irritation. The only way they will stop producing them is if you stop buying them.

SECRET FROM LOU'S ARCHIVES

At the risk of being annoying, I must again warn you to avoid, at all cost, using any lubricant containing the spermicide nonoxynol-9 during oral sex. This ingredient not only tastes awful, it will have a slight numbing effect on your mouth.

You're Never Too Old for Toys

Long associated with subjects less than respectful, sex toys and other "adult toys" have come out of the proverbial closet. Do you know how many more men and women use sex toys today than a decade ago? The numbers will probably surprise you. According to two adult-novelty manufacturers, the market has increased tenfold over the past ten years, becoming a $500-million retail business. Experts attribute this marked increase in the use of sex toys to a couple of reasons. In general, one manufacturer explains that "there is less stigma" attached to toys than there used to be. Furthermore, couples feel there is more openness in marriages to try new things. The manufacturer said, "Men and women are feeling pressure to remain monogamous and be safer about sex. As a result, they are looking for inventive ways to spice up their sex lives." Clear evidence of this turnaround is the fact that some of our grandmothers and great-grandmothers were using vibrators, showing us that they were a lot more progressive in this area than we had any idea. So keep reading.

First let me say that these products are not meant to replace passionate, connecting lovemaking. It is a given that the majority of women in the ladies' seminars genuinely like men and want to be around men. This is true despite the fact that we may not necessarily understand men at all times. So again, toys are not meant to replace either partner. They are simply meant to enhance your sexual experience and add a bit of fun to your sex life. As one man, a triathlete from Los Angeles, said, "I'm just going to design my own tool belt. I'll slap a bottle of lubricant on one side and a vibrator on the other. Then I'll be all set."

If your partner is unfamiliar with sex toys, then be respectful and courteous in how you suggest introducing them into your relationship. Women can be shy and may think of the toys as a sign of your dissatisfaction. If that thought gets into her head, she may withdraw from the toys *and* you. After her boyfriend suggested they play with a vibrator, one woman said, "I went straight to 'I'm not adequate enough as a lover.' And it wasn't until he told me he got them because he thought we'd have fun that I realized how off base I was." Another woman said, "What started out as a joke gift led us to look at other toys that are now a really fun part of what we do together."

She needs to know from you that toys are something you want to share with her. You need to emphasize that it's the freedom in your relationship that enables you both to experiment and loosen the boundaries of the tried and true.

Keep in mind, too, that neither of you is expected to know how to use these items at the outset. Look at some of them and you may think, "What on earth is it?" Every industry has its own trade show, and the one I attend happens to be the semiannual Adult Novelty Manufacturers Expo; in essence, it's a trade show for sex toys. I can assure you there are times when I see a product and think, "What were they thinking?!" (Some of these products are not really intended to work; they are simply made to sell.) Then there are other times when a product seems interesting, and I hand it over to my field researchers, who then try it and give me feedback. The diagrams and directions below will shed some light on those toys that received the highest praise. You need to give yourself permission to introduce something new and have some fun with toys—after all, isn't experiencing something new a natural part of intimacy?

Though I encourage you to use toys in any way you see fit, I do suggest some Cardinal Toy Rules:

1. Wash them in warm water and an antibacterial soap before and after use.
2. Use only water-based lubricants with any of your plastic-compound items, as oil products, massage oil, or hand lotion (anything containing lanolin or petrolatum) will start to break down the surface of the plastic.
3. Use a condom on parts that are inserted vaginally or anally; this will clean up a lot easier.
4. Keep toys used for different areas separate from one another. For example, if your partner likes anal penetration, then don't use that dildo for her vagina, and so on. Toy-savvy types have one bag for vaginal toys and another for anal.
5. Keep your toys in a safe place, away from dust and oils.
6. Don't share your toys. Why risk it?

Dildo/Vibrator Basics

There is a style and type of dildo or vibrator to suit everyone—man or woman. Some are completely lifelike, having been molded from real people, often adult-film stars.

It's important to choose a style that suits you, and one that is easy to clean. Some women prefer those made of silicone because they warm up faster than latex. Some women enjoy the heightened sensations and contractions of the vagina during climax that come from the PC muscle tightening around the dildo, creating more tension.

You have your choice of:

SIZE

➤ Sizes range from very small to full arm size. The larger are admittedly for a specialized "niche" market.
➤ With or without "balls."
➤ Double dildos for simultaneous penetration for two partners.

MATERIAL

➤ Cyberskin, plastic (hard or soft), latex, silicone, metal, rubber, vinyl, Jelee™.

SHAPE

➤ Straight, curved, lifelike, ridged, smooth, egg, telescoping, and a special design suitable for G-spot/prostate stimulation.

VIBRATING FEATURES

➤ Vibrating dildos; typically the vibrating part (which can be adjusted to different pulsations) will be aligned to stimulate the clitoris while the shaft portion is inserted vaginally. Meanwhile, the shaft portion can be doing something nifty such as rotating, twisting at the head, pulsing in and out at the same time the clitoris is being stimulated. Vibration can also be variable pulsations.

➤ Power source from battery or electricity.

COLOR

➤ Any color you can imagine: fluorescent, black, brown, pink, flesh, clear, purple, white, solids, stripes, sparkles—the list is quite endless.

HARNESSES

➤ Dildos can be used "freestyle" in your hand or attached to a harness, which is leather or fabric, and worn around your hips.

➤ Thigh harnesses can be used by a man if he wants full-body contact. One seminar attendee told of how her husband, who is paraplegic, fulfilled her beyond her wildest dreams. "He was able to penetrate me in a way I didn't think possible." You never know when these toys will work their magic.

How to Use Them

➤ **Breathe.** During any sexual activity breathing is your friend and deep breathing will heighten the sensations.

- ➤ **Apply to clitoris.** This will add a significant buzz to partner sex. You can cushion the vibration through a garment or the fleshy outer labia. Often women find direct clitoral stimulation too intense until they are more excited. Use a range of stroking motions up and down the clitoral ridge.
- ➤ **Insert vaginally.** Insert either a dildo or vibrator in the interior of the vagina; the first 1½ inches is the most sensitive.
- ➤ **Anally.** If you and your partner enjoy anal play, a small butt plug or vibrating dildo will send you heavenward. Men who enjoy this typically choose a slim little wand style that can be inserted while they are masturbating or their partner is manually touching them.
- ➤ **In combo.** On yourself or with a partner. This can be accomplished by wearing a harness, which, depending on its design, can hold more than one dildo. So, your partner could wear a vaginal-plug dildo in the harness for herself, while the "front loaded" dildo is available to penetrate you. This way everyone can have the feeling of fullness.

Types of Vibrators

There are umpteen styles, sizes, shapes, and colors of vibrators. They are powered by one of two sources—electricity or batteries. They are travel size or made to leave at home. Some have smooth surfaces, while others come with ridges—just like some potato chips. Other vibrators come with protruding attachments to stimulate more than one area at a time (see the Rabbit Pearl on page 278). The following sampling (the favorites among the women and men in my seminars) should help you begin the search for the perfect vibrator for you and your partner.

➤ "Wand style" describes the shape of the vibrator and is therefore the most recognizable of the various styles. It is usually made of hard plastic and powered by batteries.

Wand Style

➤ Coil-operated vibrators were originally designed for sore neck and muscle massage. Often electrically powered, they tend to be larger and stronger than the wand style. Some older coil-operated vibrators strap onto the back of your hand for legitimate massage work. They come with various attachments and are the easiest to disguise as being for another purpose.

➤ Fingertip and remote-controlled vibrators are distinctive for their ability to create a surprise effect. Manufacturers finally have made some that work!

Remote Style

> Waterproof vibrators are capable of accompanying you and your partner into the shower! They range in size from small, handheld ones to larger, soft, foam-covered balls four inches in diameter that can be used over the entire body (see the Pulsa Bath on page 280).

SECRET FROM LOU'S ARCHIVES

Manufacturers spend much more on the design of the box than they do on the research and development of the products themselves.

Below are some classic vibrators. If you happen to be a *Sex and the City* fan, you'll know what I mean.

THE RABBIT PEARL

The design of the Rabbit Pearl lends itself to being able to stimulate both partners at the same time. To ensure maximum

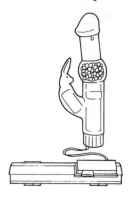

The Rabbit Pearl

stimulation for both, it's best to concentrate the vibration in the bunny section (leave the articulating option off). This way, she can have the wand section inserted vaginally and, with you lying on top of her, your hips matched with hers, turn on the (very strong Japanese) motor. The RP's nose or ears can be stimulating her clitoral area and the back of it can be stimulating the underside of your scrotum.

THE MICRO TICKLER

The small, vibrating silver bullet is encased in an incredibly stretchy sheath that holds it in place at the base of the man. The sheath has a two-textured vibrating surface that can also be used to please a woman.

The Microtickler

THE HITACHI MAGIC WAND
AND THE G-SPOTTER ATTACHMENT

The Hitachi Magic Wand vibrator is a classic for good reason. It stimulates a wide area in a big, soft way that women love. The G-Spotter is an attachment that specifically stimulates the G-spot.

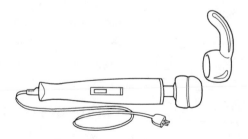

The Hitachi Magic Wand

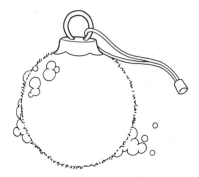

The Pulsa Bath

THE PULSA BATH

The Pulsa Bath is a Nerf-like ball about six inches across with an internal vibrating component—your showers and bath time will never be the same.

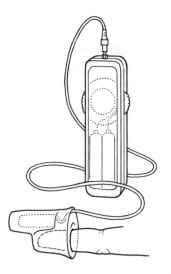

Finger Vibe

FINGER VIBE

The Finger Vibe is one of the more powerful, almost silent fingertip vibrators. It is soft, and you can pinpoint the vibration very specifically. It doesn't ever numb your finger—a terrific product!

HIP HARNESS VIBRATOR

Developed for those who like "hands-free" operation of their dildo or vibrator. The main difference between this and the regular handheld vibrators is the design feature of elastic thigh straps, which enable a woman to adjust the vibrating area to her liking. This same design is used for remote vibrators that a partner can operate from across a room. Please be aware that some remote vibrators operate on the same radio frequency as garage-door openers.

Special Playthings

The Pearl Necklace

Here's a "toy" your partner can wear to dinner and use in bed later. I recommend a 30- to 36-inch strand of 8 to 10mm round costume pearls because of their smooth, even size and shape. (She should use costume pearls, not real, natural pearls.) She starts by lightly lubricating your penis, then slowly adorns you by wrapping the pearls around the shaft. If she's worn them out for dinner, the pearls will be softly warm. When your penis looks like it is wearing a Princess Diana choker, she can start slowly stroking you up and down with the Basket Weave stroke. She then unwraps your penis and, almost like she's flossing under your testicles, slowly pulls the pearls from one side to the other, slightly lifting the testicles. And when she's done she can coil the "poils" at the base of the shaft and settle herself on top of you. No doubt pearls will start to have a new place in your repertoire!

Cock Rings

The theory behind cock rings is the law of hydraulics. An erect penis is a study in hydraulics. Stimulation causes blood to flow in and fill the penis chambers. Gravity and a drop-off of stimulation cause the blood to flow back out. Cock rings work temporarily by greatly reducing the drop-off of penile blood pressure by holding shut the veins along the sides of the erect penis that allow the blood to flow out. The result is a firmer, more long-lasting erection. And some men report delays in ejaculation.

TIPS ON USING COCK RINGS

1. To be most effective, you or your partner can apply a light lubricant on the ring and your penis. It's best to use a water-based lubricant, as it will not break down the material the way oils/lotions will.
2. The most effective position for the ring is on the shaft and underneath the scrotum. Placing it only on the shaft has some men reporting, "It was too tight just on the shaft, and yet even though I thought the other way would be more of the same, oddly I felt more supported and 'just right.'"
3. The ring can be worn during manual stimulation and/or during intercourse. Often couples will try the ring first during manual sex, and when they know what works for them, they move to intercourse.
4. Some couples have reported they enjoyed either starting intercourse with a cock ring on and then removing it prior to climax or placing it on halfway through and finishing with it in place.
5. The scrotum and penis may be a much darker color when the ring is in place. That is natural, as the blood is pooled there. The ring should not be worn for

longer than twenty to thirty minutes without removing for a few minutes' break.

6. When you're finished using the cock ring, simply wash with antibacterial soap and water and it will be ready for next time.

Shaft Sleeves

These one-size-fits-all products are made of a very stretchy, soft, almost plush, rubberlike material that can be used on the penis or fingers. The main idea behind them is that most manual stimulation is done with the fingertips, and those tend to be soft and smooth. Shaft sleeves offer a new way to increase sensation in those most delicate areas with a variety of soft-textured surfaces that are easily controlled with your fingers. Because of their expandable nature, they can also be worn at the base of the penis. In the seminars, men try them on in the palm of their hands and are always surprised by the softness of the sleeves. This versatile item can be used:

1. **By you on your partner.** Now instead of relying solely on your fingertips to stimulate your partner's clitoral area, you have help in the form of these soft-textured sleeves. Just try one on the palm of your hand. Be sure to put the lubricant on or you won't get the real sensation. Men have reported using two at a time so they can caress and pleasure both sides of the inner labia and clitoral ridge. Women say, "He was good with his hands before, and now he is amazing." When used during intercourse, you wear it at the base

of your penis for deep, slow penetration. The soft ripples and ridges are able to stimulate her. Works for both female-superior and male-superior positions.

2. **By your partner on you**—slipped like a finger sleeve over one or two fingertips. Some people report using two sleeves covering different fingers. Apply a light amount of water-based lubricant and use your imagination.

3. **Solo**—perhaps the best way to discover the sensations possible with the different textures.

Butt Plugs and Anal Beads

For men, the primary stimulation spot is the prostate gland. The sensation delivered for women is feeling more full, and if intercourse is to take place, there is an even greater feeling of fullness. Both toys require lots of lubrication, as the anal area is nonlubricating.

Butt plugs are in essence a dildo for the anus, but with a design adaptation of a flange at the base to ensure it does not fully enter the rectum. It is usually an inverted cone shape so that once it is in, the strength of the sphincter holds it in place. As I'm sure you know by now, there are actually two anal sphincters. Only one of the sphincters, the strong muscle ring that keeps the anal opening closed, is under voluntary control. The other is under involuntary control, so try as you might, you can't consciously relax it. Therefore, in order to relax both sphincters, you need physical assistance. One man suggests "inserting one finger for one minute, two fingers for two minutes." But remember to keep the fingers still—don't move them.

Anal beads are plastic or metal balls on a string. All but one of the beads are inserted into the anus, then pulled out before or at the moment of orgasm, as the PC muscle is undergoing orgasmic spasms in the anus. "When it gets pulled out, I have another orgasmic wave," reported a thirty-seven-year-old woman from Beverly Hills.

Crystal Wand

This is one of the better G-spot stimulating devices, and it makes sense—a woman designed it. Made of solid, clear acrylic, it can be angled and rested on a pillow so that the woman can maintain the pressure she prefers while masturbating. You can use it for prostate stimulation.

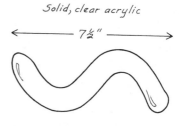

Solid, clear acrylic

←——— 7½" ———→

Crystal Wand

HISTORICAL AND HYSTERICAL FACTS	The ever-ingenious Chinese created sexual toys in the twelfth and thirteenth centuries such as the double olishos, a dildo that could accommodate two women at once. The device was contained in an ivory or wooden phallus with two silk belts in the middle of it. The movement of one woman created pleasure for the other. Another device was a dildo that could be manipulated by moving the heel of the foot. This kept the hands free for other amorous activities, or perhaps household duties.

Sportsheets™

Like all great ideas, this one began small and then grew. Sportsheets™ were invented by a marine officer whose inspiration was watching David Letterman attach himself to a wall of Velcro. He said to his officer buddies in the mess, "Wouldn't it be great if you could do that with your girlfriend?" The wife of one of the officers made sheets out of fabric and created Velcro attachment pads with cuffs, and then they had a party to see if this would work. Sportsheets™ were born.

Sportsheets™ are a kind of sex kit, made up of a very soft, plush, yet durable velour-type sheet that fits from a full up to a king-size bed. Four anchor pads that are attached to cuff straps anchor you or her to the sheet and the bed. The idea is that one partner is secured to the bed with the cuffs in whatever position you or she desires. And you can increase the playfulness of sex without the more serious tone of other bondage products. I call this the Boy Scout introduction to bondage, for those of you who want to test the waters in safety.

The fitted sheet is very soft and can be left in place on your bed. The Velcro pads are not at all menacing. For women who like to be "grounded," this is the next best thing to being tied up!

Secret from Lou's Archives

For the true bondage beginner, try using toilet tissue to give the feeling of being held hostage, with no real threat.

The Bungee Weightless Sex Experience

This product may provide you and yours with a truly new experience. Designed by a bungee enthusiast, it is essentially a modified bungee jumping harness, made up of a series of straps that you hang from a stud beam in the ceiling. A photo reference chart for the myriad positions is included in the package.

With her cradled in the harness, you can penetrate her with no back or leg strain. Women and men like the weightlessness. This is the perfect addition to your playground—especially for those of you who like hammocks and swings. There's something about the movement aspect that is exciting and pleasurable. As the designer/inventor said, "Never again will you have a crick in your neck." (Be careful of your drywall. It's best to check before anchoring, or you'll tear part of your ceiling out.)

This is also a great way to give her oral sex. With a flick of your finger, you can move her around and never have to crane your neck or move your head again.

Surgical Procedures

There are certain surgical procedures that promise to enhance your sexual experience. And while some of these are gaining popular attention, I can only recommend a few, as the others are quite dangerous or create very serious side effects.

The surgical enhancement procedures for men concern penis enlargement, and there are two main types: (1) cutting the suspensory ligaments that attach the root of the penis to the pelvis, which causes the penis to drop and hence have a longer look when flaccid. Unfortunately, this makes the erection less stable because its support structures have been cut; (2) injecting adipose (fatty) tissue harvested from another area of the body into the penis to increase its width. The problem with this procedure is the body's tendency to reabsorb the adipose in an irregular fashion, resulting in a lumpy penis. One woman referred to a penis that underwent this procedure as "a swollen, angry sausage."

I agree with Drs. Milsten and Slowinski, who approach these types of procedures with an "if it ain't broke, don't fix it" attitude. As described above, these procedures are often fraught with problems, and may not be worth the pain of surgery.

SECRET FROM LOU'S ARCHIVES

Because of the high number of malpractice cases resulting from botched male sex-enhancement surgeries, a new area of legal expertise has developed.

Exercises

There are different exercises that will increase your degree of pleasure. The most common and talked-about exercise is of course the Kegel, which directly strengthens and tones your pubococcygeal, or PC, muscles. The PC muscle is your sex muscle.

How to Do Kegels

➤ Contract and internally lift the region between your genitals and anus, squeezing your muscles inward, toward the center of your body.

➤ Breathe in and out as you squeeze and release the muscle.

SECRET FROM LOU'S ARCHIVES

The PC muscle is a small muscle, so when you first start out building it up, a number of reps will make it sore. According to Bryce Britton, author of The Love Muscle, *tie your exercise schedule of three times a day for five minutes to something you already do regularly—foot on the brake while driving, sitting at a light, brushing your teeth after each meal. And do a variety of moves. After all, you wouldn't go to the gym and do only biceps curls would you?*

As Dr. Beverly Whipple attests, there is a direct correlation between a well-toned PC muscle and the intensity of orgasms. And strengthening it can also increase potency. While erect, contract your PC muscle and watch it jump. To increase the resistance (as a strengthener), you can use a wet washcloth draped over your erect penis, in the shower or afterward.

CHAPTER THIRTEEN

Sex and the Spirit

Following an Enlightened Path to Ecstasy

Transforming Sexual Energy into Spiritual Love

Sex can be fun. Sex can be passionate. Sex can be physically pleasurable. Sex can also be spiritual. If you think about it, every event or activity in our lives—whether it be driving in the car, playing a game of golf, or making love—can be experienced three ways: physically, emotionally, and spiritually. Sometimes these elements fuse together, making an event that much more meaningful. Yet, for many of us, and I include myself in this category, spirituality was considered the domain of organized religion, and in most cases that didn't include an open, passionate view of sexuality. The main message about sex that came through these channels tended to be that sex and religion simply don't mix. A bit like dogs circling each other, each camp saw the other as an adversary, possibly acknowledging the existence of the other, but staying distant.

This chapter is for those of you who want to feel connected with your partner in a spiritual way—perhaps not all the time, but at least once in a while. Have you ever felt so close to your lover after making love or during an orgasm that your surroundings seem to disappear? Or that you and your lover felt so connected and in tune with each other that the rest of the world ceased to matter?

Many of us may have one memory of such an experience when sex transported us to another realm. This sometimes occurs only with one person and fleetingly, but it is experienced as a hugely different connection and state during lovemaking. Some of the masters of spiritual sexuality refer to this state as ecstasy and think of it as the supreme form of making love. But how and why does this happen? For those of us who have had this experience, it seems to have come out of nowhere, a spontaneous event that is completely out of our control. Or is it in our control?

SECRET FROM LOU'S ARCHIVES

According to author Margot Anand, the five virtues of the ecstatic lover are: Patience, Trust, Presence, Compassion, and Clarity.

Sexologist Jack Morin, in his book *The Erotic Mind*, succinctly summarizes why peak erotic experiences are perfectly suited to spiritual experience and transcendence: "They engage us totally, enlarge our sense of self by connecting us with another or with normally hidden dimensions of ourselves or both, and expand our perceptions and consciousness" (as quoted in *Liberated Orgasm* by Herbert Otto). Therapists Jack Zimmerman and Jaquelyn McCandless have termed this "expanded state of awareness" the Third Presence. In their own relationship, they experienced a distinctive state of awareness made possible by the transcendent spiritual dimension of their relationship. As they describe in their book, *Flesh and Spirit*, "What we are really talking about [is] an expanded state of consciousness that is co-created by two partners together, with something unconditional and ultimately mysterious that is not of the ordinary world."

In this country, there has been interest in a sacred form of sex since the 1960s, and this growing interest in the spiritual evolved into the New Age movement. The desire to learn about Eastern philosophies and religions was fueled by two forces: a quest for spiritual knowledge, coupled with a rejection of past social and religious limitations on sexual expression. The 1960s radicals who were becoming champions of "free love" wanted to redefine sex and disassociate it from guilt and the concept of sin. They saw sex as an event that celebrated life.

In many ways, this emerging American vision of the new sexuality was borrowed from and built upon what the ancient Eastern schools had believed in for centuries. Specifically, the philosophic schools of Chinese Taoism and Buddhist Tantra had been practicing a sexuality that was very tied to the spiritual realm. These ancient Eastern systems of spiritual enlightenment had their beginnings about 5000 B.C., according to scholars. These groups insist that getting to the spiritual realm through sex is not only possible, it's also probable, and a goal one should seek to attain. In fact, they have come up with elaborate ceremonies (over sixty-five different positions) that basically teach you how to enter the "holy realm."

The starting premise is twofold: (1) men and women have different natures and (2) sexual acts have the capacity to be not only physiologically transporting, but psychologically and emotionally enlightening as well. The only requirements are that both partners are in agreement and they proceed in a meditative, studied way.

All Tantra Is Not Created Equal

In the past few years an East-meets-West zeitgeist has brought everything from yoga to Zen Buddhism into mainstream American culture. It seems only natural, then, that we Westerners should also be curious about the Eastern approach to sex, which has as its hallmark a more spiritual point of view. Specifically, Tantra, which developed as a form of yoga practice, embodies this Eastern (both Buddhist and Hindu) ideal. The focus of Tantra is not on transformation of sex, but on the use of sexual energy to develop and create a spiritual experience. Tantric sex uses traditional rituals and specific sex positions to help practitioners achieve mystical union. Tantric practitioners believe in combining relaxation with high states of sexual excitement. Sexual energy is recirculated for an extended time. As a result, practitioners sometimes experience long-lasting orgasms, which are not genitally focused.

However, as with most things we import from faraway lands and cultures, some things about Tantra have been lost in translation. As a result, there are many misconceptions about Tantra, ranging from people thinking it's a form of "naked yoga" in which "couples have sex," to people believing that it's merely a form of sexual massage.

Tantra is viewed as a spiritual exercise and path to enlightenment. Its movements and postures are based on yoga principles of body alignment, and breathing exercises to cleanse the body, mind, and soul. Yet its overall goal maintains that sex leads to achieving a higher level of awareness and connection to the universe, or God. Doing Tantra with your partner becomes a spiritual exercise in which together you bond so deeply that you become one, and nearer to the essence of life.

Secret from Lou's Archives

In Chinese culture, sexual energy or Ching-Chi is one of the most obvious and powerful types of bioelectrical energy. According to Mantak Chia, what we in the West call getting aroused or horny, the Taoists thought of as the generating of sexual energy.

Tantric students fine-tune their senses so that each becomes one with the universe and with their partner. The exchange of secretions between the man and the woman plays an important role in this process. Three distinct types of sexual secretions or elixirs are produced by the woman—from the breasts, mouth, and yoni (vagina). Absorption by the man of these elixirs is said to be spiritually nourishing and compensates him for the loss of semen, which he gives to the woman. In Tantric practices, the man becomes the Shiva (the Divine Will), which manifests in the creative union with the Shakti (representing pure energy). The woman becomes the Shakti, and embodies the fundamental secret forces that control the universe.

Orgasm is usually understood only in physical terms: as a highly pleasurable, explosive experience with muscular pelvic contractions, most often resulting from stimulation of the genitals. As I've pointed out in the preceding chapters, you don't have to be stimulated genitally to have an orgasm. And just as the genitals should not limit the source of your orgasm, neither should your body limit your experience of an orgasm. The main requirement for accessing this spiritual realm is that you are open and willing to let go of any attitudes that may be holding you back. I promise, this is much easier than it may seem to you at first.

When you approach sex as a spiritual activity, you view orgasm as an exchange of energy between lovers. This exchange creates yet another form of energy that can transform you and your experience, making you feel one with your lover. At the physical level, most of these practices maintain that if a man controls his ejaculation, he will be able to prolong and heighten pleasure for both his partner and himself. Sexologists Marilyn Fithian and William Hartman speculate that the quick intercourse couples often experience "does not allow enough time for the natural chemicals that accompany touch and sexual arousal to be released into the bloodstream, which then short-circuits the general sense of well-being that usually accompanies lovemaking" (as quoted in Chia). In other words, when sex is "hasty," the man and the woman are not able to exchange sexual energy and harmonize with each other, and may even drain each other of energy.

Meditation and breathing techniques are used to control and extend the arousal period so that the penis stays functional for nearly an hour. Now, that might be a nice thing to learn, don't you agree? Based upon these general premises, a couple then has many positions with which they can regulate the flow of energy between each other, and I will address these positions later in the chapter. It's also important to maintain eye contact and match breathing in order to further connect with your partner. As you may imagine, this is a very subtle process and one that requires both people to be in a calm, relaxed state of mind.

For me, there's a lot about Tantra that is wonderful, transforming, and simply practical. So, here I've boiled down what I think is the best of Tantra. I've streamlined this presentation and left out a lot of the overly "woo-woo" language, without, I hope, losing its spiritual essence. My reason for this is twofold: Many of the books out there on Tantra seem weighted down by too many ideas and New Age gobbledy-gook, which keep women and men from experiencing, understanding, or using the very practical suggestions for how to improve their sex lives, specifically in the orgasm department.

HISTORICAL AND HYSTERICAL FACTS	Extraordinary sexual positions and entanglements can be seen frozen on ancient Indian temple walls. These positions were created and performed by Tantric holy women trained from childhood in the art of love. For Western Tantrikas, without such a background, these complex positions are difficult and less than comfortable.

Second, though classic Tantra is a form of yoga practice, you don't have to become a yogi to benefit from the movements and exercises. It's my feeling that the more practical, accurate information you have about sex, the more you are likely to grow, explore, and discover sexual satisfaction. So consider this information on Tantra and go to town. To those who are open to new ideas, I guarantee you will learn something about yourself, your body, and how to increase your own and your partner's pleasure quotient.

Lou's Practical Guide to Spiritual Sex

Whatever your personal philosophy or religion, you can still take advantage of the underlying concepts and practice of spiritual sex. That is, if you have the right attitude. As I say above, the "right attitude" is one that is open and willing to the *possibility* of spiritual sex. So before I give you the techniques and positions, I would like to share with you the guidelines that experts say will enable you to reach a heightened and expanded state of awareness and sensation. These guidelines are made up of ideas, which in turn make up the open-minded attitude:

1. Have the same intention. As this is more of a mind-body connection, ideally both partners should have the same intention about their sexual joining. If not, a transportive connection cannot be achieved.
2. Accept your vulnerability. This approach to sex tends to make women and men feel more emotionally vulnerable because it stresses a more passive, receptive state. This is especially true of the man's role to encourage and give to the woman.
3. Set aside enough time during which you will not be interrupted. Maintaining a soothing, open ambience is crucial to the spiritual-sexual connection.
4. Know that like any new venture it will take time to

become proficient. For those who are already comfortable and safe emotionally, you may enter this realm overnight. For others, it may take some time, confidence, and reassurance with your partner.

5. Keep in mind the goal of spiritual sex: connecting spiritually with your partner through sex. This is a sexual attitude and style, not a sexual performance goal. If your only reason to study these philosophies is to discover the way to be multiorgasmic, then you are missing the larger point!

For those who feel these states may not be possible for them, I would like to point out it is easier *done* than *said*. In other words, you may find the language of Tantra a bit new and therefore off-putting, but in practice the actual positions and techniques are quite simple and straightforward. You might also be interested in knowing that the benefits of Tantra are quite real and concrete. Margot Anand points out in her book *Sexual Ecstasy* that Tantric sex can help men:

➤ Learn to increase the ability to control ejaculation in states of high arousal.
➤ Learn how to experience extended, whole-body orgasm without ejaculation.
➤ Experience their full orgasmic potential, as shown in the diagram on page 300.

And it can help women:

➤ Learn the ability to become sexually aroused more quickly and fully.

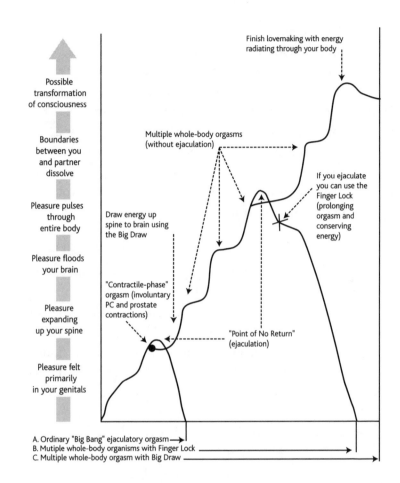

Possible
transformation
of consciousness

Boundaries
between you
and partner
dissolve

Pleasure pulses
through
entire body

Pleasure floods
your brain

Pleasure
expanding
up your spine

Pleasure felt
primarily
in your genitals

Finish lovemaking with energy
radiating through your body

Multiple whole-body orgasms
(without ejaculation)

Draw energy up
spine to brain using
the Big Draw

If you ejaculate
you can use the
Finger Lock
(prolonging
orgasm and
conserving
energy)

"Contractile-phase"
orgasm (involuntary
PC and prostate
contractions)

"Point of No Return"
(ejaculation)

A. Ordinary "Big Bang" ejaculatory orgasm
B. Mutiple whole-body organisms with Finger Lock
C. Multiple whole-body orgasm with Big Draw

MALE ORGASMIC POTENTIAL

Instead of the ordinary "Big Bang" ejaculatory orgasm (A), with sexual kung fu you can draw your sexual energy up during contractile phase (before ejaculation) and have multiple whole-body orgasms. If you ejaculate, you can use the Finger Lock, which will prolong your orgasm and conserve energy (B). If you avoid ejaculation, you can use the Big Draw to finish lovemaking with energy radiating through your body (C).

➤ Learn how to experience whole-body orgasm through sexual intercourse.

The Basic Positions

Many of the truly ancient Tantric positions are complicated and elaborate and would be difficult to practice by ordinary people on an ordinary day. Charles and Caroline Muir, who have spent years studying and adapting Tantra for Western women and men, have developed five basic sexual positions for people wanting to try Tantra. Within these five positions, hundreds of variations are possible. The five are:

1. Yab Yum, which is unique to Tantra
2. Horizontal with man on top
3. Horizontal with woman on top, or Swooping Shakti
4. Completing the Circuit
5. Man behind the woman, or Piercing Tiger

Regardless of how many positions you choose to do, the main credos of spiritual lovemaking hold for them all: This is a blending of mind, body, and spirit and your aim is connecting into oneness, not just getting off.

Yab Yum

According to Margot Anand, the Yab Yum position is "the ultimate form of Tantric union." In this position, the position of the man and woman allow the chakras, or energy centers, to be more aligned so that the energy can flow more easily up and down and through the partners.

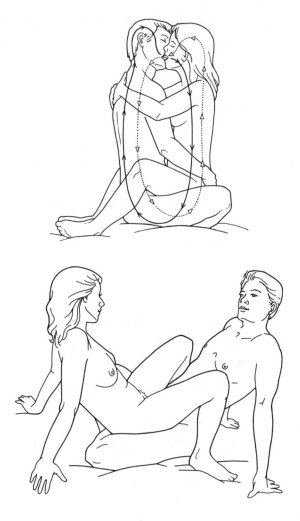

Yab Yum

In Yab Yum the spine is aligned with gravity, which is an essential ingredient for drawing energy to the higher chakras and for stimulating the pineal and pituitary gland, which is considered critical for enlightenment to occur. Both of you sit erect and facing each other. You sit cross-legged and she sits astride you, while you support her weight on your thighs. Her legs are open and around you, with the soles of her feet touching. Note that her slight elevation brings your chakras into alignment. If necessary, to alleviate the stress on your thighs, place a pillow under her hips.

Before going into formal Tantric practice, you may want to consider a more relaxed starting position such as in the lower illustration on page 302. It lets you find your comfort place, and you can initiate small pelvic rocking to build sensation before moving to the more connected illustration (shown at the top of page 302).

Horizontal with Man on Top

According to the Taoists, the horizontal position (with the man on top), "respects the woman's innate nature—her qual-

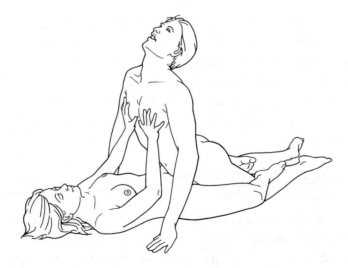

Man on Top, with Tongue Press

Push-Pull

ities of water, coolness and slow rhythm. The posture allows
the woman to be passive at first, giving her time to unfold, receive, open, and slowly change from water to fire." Also, the
tip of the tongue held against the roof of the mouth completes the energy circuit and is crucial to allow the energy
flow. In the illustration above, you can see the push-pull
emphasis.

Horizontal with Woman on Top,
or Swooping Shakti

With the woman on top, she is now the initiator. You take
a backseat and relax. And you can more easily channel and
circulate your energy up through your body and toward your

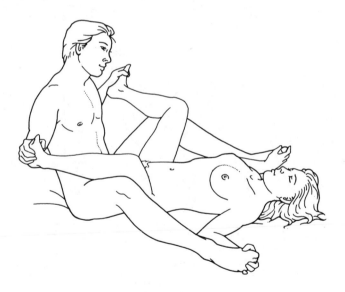

Circulating Sexual Energy

partner. This is the ideal position to initiate her Pompoir power (i.e., Kegel exercise) on her lover. As I discuss later, this is crucial in creating the Wave of Bliss. A variation of this (illustrated above) shows the energy circulating between the couple along the chakra pathway.

Completing the Circuit

Completing the Circuit

Facing each other, the couple are completing and holding the energy circuits closed by holding each other's feet in their hands while maintaining connection and penetration. See the illustration on page 305.

Man behind the Woman, or Piercing Tiger

With you behind your partner, she can tighten her vaginal channel with the PC pump muscle (this is what the Kegels work) to heighten the sensation for both of you. Also, the tightness of entry between her thighs is good if you are long and she is shallow.

Man behind the Woman, or Piercing Tiger

The Techniques

As Kenneth Ray Stubbs, Ph.D., points out in his book *The Essential Tantra*, Tantra can be broken down into three essential ideas that should direct your approach:

> ➤ Time: Be present and let go of future expectations.
> ➤ Contact: Maintain contact with your partner at all times.
> ➤ Flow: Allow a natural flow from one movement to another, one moment of stillness and concentration to another.

If you keep these three concepts in mind as you begin to practice these techniques, you will greatly increase your ability to reach a spiritual or ecstatic state with your lover. Here are some other considerations to keep in mind before you choose a position. I've borrowed these steps from the wonderful Stephen Chang book *The Tao of Sexology*:

1. To harmonize and relax better with your partner, place similar body parts together: lips to lips, hands to hands, genitals to genitals.
2. To stimulate and excite each other, place dissimilar parts together: lips to ears, mouth to genitals, genitals to anus.
3. The person who is doing the most moving (generally the person on top) gives the most energy to the other partner. The person underneath can move as well to

complement the movement of the person on top. This will help expand, circulate, and exchange sexual energy more quickly.

SECRET FROM LOU'S ARCHIVES

According to Charles and Caroline Muir, the potent kiss is a Tantric technique that uses an energetic conduit between the valley of a woman's upper lip and her clitoris. "The lover gently sucks on her upper lip, using his tongue and lips to draw in on the frenulum which stretches from the inside of the upper lip to the point on the gum directly above the two front teeth. As he sucks her upper lip, she sucks his lower lip and visualizes the subtle channel that runs from her frenulum to her clitoris. Once that channel opens as a conduit for sexual energy, a woman may be able to experience deep clitoral stimulation—even orgasm—from the kiss alone."

Once the couple has decided the flow of a lovemaking session (you can make it either relaxing or exciting), then they can try the different techniques. In a general way, the approach to intercourse in a Tantric manner is about a shift in attitude: being open and relaxed and in touch with each other at a very deep, subtle level.

In terms of what you're actually doing, nothing is changing all that much. It's about where you consciously put the emphasis. For instance, the in-and-out thrust, in which the penis is thrust deeper into the woman, is the more vigorous style. You can make it more slow and gentle by literally slowing your thrust. The up-and-down thrust is more for the slow, relaxing mood as the man will have to remain fairly close to the woman

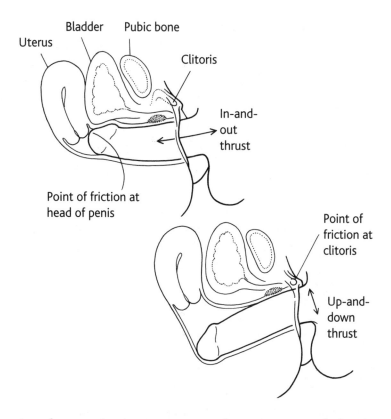

Uterus
Bladder Pubic bone
Clitoris
In-and-out thrust
Point of friction at head of penis
Point of friction at clitoris
Up-and-down thrust

in order to maintain constant stimulating contact with the clitoral area. Keep this in mind as you move through the various techniques described on page 310. In the illustrations you can observe the various techniques to easily adjust the stimulation area with one subtle position change.

The Kabazzah

Kabazzah, which is also known as Pompoir (by the French), Quivering Butterfly (Eastern), Kegels (by us North Americans), and Snapping Pussy (by some who prefer a flair), refers to the Eastern technique where the male partner is

Woman's Feet on His Shoulders | Woman Riding | Rear Entry

Deepest—
stimulates cervical
area

Woman moving
up and down—
deepest, cervical

Deepest—
straight in

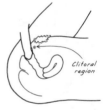
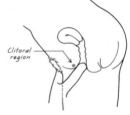
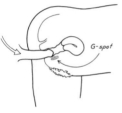

Man on tiptoe—
stimulates clitoris

Woman leaning
forward—clitoral

Man on tiptoe—
shallow G-spot

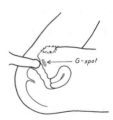

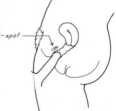
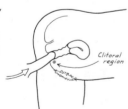

Man crouching—
stimulates G-spot
front wall

Woman leaning back
with up-and-down
action—G-spot

Man crouching—
shallow thrust—
clitoral

passive and the female uses only abdominal and vaginal muscle contractions to "milk" his penis. This is basically what I've described previously as a Kegel exercise, but used as a form of sexual expression, the move goes beyond strengthening and toning the PC muscles, and becomes a technique a woman can use to stimulate her partner's penis while it is inside of her.

While the woman moves her muscles, both partners should try to relax and enjoy the sensations of the union. Remember, this is slow, subtle sensation. The more in tune both of you are to the internal movement, the more stimulation can build, and the more pleasure you will experience.

The Big Draw

This technique stems from a branch of Chinese medicine, and is popularly referred to as sexual kung fu. Its goal is to increase your orgasmic potential. This process takes learning and practice, so don't be discouraged if you feel awkward or uncomfortable as you begin to test the waters. But believe me, the results are real and quite enjoyable—for both your lady and yourself.

In the Big Draw, you practice stopping thrusting as you feel orgasm is imminent. When you feel you are about to come, you pull out, to within an inch of withdrawing from her vagina. The most important part of the move is the change in depth of thrusting. You never totally withdraw, so you maintain a vacuum-like feeling with strong, deep penetrations. The Big Draw itself refers to your ability to move energy up through your body and use it to keep your PC muscles strong so you can control the emissions if you should choose to do so.

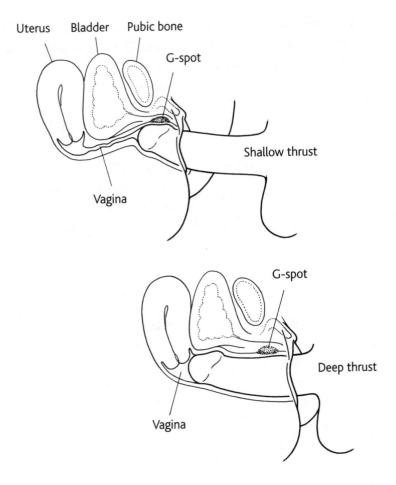

Uterus   Bladder   Pubic bone

G-spot

Shallow thrust

Vagina

G-spot

Deep thrust

Vagina

The Big Draw

The goal is actually represented in the illustration above, indicating how it can maximize the orgasmic potential.

To enhance this technique you can use the Three Finger Draw. In this technique you (or your partner) put pressure on the mid-perineal area to stop ejaculation. This will help you become familiar with the sensation of controlling ejaculation and know your timing more accurately. If your lover gets involved, this also can be a shared, intimate moment.

The Wave of Bliss

The Wave of Bliss is a stunning technique that has the power to bring a couple together at the most intense, spiritual level. This is Margot Anand's favorite technique to use in the Yab Yum position, and I've used her description here because of its clarity and simplicity. You will both need a supportive cushion or pillow. According to Ms. Anand, there are seven essential steps:

1. PELVIC ROCKING

You begin by kneeling down on your cushions and facing each other, not touching. Gently move into a seated position, with your legs comfortably crossed. Close your eyes and focus on what is happening inside of your body and your heart. Begin to rock your pelvis forward and back, toward and away from each other, gently brushing your genitals and anus against the pillow. Do this for about five minutes and pay attention to the growing sensation in your genitals.

2. CULTIVATING AROUSAL

In this same position, keeping your eyes closed, continue the pelvic rocking and emphasize sensations in your genitals by squeezing your PC muscles. As you rock backward, tighten the genital muscles; as you rock forward, relax them. You are creating a sensual rhythm here that continues to build sensation and stimulation; in fact, you might feel a warmth and tingling in your genitals and pelvis.

3. OPENING THE INNER FLUTE TOGETHER

Now you are warm and ready to open your eyes and look at each other. Try synchronizing your rocking movements. Continue squeezing your PC muscles and being aware of your genital sensations. It's also important to maintain eye contact with each other so your connection stays alert and continues to deepen.

As you rock your pelvis backward and tighten your pelvic muscles, inhale deeply, imagining that you are pulling the sexual energy upward and out through the top of your head. As you rock your pelvis forward, relax the genital muscles and exhale, imagining the sexual energy moving back down through your body and out the genitals.

Stay in tune with each other as you breathe. Keep looking in each other's eyes, stay relaxed, and gradually let yourselves synchronize your rhythm. Try it fast, then try it slow, playing with the pace that is right for you. Even though your lips are not touching, imagine that you are kissing each other through your breath.

4. THE PLAYFUL WAVE

This step requires some "dynamic dance music," suggests Anand. I would choose any kind of music that has a sensual, rhythmic beat and an upbeat or playful tone. Maintain eye contact and remain seated on your cushions and turn on your music. Slowly reach out toward each other with your hands

The Playful Wave

and touch your palms playfully, following the music as if your hands were dancing. Now you each bring your entire body into the dance, moving your arms, upper torso, and pelvis. Let your bodies move to the music and let your breath carry the movement. Be aware of who is leading and who is following, who is pushing and who is yielding. Then switch roles and feel the difference between the two.

Anand suggests introducing massage oil and gently massaging each other, sliding your hands over each other's skin. When you are ready, oil and caress each other's genitals, as you continue the slow, undulating movement of your bodies in the rocking rhythm. Then approach each other and "assume the position of the wave." In other words, your partner moves on top of you, while you guide your penis ("vajra") into her vagina ("yoni"). Even if you do not have an erection, you can still assume this position, pressing your penis against her.

5. CONNECTING BREATH TO BREATH

Now your partner wraps her legs around you, while you remain seated in a cross-legged position (this is called the Lotus Position). Feel free to use pillows to make the position more comfortable. Once you are both comfortable, take a few minutes to relax and feel each other's breath. Begin the gentle rocking again, along with the squeezing of the PC muscles. Move against each other and harmonize your rhythms.

When you are ready, begin to kiss and imagine that you are exchanging breath with your partner.

6. OPENING TO YOUR INNER LIGHT

At this point, you and your partner are becoming more and more aroused, nearing orgasmic sensations. As Anand says, "This step is key to moving orgasmic energy from the genitals and transforming it into an ecstatic and meditative experience." Continue kissing and exchanging breath. Close your eyes and let your eyes roll slightly upward and focus them on the Third Eye, that place in the center of your forehead, between your eyes. Tantrikas believe this is the seat of soul awareness. Draw all your sexual energy upward toward this point. Think of moving the sensation from your genital region through your pelvis, up through your belly, through your throat, and up through your Third Eye. Once you arrive at the Third Eye, hold your breath and keep squeezing your genital muscles. Now try to relax the rest of your body.

After a while, Anand states, "you may have the feeling of an explosion of light or a shooting star or fireworks." All along, continue kissing and exchanging breath. While you have been inhaling, your partner is exhaling, doing so very slowly and consciously, holding *your* breath as a way to slow *your* rhythm and accentuate the control of energy. Continue this exercise for several minutes, and when you want to stop, bring your focus and energy down from the Third Eye to the genitals.

7. THE INFINITE CYCLE

In this final step, you stay locked within each other and continue breathing together. As the woman inhales and then ex-

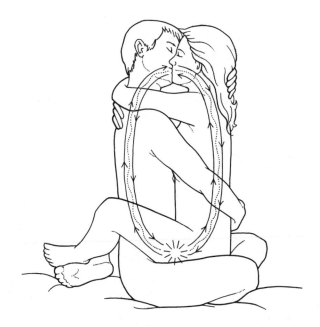

The Infinite Cycle

hales into her partner's mouth, she concentrates on moving the energy from her genitals up through her body and into her lover. The man receives her breath (when he inhales) and moves the energy down through his body, out his vajra (penis), and into her yoni (vagina). This is a flowing, rhythmic movement, different from step 6 above in that there is no holding of breath.

The intensity of this last step can lead to orgasm, if either or both of you want to share that pleasure. You can also choose to relish in this wave of bliss that the rocking, breathing, kissing, and pure rhythm of sensation has created.

The Tantric Orgasm

You've waited, and waited, and now it's time. Here is the step-by-step description of achieving the ultimate orgasm, Tantra style. I've borrowed from the description that David Ramsdale uses in his book *Sexual Energy Ecstasy*. The road to orgasm begins with you and your partner in the Yab Yum position, with you penetrating her.

1. She contracts her PC muscles while you remain still, not moving your pelvis at all.
2. She is only squeezing her PC muscles, not moving her hips or pelvis.
3. You can caress and kiss and gaze into each other's eyes, but remain motionless below your hips.
4. Keep in mind that she is the actor or giver of energy in this exercise, and you are the receiver and therefore in a more passive role.
5. Maintain a calm, relaxed state of mind and body.

6. By this point, you are responding to your partner's genital squeezing of your penis. Both of you are becoming highly aroused from the genital sensations.
7. After a while, this stimulation may become very intense, and you might feel the urge to orgasm. She should back off the intensity of her squeezing so that the orgasm can be delayed.
8. After about fifteen minutes, Ramsdale says, you "will experience a bioelectrical force-field effect." In other words, the sensations the two of you have created are so intense that you feel alone and separate from your surroundings, as if joined as one. This is an electric, transcendent feeling of bliss shared with your lover.
9. Stay with this feeling as long as you wish. Ramsdale recommends staying in the "electrical force field" another fifteen minutes in order to come to full Tantric orgasm. When you do choose to release into the pleasure of orgasm, you may feel exuberant and expansive, transported to another level of consciousness—that is, a state of spiritual ecstasy.

Spiritual sex is by its nature a very personal, subtle experience. It taps into a deep reservoir of powerful emotion between two people, and when this emotion is expressed and shared between two people who love each other, they can transport themselves to another realm that has no other name than the spiritual.

This kind of experience may not be for everyone, but those with the curiosity to try it may discover new limits and potential for sexual pleasure, beyond what they had previously imagined. So enjoy!

PART IV

Healthy
Ecstasy

CHAPTER FOURTEEN

Avoiding Physical Roadblocks

Medical Concerns That Impact Sexuality

Take Care of Your Body

The point of this chapter is to expand your knowledge of medical issues that impact your ability to enjoy your sexuality. How fabulous that as human beings we have so many different facets by which we can experience sex—mentally, physically, and spiritually! However, there are also many different ways that the sexual flow can be interrupted or derailed. When our bodies are operating well, everything in our lives operates well, including our sex lives. Like a finely tuned motor, we hum. However, if just one cylinder is misfiring, we are out of sorts and can't complete the course.

For men, the many medical and physical issues that affect sexuality revolve around the penis, most especially the fear of premature ejaculation or impotence or the inability to attain an erection firm enough for penetration. In this chapter I also address other medical conditions that impact sexual functioning.

As you probably know, many of the medications for such conditions as high blood pressure, diabetes, depression or anxiety, and heart disease do impact both desire (i.e., libido) and full physiological sexual functioning. The first step to addressing medication issues is to become aware; the second is to consult your physician and see if there are any alternative medications that have fewer or no negative sexual side effects. Also, I will present some suggestions that may help "skirt" the problems, so to speak. Medical concerns are real, but most are treatable if you take the time to address them thoroughly. You should take your sexual health seriously, and the first step is learning what might affect you—either now or in the future.

HISTORICAL AND HYSTERICAL FACTS	I agree with Dr. Gloria Brame, who writes, "What if all this 'dysfunction' is not so much a lack of interest in sex, but a lack of interest in the type of sex that society considers normal?"

Let's Ban the "Dys" of Sexual Functioning

One of my real pet peeves when it comes to dealing with sexual functioning is how quick the media and the medical establishment are to jump to conclusions and label a problem or difficulty with orgasm as a "dysfunction." The language alone is enough to deter people from seeking help, asking questions, and becoming creative in their search for solutions. I think we already have established that what we tend to call "normal" isn't all that broad or accurate—especially in terms of sexuality. To tell people they have a *dys*function sets people back, increasing their hesitancy to speak up about their problems.

The following list of the normal changes in male sexual function that come with aging is from the book *The Sexual Male* by Drs. Richard Milsten and Julian Slowinski:

1. It takes longer to achieve an erection.
2. The duration of ejaculation decreases from between four and eight seconds to approximately three seconds.
3. The volume of ejaculate decreases from approximately one teaspoon to less than half that amount.
4. The force with which the semen is expelled decreases so that it is projected from the end of the penis a distance of only two to twelve inches instead of twelve to twenty-four inches.
5. The time from erection to ejaculation may increase.
6. Following ejaculation, the penis becomes softer much more rapidly.
7. The time before the next erection can be achieved is prolonged.
8. The weight of the testicles decreases.
9. The tactile sensitivity of the penis decreases.
10. The intensity of the orgasm may decrease.
11. The angle of the erection may decrease.

As you can see, in these normal changes there is nothing about impotence. As Milsten further comments, "Erectile ability is in fact associated with a male's general health status."

I believe that the more you accept your body, your age, and your own desire level, the more comfortable you will be with your sexuality in general. Further, the more comfortable you are, the more likely you will be to explore and discover the absolute heights of your own pleasure.

> ## SECRET FROM LOU'S ARCHIVES
>
> *The truth is that erectile insufficiency is not caused by aging. It is a phenomenon that occurs with the onset of other illnesses, and since the likelihood of illness increases with age, so does impotence. As males grow older, certain alterations in sexual functioning do occur.*

Do You (or Does Your Partner) Have Low Desire?

My problem with the phrase "low desire" is its ubiquitous nature. It seems that every publication you pick up—whether it is a men's or women's magazine—there's an article stressing how Americans, especially women, "suffer" from low sexual desire. In an issue of O (Oprah's magazine), the editors claimed that more than 25 million women have experienced low sexual desire. Now, if someone asked you whether you had low or high desire, how would you answer? I would guess that many people have high desire some of the time and low desire at other times. When you're in a new relationship, don't you experience a rush of desire? Don't you feel more passionate? Once a relationship has a few years on it, wouldn't you agree that it's natural that the lust factor can wane? What about the stresses of work, family, and personal issues? Don't you believe that the day-to-day demands of life in general take their toll on our feeling sexually open and wanting?

It is my observation that the pharmaceutical industry is looking for a new cash cow, and that cash cow would be a drug to treat the "sexual dysfunctions" they have "discovered." The medical establishment, spearheaded by the pharmaceutical industry, has begun to define low desire as a disease, and one that can only be treated by prescription drugs. Now, I am not arguing the merits of Viagra, but I am questioning the drug companies' underlying motivation and definition of low desire. Low desire is an experience many women and men have that is the result of more than one factor. It's my conviction that as we know more about our own bodies, and connect our bodies to what is happening in the rest of our lives, we will begin to unravel the reasons why we may have become disconnected from our libidos. After all, why do we need drugs to get in touch with what is the most natural thing about us—our sexuality?

And while I don't deny that low desire exists, I regret that doctors, counselors, other women, men, and the media in general alarm people about this. Low desire is neither a fact of life nor an unchangeable medical condition. Rather, low desire is often transient, often subjective, and often a reaction to stresses in our lives, including fatigue and everyday pressures of home, family, and work. I prefer to address low desire less as a problem and more as an experience, one that needs to be recognized and acknowledged, certainly, but one that also needs to be understood in order to deal with it.

That said, there are cases where low desire can be directly linked to physiological causes, such as men or women experiencing hormonal imbalances or going through serious illnesses. And it makes sense since stress is one of the biggest interrupters of sexuality, and whether we are emotionally or physically stressed, our sexuality usually takes a holiday.

Healthy Body/Healthy Sex

Let's first take a look at the physiological issues that impact your sexual health.

When men are bothered by problems affecting their genitals, they often don't have the built-in "let's talk about it" response that women have. Yet when this sensitive area of your anatomy is having problems, you do want to deal with it quickly. As one man told me, "I do not want Johnny having problems. When he has something wrong, I have something wrong."

If it is pain or an infection, invariably men head to the doctor. Unlike women, men rarely have a problem with telling a doctor they had sex and think they may have "caught something." Symptoms that will bring a man in for an exam can be a burning sensation during ejaculation, or pain in the testicles or around the anal opening at or shortly after ejaculation. What I've gathered below is the most current information about sexual health considerations.

There are many health conditions that can negatively impact sexual functioning in men. Here is a list of those to be aware of:

Addison's disease (adrenal insufficiency)
Alcoholism
Anemia (severe)

Anorexia nervosa
Chronic active hepatitis
Chronic kidney failure
Cirrhosis
Congestive heart failure
Cushing's syndrome
Depression
Drug addiction
Drug ingestion: antiandrogens, antihypertensives,
    digoxin, estrogen, tranquilizers
Excessive prolactin secretion (drug- or tumor-induced)
Feminizing tumors
Hemochromatosis
Hypothyroidism
Kallmann's syndrome
Klinefelter's syndrome
Male climacteric (with testosterone deficiency)
Multiple sclerosis
Myotonic dystrophy
Nutritional deficiencies
Parkinson's disease
Pituitary insufficiency
Pituitary tumors
Testosterone deficiency
Tuberculosis

(Source: W. H. Masters, V. E. Johnson, and R. C. Kolodny, *Heterosexuality*, 1994, p. 86)

If you suffer from one or more of these conditions, know first that your sexuality may be affected. You should consult with a physician to see about necessary treatment.

The following conditions more directly relate to the

genitals and therefore impact sexual functioning more immediately.

Prostatitis

Prostatitis is an inflammation of the prostate gland caused by a bacterial infection. It is often accompanied by fever and back pain, a general overall feeling of being ill, and a searing sensation in the penis and urinary tract. An aggressive use of antibiotics can treat the infection.

Chronic Prostatitis

This somewhat more rare but more serious condition is caused by a chronic infection to the prostate gland that ends up affecting the seminal vesicles as well. When both these glands are chronically swollen, they press on surrounding nerves and thereby short-circuit during urination and sexual arousal. One researcher said it's like angina, in the characteristic way it spreads. There is no certain cause for this infection; boys who have never had sex can suffer from it as well as sexually active adult men.

Impotence or Penile Erectile Dysfunction

Getting an erection is the essence of many men's sexuality, and therefore an inability to become erect or maintain an erection for a desired length of time can be an enormously burdensome experience. Although impotence can strike men of any age—including teenagers—it is often associated with men over age fifty-five. Here are some numbers:

> ➤ At age fifty-five, 8 percent of healthy men suffer from it.

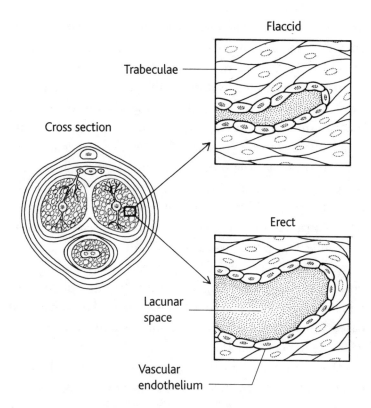

Flaccid

Trabeculae

Cross section

Erect

Lacunar
space

Vascular
endothelium

Bloodflow to Flaccid and Erect Penis

> At age sixty-five, 25 percent of men.
> At seventy-five, 55 percent.
> At eighty, as many as 75 percent of men experience
  the frustration of impotence.

According to Dr. Irwin Goldstein, there are three main
physiological causes of erectile dysfunction: (1) failure to initiate, (2) failure to fill, and (3) failure to store. Failure to initiate is a fancy way of describing what happens when

important nerves in the penis fail to function correctly in response to sexual stimulation, which may be caused by low hormone levels. Failure to fill means just that—not enough arterial high-pressure blood gets to the penis to expand the penile tissue. Failure to store indicates that the erection-storage mechanism is unable to expand to its maximum against the tunica, or fibrous coat, to maintain the blood in the penile tissue.

As many psychologists can confirm, one of the first organs to be adversely affected by stress and overwork is the one between the thighs. However, enough research has been done to suggest that male and female dysfunction may have a common molecular and physiological link. Traditionally it has been viewed that most cases of female sexual dysfunctions were purely psychological in origin. This was true as well for male impotence—at least until the 1980s. Now we know that most cases of male dysfunction are physiological in cause, specifically due to poor bloodflow.

Also, there are clear physiological links to men's difficulties getting and staying erect, including most physical illnesses. As I mentioned in chapter 2, erection is dependent on a man's nervous system sending electrical signals that cause blood to engorge the vessels, making the penis erect. Many illnesses can cause temporary or permanent damage to these electrical circuits. Men with diabetes are particularly prone to this problem; in fact, 50 to 70 percent of men with diabetes (2.5 million men in the United States) suffer from impotence. This is partly because of damage to nerves, but it's also due in part to disturbances in their metabolism.

A prolapsed disk, any operation to pelvic organs (including hernia surgery), and multiple sclerosis can also cause erection problems. Aging, as we see above, is a natural, overall factor affecting erectile functioning. And as I point out below in the section on hormones, hormonal changes weigh heavily here.

According to Taoist physician Dr. Mantak Chia, erection trouble is caused not only by physiological and psychological problems, but also by an energetic problem—specifically, weak sexual energy. Difficulty in getting or maintaining an erection is understood as resulting from a man's physical and sexual exhaustion. The general Taoist approach to sex emphasizes energy currents.

It should make plain sense that if you are doing something that is going to impact your circulatory system either positively (i.e., working out) or negatively (i.e., smoking and drinking), your sexual functioning will be affected. Why? Because blood and good circulation are the two things that power orgasms. You smoke? That, gentlemen, is one of the quicker ways to reduce penile functioning. The majority of blood vessels in the penis are tiny, and the tinier they are, the faster blood impairment will weaken an area. There was once a great billboard advertisement with several men standing around in tuxedos smoking. As a pretty woman walks by all their cigarettes droop over like wilted flowers. The message was clear: If you smoke, you reduce your most masculine function. As Drs. Milsten and Slowinski point out, "The evidence is overwhelming that the use of tobacco causes impairment of bloodflow not only to the heart but also to the penis. Recent data suggest these changes may not be reversible, so it is important to avoid damage in the first place."

This is also true of significant alcohol consumption. As Dr. Irwin Goldstein says in his book *The Potent Male*, "[H]eavy drinking of alcohol, over time, may destroy the ability of a man to make love. Too much alcohol may reduce the production of the testosterone in the testicles. Since heavy drinking also impairs liver function, and the liver is responsible for metabolizing hormones, the reduced amount of hormones may not be enough for proper penile functioning. Heavy drinking may also damage a man's nervous system, which is vital to sexual functioning. . . . Prolonged use of cocaine and marijuana also result in erection problems." Frankly, I would think these warnings about using any kind of drug—legal or otherwise—would convince men to be careful and be moderate in their behavior. Lifestyle changes aren't necessarily easy, but if potency and sexual health is important to you, you may find the motivation.

There are ways of learning how to stimulate and maintain stimulation in order to stay erect longer (if that's your wish) and to better control ejaculation. I describe and discuss these in chapters 7 and 13, where I address ways to enhance orgasms through better erection and ejaculatory control, and Eastern Taoist and Tantric techniques.

Premature Ejaculation

Premature ejaculation occurs when a man ejaculates either before entering the vagina or shortly thereafter—in either case, before he wants to. Traditional teaching has been that psychological issues are at the root of this problem, but another school of thought is that it is just another of many physical differences between men. The American Psychiatric Association defines rapid (a.k.a. premature) ejaculation as "persistent or recurrent ejaculation with minimal sexual stimulation before, during, or shortly after penetration and before the person wishes it." Despite these slightly different definitions, rapid ejaculation remains a frustrating circumstance for both the men and the women involved. As sexologist Helen Kaplan states, "It simply isn't known how long the average male takes to ejaculate. Given the naturally competitive nature of men, if an actually well-adjusted man reads he should take X amount of time and he takes Y, he may start to feel inadequate, even though his partner is satisfied." That aside, women do get frustrated. One woman told me, "He was the best guy, but he would come as soon as he was inside me, and I needed more. He's now married to a great woman and said the timing that was a problem for us is the ticket for the two of them." (The other side of the coin is delayed ejaculation, which can be as difficult to deal with. The woman can get very sore vaginally or orally, and still he is unable to orgasm. In this kind of situation, a woman can feel that no matter what she does, she isn't doing "something" right.)

Secret from Lou's Archives

According to Dr. Milsten, "Erectile failure can occur as a result of any of the following: too tired, too rushed, too annoyed, too bored, too preoccupied, too ambivalent, too guilty, not sufficiently interested or aroused, too little privacy, too much to drink or eat."

According to some experts, as many as 40 percent of men have had problems with ejaculation. Especially when a man is young and virile, premature ejaculation can cause anxiety and noticeably affect his enjoyment of the climax.

Since an erection and the ability to control ejaculation are associated with feelings of strength, control, and power, many men often experience tremendous feelings of inadequacy when premature ejaculation happens. As men age, and they expect some of their physical functioning to wane, they take it less to heart.

SECRET FROM LOU'S ARCHIVES

Premature ejaculation varies in degrees; some men ejaculate upon seeing a woman—naked or clothed. For most men ejaculatory control increases with experience.

There are three different approaches to the treatment of premature ejaculation. The first approach utilizes counseling as a way to deal with and address the psychological dimensions of the behavior. Let's be honest: If you feel that the part of your anatomy that most identifies you as a man is out of your control, you will definitely have some psychological issues.

The second approach is behavior modification. A popular method is the "stop-start" technique, which boils down to exercises you can learn to do to control ejaculation—either with a partner or solo. The Kegel exercises discussed in chapter 12 are an example of this approach.

The third approach is the recent use of pharmacological drugs. Most of these drugs were found to work on premature ejaculation secondarily. For example, Prozac, which is used for depression, delays ejaculation. The same occurs with the drug Anafranil, normally used for obsessive-compulsive behavior.

For any man (or couple) who is bothered by premature ejaculation, I suggest you consider all three approaches to see what is most suitable for you.

Our Hormonal Soup and Its Sexual Ingredients

Hormones are those elusive, fascinating body chemicals that make you a sexual being. They are powerful and have a tremendous effect on your body and mind. Therefore, when hormone levels in the body are unbalanced, the body will respond, and often negatively, especially in terms of sexual functioning. The main hormone that affects your sexuality is testosterone.

The Power of Testosterone

Often referred to as the hormone of desire, testosterone has the power to make you feel sexual and lusty. Sexually, the presence of testosterone is not only linked to sexual desire, but also to feelings of well-being and a sense of energy in men and women. When you don't have enough testosterone, you often feel sluggish about sex, or lose interest in it completely.

When testosterone levels are high or adequate, men feel alive, vigorous, and sexually tuned in, and frequently turned on. However, testosterone, which is produced by the testicles, decreases gradually and variably with age. When its levels are low, not only can men experience diminished libido, but also difficulty attaining an erection. Of course this is not the sole cause or even the most frequent reason for loss of erections, but measuring levels of testosterone in the blood or saliva is an important step in understanding any kind of erectile problem. Treatments for low testosterone levels include skin patches and creams that are applied to hairless areas of your body (such as the back, abdomen, and buttocks) since testosterone cannot be readily absorbed from the stomach in pill form.

However, it is important to keep in mind that replacement of testosterone requires a careful analysis of the libido and/or the erectile problem. Because testosterone can stimulate prostatic growth, an evaluation of the size of the prostate as well as measurement of the prostatic specific antigen (PSA) is required before a man is given this hormone. Another concern is the correlation of testosterone with levels of cholesterol in the blood. If your total cholesterol and LDL cholesterol (the "bad" lipid) are high, you need to remain observant and check in with your physician regularly. This is also true of watching liver function—your physician may recommend a liver-function test during treatment. If you suspect you have a hormonal imbalance, contact your physician.

Medications that Impact Sexual Functioning

The list of drugs that adversely affect sexual functioning is huge. Almost any and all medications have been reported at one time or another to cause sexual difficulty. So, if you were doing fine until you started a new drug, be sure to ask your physician if there is a history of similar problems linked to this drug, and/or see if there is another drug that you could try for the problem.

STDs (Sexually Transmitted Diseases)

Sexually transmitted diseases wreak havoc on our sexuality. They can be contracted by anyone having unprotected sex. In fact, one in every fifteen Americans will contract a sexually transmitted disease this year, and one in every four Americans already has one. You are not immune by virtue of your age, ethnicity, education, profession, or socioeconomic status. What further complicates matters is the fact that it is often difficult to tell who has an STD; many people who are infected look and feel fine and can be blissfully unaware they are infected.

STDs can be spread through vaginal, oral, and anal sex. Some can also be spread through any contact between the penis, vagina, mouth, or anus—even without intercourse. If your physician confirms your suspicions, follow the medication instructions to the letter, and tell your partner or partners immediately. There is no question that this can be difficult. But, if your partner is not treated, too, she can easily give it back to you or give it to someone else, as well as be at risk of irreparable damage herself.

It is not wise, under any circumstances, to self-diagnose when it comes to personal health. Several of these symptoms can be caused by things other than an STD, and many STDs can exist for a very long time before *any* symptoms are noticeable. If you think you have an STD, see your doctor.

In the next chapter I discuss the most common sexually transmitted diseases along with their symptoms, potential dangers, and treatments and/or cures. This list is for your general information. For more information about these and other sexually transmitted diseases, you can call the CDC National HIV/AIDS and Sexually Transmitted Disease Hotline at 800-342-AIDS or 800-227-8922.

Maintaining your sexual health should be equal in importance to maintaining your overall physical and emotional health. Stress is unavoidable, but there are ways to keep the channels of awareness open. If you are not functioning at your sexual peak, you can at the very least feel confident and assured that you can achieve this necessary health. Sex is too important to give up or compromise.

CHAPTER FIFTEEN

Safe Sensuality

Keeping Yourself Protected

Knowledge Is Power

Safe sex doesn't have to mean boring sex. On the contrary, I like to think of it as a challenge to be creative. It's also a call for you to be considerate not only of your partner's comfort and protection, but of your own as well. Bringing the subject of safety into your relationship can be a way of saying, "I care about you, I care about us." Furthermore, feeling protected, comfortable, and well taken care of is a crucial foundation for having great sex.

I realize this information is mainly needed by those people who are single and/or with new partners. However, before married people or those in long-term, committed relationships ignore this chapter, let me remind you that with the divorce rate being what it is, we should all be careful and forewarned—to some degree, even the most married among us experience some serial monogamy. For those of you who are parents, these facts are just as crucial. You may not want to

341

scare your children, but you do want to give your children information that prepares them for life, and sexually transmitted diseases (STDs) and sex are a part of life. You may want to consider two statistics: first, that the average age of those newly infected by HIV has dropped from twenty-six to twenty; and second, that one in five people living with HIV were infected as teenagers.

It is crucial that you know what diseases are out there, what the figures are, and what you can and should do to prevent contraction. I understand that reminding you of the dangers may temporarily mute your sexual desire, but I trust you'll thank me later. Better your desire be extinguished for a few moments than have your sex life, or even your life, extinguished in the long term because of ignorance.

In this day and age, safety is essential. It would be irresponsible of me to offer advice on sexual interaction without discussing safety. To begin with, you may be surprised to know that as a man you are typically at less risk than your lady for contracting a sexually transmitted disease. Why is your lady at greater risk? It is partly a square-footage issue. The tissue most at risk during sexual encounters is the highly vascularized mucosal tissue of the vulva and vaginal barrel (for men this tissue is in the urethra) because it is easily abraded during sex. And there is more mucosal tissue in the vaginal barrel than in the urethra. A second reason is that since women are typically the receptive partner during sex, and your body fluids are left *inside* her, she is more vulnerable to infection. The corollary for women being more at risk is the need for men to take on greater responsibility to keep both partners safe. I know of a man who, upon entering a relationship, struggled with telling his new love about having herpes. Although she wasn't thrilled with his news, she very much appreciated his being honest and straightforward. She said it actually brought them closer. He was scrupulous about his hygiene and vigilant about any possible outbreaks. He also insisted on using condoms even when his lesions were inactive, and he avoided intercourse when they were. Meanwhile, he took suppressive antiviral therapy to reduce asymptomatic shedding. They've been together for six years and she has never developed herpes.

Now, before you think you don't have to worry about getting infected, think again. From what I've observed in my seminars and other research, I've come to realize that many men assume they are practicing safer sex when they (or their partners) use birth control. Safer sex is not merely about precautions against unwanted pregnancy. You must realize not only that although you share responsibility to use protection against pregnancy, even with those protections, you are still at risk of becoming infected by an STD. Men as well as women very often can be asymptomatic of disease. In other words, you may not show any physical symptoms of being infected by a number of sexually transmitted diseases, but you can suffer long-term damage and unknowingly pass on infection. This is especially true of chlamydia, human papilloma virus (HPV), and herpes (see below for more specific information on these and other diseases). So feeling well and not noticing a problem with your penis does not mean that you do not have a dangerous STD. Also be aware that the older you are, the greater the likelihood that your partner will have a sexual history, and chances are people will "adjust" the details of their sexual history. So please be cautious and take the necessary preventive measures.

It wasn't too long ago that the term "safer sex" referred strictly to being kept safe from an unwanted pregnancy. And yet there is still misunderstanding in this area. As a 49-year-old Episcopalian minister said, "Oh Lord, we used the rhythm method, and after our third unintended pregnancy, my wife and I thought we couldn't count." But after all this time, in which many different forms of birth control have become available, unwanted pregnancies are still highly prevalent in this country. What this tells us is that despite the information and products available for birth control, we as a culture are still behaving irresponsibly. Is there any excuse for this neglect?

SECRET FROM LOU'S ARCHIVES

There is no absolutely "safe" period for sexual intercourse insofar as conception is concerned. Mother Nature is no fool in this regard. When a woman is highly sexually stimulated, she can ovulate out of cycle.

In today's lexicon "safer sex" is often associated with HIV and AIDS. There is no question that AIDS (acquired immune deficiency syndrome) deserves every bit of the attention it has received. This disease not only kills, but often strips people of all their hope, dignity, and quality of life. Happily, several advances have been made in medicine that allow persons infected with HIV to live longer and healthier lives. However, since positive response to treatment is not a guarantee, prevention is a lot more effective.

Even if you are not in a high-risk group for HIV or AIDS, you may still be susceptible to infection. I asked Dr. Eric Daar, an immune disorders and AIDS specialist at Cedars-Sinai

Medical Center in Los Angeles, about men being infected with HIV by women, and he said, "I am currently treating a young man whose only risk factor was unprotected sex with a woman." The woman his patient slept with was not a prostitute. Dr. Daar then went on to discuss the thousands of women unwittingly infecting men in Africa and Asia, where HIV infection and AIDS exist mainly in the heterosexual, not homosexual, population.

The Numbers

The sheer number of men and women who have or have had one or more sexually transmitted diseases is quite astounding. As previously noted, one in every fifteen Americans will contract a sexually transmitted disease this year, and one in four Americans already has one. I cannot stress enough the importance of knowing the person you are sleeping with.

As I mentioned, many STDs have no obvious symptoms. A woman may only become aware of an infection when she takes steps to start a family, and by then, the damage has already been done: A sleeping STD has robbed her of her ability to conceive a child. (Admittedly, sometimes the damage can be addressed and a woman can get pregnant through reproductive technologies, such as in vitro.)

Unfortunately, not knowing about a disease does not prohibit one from passing it on to somebody else, and this lack of awareness can go both ways. Men, too, can be asymptomatic of an infection and pass it along to their partners. Therefore, it is as much your responsibility to get tested as it is your partners'. No one is immune from acquiring a sexually transmitted disease. Your age, race, ethnicity, or socioeconomic status will not protect you. The best agent of protection is yourself, so it's up to you to know the information, to be aware and considerate, and to take the time to ensure the safety of both of you.

Transmission

STDs can be spread through vaginal, oral, and anal sex. Some can also be spread through *any* contact between the penis and vulvar area, mouth, and/or anus. Sexually transmitted diseases can be spread from man to woman, woman to man, man to man, and woman to woman. Several STDs can be spread from mother to child at birth or through breast milk. And, as you are probably already aware, sharing needles can spread STDs, including HIV.

There is really only one way to be 100 percent sure you don't get a sexually transmitted disease: remain abstinent. But I think most of us (I'm including both men and women here) would feel a bit constrained if we gave up sex. The next less risky way to be sexual is to use your hands. Don't shrug off the fun you can have with your (or her) hands. You might be very surprised and eager to explore this territory of sexual delight. Make sure that your hands have no open wounds, abrasions, or cracked skin. Herpes and HPV, however, can be transmitted from genitals to hands (see below for more specific information on herpes and HPV). If you or your partner has either of these two viruses, you can protect yourselves by using latex gloves.

It's also true that genital-to-genital contact *without* intercourse can transmit some STDs, such as herpes and syphilitic lesions. With these types of infections any kind of genital contact *at all* without condoms can be a problem. However, sometimes herpes is not restricted to the genitals and can manifest at the end of a nerve ganglion on the thigh or buttocks. Meeting that gorgeous stranger on the plane and inviting her for a few adult beverages, which you then follow with falling into the hotel bed, arms and legs in heated disarray, may not be the smartest move in this day and age. Instead, should you find yourself lusting after someone you just met, and neither of you want to stop the inevitable, take a moment to talk about safer sex. I promise you, she will be grateful—and if not, you should be grateful you took care of you.

Responsible adults talk about sex beforehand. And after exchanging information with a new lover, they use a condom. Until you've both tested negative for *all* sexually transmitted diseases, and waited the appropriate incubation period to ensure a clean bill of health (without engaging in any risk behaviors in the meantime), you should continue to use condoms every single time you engage in vaginal, oral, or anal sex. As I am sure you're aware, condoms are available everywhere, in all sizes, styles, colors, and textures (there is a bounty of information on condoms at the end of this chapter).

For you roving males—you may not want to hear this, and I apologize in advance for sounding like your mother—but you can also reduce the risk of contracting an STD by limiting your number of sexual partners. The facts are plain: You are more likely to get a sexually transmitted disease if either of you has more than one partner at a time or has had a lot of previous partners. That's why the value of trust should never go underestimated in a relationship. What is often brushed aside or chalked up as one little indiscretion could have very serious health side effects. It's your choice, but I suggest being safe rather than sorry. Is one night of passion worth a lifetime of having lesions break out on your penis every month—or worse?

The Diseases

The following is a list of the most common sexually transmitted diseases along with their symptoms, potential dangers, and treatments and/or cures. This list is for your general information. It is not wise to self-diagnose when it comes to personal health. Several of these symptoms can be caused by factors other than an STD, and as I said earlier, many STDs can exist for a very long time before any symptoms are noticeable. If you think you have been exposed to an STD, see your doctor.

If your physician confirms your suspicions, follow the medication instructions with accuracy, and tell your partner or partners immediately. There is no question that breaking the news can be difficult and awkward. But she needs to know for her own health in order to get treated, and so she doesn't potentially re-infect you. For more information about these and other sexually transmitted diseases, you can call the CDC National HIV/AIDS and Sexually Transmitted Disease Hotline at 800-342-AIDS or 800-227-8922 (see the end of this chapter for further resources).

Chlamydia

Chlamydia is caused by a bacterium that is also a parasite, meaning it needs other cells to exist and survive. It is often called the silent STD because there are usually no symptoms until the disease is in an advanced state. Men's symptoms include burning during urination (due to infection in the urethra) and epididymitis (inflammation and swelling of the epididymis on the testicles). By the late 1980s chlamydia had become the most common sexually transmitted bacterial infection in both North America and Europe. An estimated 4 million new cases will occur annually. And 40 percent of nongonococcal urethritis (NGU) in men is caused by *Chlamydia trachomatis*.

SECRET FROM LOU'S ARCHIVES

Epididymitis, as a result of chlamydial infection, can lead to male infertility.

Chlamydia is spread through oral sex and intercourse. In women it can cause a bacterial infection deep within the fallopian tubes, causing chronic pain, tubal pregnancies, and/or infertility. With oral transmission, chlamydia can give you an upper respiratory infection. It can also be passed from mother to child during birth, causing eye, ear, and lung infections in newborns. The good news is that chlamydia is easily cured with antibiotics, but it must be tested for specifically.

SECRET FROM LOU'S ARCHIVES

Although chlamydia and gonorrhea don't manifest in the same way in women as they do in men, the results are often similar.

Gonorrhea

Also referred to as the clap, gonorrhea is often associated with another century. However, the disease is still rampant in our country today. An estimated 600,000 new cases of gonorrhea will be contracted in the United States this year. Similar to chlamydia, it is a bacterial infection that can be completely asymptomatic. In women it often goes undetected until permanent damage has already occurred, including sterility, tubal pregnancies, and chronic pain. However, in men the symptoms can include a yellow puslike discharge from the penis, pain while urinating, the need to urinate often, and pain in the lower abdomen. This STD is highly contagious and can be spread through any contact with the penis, vulvar area, mouth, or anus, even without penetration.

If left untreated, it can cause sterilization, tubular pregnancies, and chronic pain. It can also lead to pelvic inflammatory disease in women. Gonorrhea can be passed from mother to child during birth, causing eye, ear, and lung infections.

The good news is that if detected early, gonorrhea is easily curable with antibiotics.

Secret from Lou's Archives

Epididymitis among sexually active men under age 35 is most often caused by Chlamydia trachomatis *and* Neisseria gonorrhoeae.

Syphilis

Syphilis is a very dangerous bacterial infection, and an estimated 104,000 new cases in men and women will be contracted in the United States this year. If left untreated, syphilis can be fatal and/or cause irreparable damage to the heart, brain, eyes, and joints. Forty percent of all babies born to mothers with syphilis die during childbirth. Symptoms are painless sores, rash on the palms and feet, and swollen lymph nodes. This disease is highly contagious through oral, vaginal, and anal sex, as well as through open wounds on the skin. When detected early, syphilis is curable with strong doses of antibiotics. Syphilis is common in heterosexual men in certain parts of the United States and very rare in others.

Herpes

It is estimated that somewhere between 200,000 and 500,000 new cases of genital herpes will be contracted this year, and 30 million Americans are infected already. Even more frightening is the number of people who are not aware of already being infected.

Two viruses cause genital herpes: herpes simplex 1, which occurs orally, and herpes simplex 2, which occurs genitally. Herpes simplex 1 is what we refer to typically as cold sores on, around, or inside the lips and mouth. The visible symptoms of herpes simplex 2 include painful and/or itchy bumps or blisters on the genital area; in men, typically on the shaft of the penis at the end of the foreskin or near the head of the penis. In women, the outbreak occurs near or inside the vagina and/or rectum. Men can also get herpes near the anus even if they've never had anal intercourse. Sometimes herpes lesions first appear in areas related to the genitals by nerve endings. In this case, the buttocks and thighs are common sites.

Herpes is highly contagious when physical contact is made during an outbreak, but it can also be contagious when the virus appears to lie dormant. This is because in most people with herpes, it can reactivate without symptoms. Lab studies have found that in cases in which a person feels that herpes is not active, 5 percent of the time evidence of the infectious virus can be found on the skin.

The first outbreak of genital herpes usually lasts between twelve and fourteen days, while subsequent outbreaks are shorter in duration (four to five days) and are milder. There is no cure for this virus, though anti-viral medications have proven highly successful in both minimizing the symptoms of current outbreaks and suppressing future recurrences. What, precisely, determines a herpes recurrence has not been determined; however, studies indicate there is a strong association between herpes outbreaks and stress.

While the symptoms of the herpes virus can be very uncomfortable to those who have them, the real danger of this sexually transmitted disease is to an unborn child, or to an immune-suppressed individual (with HIV or AIDS, for example). Newborn (neonatal) herpes is also a worry, but recent information shows that this is very unlikely in cases where the mother has herpes prior to becoming pregnant. Neonatal herpes almost always is caused by men: The woman at greatest risk for giving birth to an affected baby experiences her transmission and first herpes episode late in pregnancy. It is most often transmitted to the infant during delivery and can cause painful blisters and damage to the eyes, brain, and internal organs of a newborn baby. One in six will not survive at all. Therefore, if you and your partner are working on getting pregnant, and you have herpes and she does not, it is paramount for you to use proper safe-sex practices during pregnancy and consider suppressive antiviral treatment.

The good news is that when genital herpes has been diagnosed in the mother, a cesarean delivery can generally prevent damage to the child. In fact, the risk is so low these days that women who have recurrent herpes episodes are only given a cesarean section if there is an active symptomatic lesion present.

If you think you have been exposed to herpes, there is only one test, a blood test called the Western blot, that can make this diagnosis without symptoms. Doctors more often perform viral culture tests by swabbing a lesion when it is in a very early stage of blistering or erosions.

I understand that it is awkward and difficult to tell your partner that you are infected, especially in a new relationship. As one man, a math professor from Los Angeles, told me, "I had met this terrific woman and I was terrified to tell her I had herpes. I remember lying in bed with her; we hadn't done anything at this point, and I knew I had to tell her. I was afraid that once she knew, she wouldn't want to continue the relationship. When I told her, she wasn't pleased to hear the news, but I told her that I had got it from a woman who hadn't known she was infected. We didn't have sex that night. After a day, she came back to me and said that she did want to continue our relationship, and that it was how I told her the news that made the difference. I was thrilled."

Human Papilloma Virus (HPV)

The human papilloma virus, also known as condyloma, represents a family of viruses that consists of more than 170 different types. There will be an estimated 1 million new cases of HPV diagnosed this year. All sexually active men and women are susceptible to contracting HPV. It is spread by direct contact during vaginal, oral, or anal sex with someone who has the virus. Though rare, infants can be infected during childbirth. Certain strains of HPV can cause cervical cancer.

Some forms of HPV cause visible genital warts, though some strains cause no warts at all. Genital warts are growths that appear on the penis, scrotum, groin, or thigh, and in women on the vulva, in or around the vagina or anus, and on the cervix. They can be raised or flat, single or multiple, small or large. Genital warts can be treated in several ways including freezing, laser surgery, chemical peels, and topical creams.

HPV is a virus that can lie dormant for years, and there is no known cure for this disease. Worse, the strains of HPV that don't produce visible warts can go undetected. For this reason it is imperative that all men and women have regular checkups. The disease is manageable with proper diagnosis. In the meantime, since there is no cure, I suggest limiting partners and using safer sex.

SECRET FROM LOU'S ARCHIVES

In a Seattle study of eighteen-year-olds, 25 percent of girls who had been sexually active for one year had already been infected with HPV.

Hepatitis B

Infection caused by the hepatitis B virus is not usually considered an STD; however, it is spread through infected semen, vaginal secretions, and saliva, and it is one hundred times more infectious than HIV. You can get hepatitis B from vaginal, oral, or—especially—anal sex. You can also be infected through direct contact with an infected person via open sores or cuts. This means that if someone in your home is infected, you can contract hepatitis B by using the same razor or toothbrush.

Hepatitis B attacks the liver. In its mildest form, you may never know you have it, but some carriers develop cirrhosis and/or liver cancer. Your chances of contracting liver cancer are two hundred times higher if you're a carrier of hepatitis B. Symptoms, when they appear, can be very much like those of the stomach flu. See your doctor immediately if you have nausea, unexplainable tiredness, dark urine, and/or yellowing of the eyes and skin. The only treatment for the disease is rest and a high-protein, high-carbohydrate diet.

There is a vaccination for hepatitis B. It is a series of shots, given in the arm. You must have all three shots to be safe. If you know your partner has hepatitis B, the vaccine will protect you after you have completed the shots, but you should have a test to make sure you've responded to the vaccine. People with no known special risk (such as an infected partner) probably do not need the test—just the shots. This is the only STD vaccine that works and it is widely available.

Hepatitis B mainly attacks young men and women in their teens and twenties, and once you contract it, you're a carrier for life. This year in the United States, there will be between 140,000 and 320,000 new cases of hepatitis B documented. Not all doctors and nurses are aware of this fast-growing problem in their communities, so don't hesitate to ask for your vaccination—especially if you change partners frequently. Hepatitis B is easily passed from mother to unborn child. It is also transmissible to young children and infants, but can be largely prevented by vaccination of infants at birth.

HIV/AIDS

The expected number of people in the United States who will contract HIV this year is 45,000, and the number of new infections is not yet declining. The chilling part of this statistic is that even though we know how to prevent HIV transmission, and have aggressive new antiviral therapies to deal with it, we are not taking the most important step: preventing the spread of it.

Centers for Disease Control and Prevention figures documented in February 1999 show that in the United States the majority (51 percent) of HIV-infected individuals are heterosexual. Does this get your attention, gentlemen? I hope so. I don't mean to use scare tactics here, but I do feel obligated to give you the real information. In addition, the average age of those becoming infected has become younger, with a marked increase in the number of infected adolescents.

HIV and AIDS are not the same thing. Unfortunately, one is the precursor of the other. Acquired immune deficiency syndrome (AIDS) is a diagnosis resulting from infection with a virus known as the human immunodeficiency virus (HIV). If you test positive for HIV, that means your system has been exposed to the virus and your body is presenting an immune response to it.

You cannot get AIDS without having HIV. You can, however, be HIV-positive without having an AIDS diagnosis. HIV attacks the immune system, leaving the body unable to fight off disease. It is a sexually infectious virus spread through bodily fluids that are high in white blood cells: blood, semen, vaginal fluids, and mother's breast milk. It is not airborne and cannot be spread by casual contact. Touching, kissing, sharing food, coughing, mosquito bites, using common toilet seats, and swimming in pools do *not* spread HIV. Though, in very rare cases, HIV has been transmitted from a highly infected person through kissing or biting, it resulted from poor oral hygiene that caused open bleeding gums or mouth sores. It is the high vascularization (i.e., a lot of blood supply close to the surface) of mucosal tissues of the anus, mouth, and vagina that makes these areas the most vulnerable to infection.

There are usually no symptoms accompanying HIV. People can get the virus and feel terrific for many years. A small percentage of people will develop an acute mononucleosis-like illness when initially infected. Left untreated, HIV almost always leads to AIDS, and because it is the immune system that fails, the symptoms for AIDS can look like anything from a cold to cancer.

Although there is no cure for AIDS, there are drugs that dramatically slow down the effect that HIV has on the immune system. It can take up to six months for your immune system to show antibodies, which means that you have tested positive for exposure. Every sexually active man and woman should have two HIV tests—one after risky behavior, and another after waiting six months. The six-month waiting period will ensure you have a clean bill of health before having unprotected sex with any new partner. Sadly, in this day and age, it isn't always enough to accept a verbal declaration of good health. Many, many people have been deceived by lovers who claimed to be HIV-negative and weren't.

In one reported case, a young mother didn't realize she was infected with HIV until her daughter was born. When her physician gave her the terrible news, she was shocked. Immediately, she and her husband were tested and both were found to HIV-positive. As you can imagine, each suspected the other of not having been truthful about a past experience. It turned out that before they were married, the husband had had a fling with an old girlfriend. Since the two knew each other well, neither bothered to use safer sex (she was on the pill). Unfortunately, the woman didn't know she had been infected, and unwittingly passed it on to the man, creating a domino effect of infection.

It is very important that you ask to see the results of your lover's HIV test and all tests for sexually transmitted diseases, especially in the case of (but not limited to) women you don't know well (consider going together to get tested). It is also important that she see the results of yours. In fact, rather than make her ask to see yours, offer your results as a show of good faith, opening the door for her to do the same. If your lover refuses to show you her test results, it may be wise to refuse to have unprotected sex with her. Remember, she is being secretive about something that affects *your* health and quite possibly your life. No one should want to keep her/his good health a secret.

When obtaining an HIV test, be mindful of the difference between confidential and anonymous testing. They are not the same. When you have an *anonymous test* you are identified by a number or letter only, not by your name, Social Security number, or any other identifying information. After the blood sample is taken, you confirm that the numbers/letters on the vial and the numbers/letters on your identification slip are the same. A week later you go back to the clinic where the test was taken and get the results. Typically, no results are given over the phone. A *confidential test* means that the results are confidential and limited only by the integrity of those who have access to the information. In other words, you are using your name and placing your trust in the doctor, nurse, or clinic where you get tested. Several years ago an employee at a southern clinic copied the names of all those who had tested positive for HIV and sold the list for fifty dollars a page at a local bar. Clearly, this was a completely unethical act by an amoral person, and it is not commonplace. You can never be 100 percent sure with confidential testing, however, and may be better off with anonymous testing.

There is a new method of testing for HIV, called Orasure, an oral specimen collection device that requires no blood collection and is 99 percent accurate. Like a blood test, it tests for the presence of HIV antibodies.

Finally, I'd like to make several important points about HIV/AIDS:

Point #1: There are several clades (or types) of the HIV virus: A, B, C, D, E, F, M, and O. And within each clade there are different strains. So even if a man or a woman is already positive, he or she can still become infected by another form of virus and is even more susceptible, given the weakened state of the immune system.

Point #2: The most common clade in North America and Europe is B, and for Southeast Asia it is E. Central Africa is a melting pot of different clades.

Point #3: Some strains appear to be more virulent than others. Depending on the virulence of the strain one is exposed to, you could have an almost immediate AIDS diagnosis.

Point #4: "HIV-positive" means you have been exposed to the virus that causes AIDS. Your body shows a positive immune response to HIV.

Point #5: In 1993 the CDC created a definition benchmark for an AIDS diagnosis. This enabled physicians to diagnose AIDS in a uniform manner and also better qualify people for health insurance coverage and drug programs.

Point #6: It is suggested that you wait six months after risky behavior before getting tested. This is because it can take up to six months for antibodies to show up in a test, although most people (95 percent) test positive within three months of exposure, using the antibodies testing methods.

Point #7: A test called a PCR (Polymerase Chain Reaction) tests for the actual virus in your blood. Estimate that someone who is going to seroconvert (go from HIV-negative to HIV-positive) can start to have the virus in his or her system within five to seven days of exposure; on average it takes two weeks for seroconversion. This is an expensive test. It is not an accepted screening test but is occasionally used by groups at very high risk, such as pornography actors.

Point #8: Some years ago there was hope that with the powerful antiviral medications that had HIV-positive people walking around with little to no detectable viral load, these people could stop their drug-therapy at some point. That no longer appears to be the case, as there seem to be reservoirs of HIV in the body. Still, there is a small amount of hope that even more treatments might clear the virus completely in some people in the future. Right now, these treatments are just experimental. The better we get at detecting the virus in the laboratory, the better we are at successfully treating those who are infected.

Point #9: Just because someone has no detectable viral load does not mean he or she cannot infect someone else.

Point #10: In 1998 the CDC estimated that 80 percent of people who are HIV-positive do not know they are infected because they have never been tested.

Point #11: An opportunistic infection is one that would not be a threat to a healthy, normal immune system but takes the "opportunity" to attack a compromised immune system. For example, a person who is undergoing cancer treatment such as chemotherapy is at risk for an opportunistic infection. Every infection, however, isn't an opportunistic one.

While I've discussed the most common of the sexually transmitted diseases, there are more than 50 known STDs to date. Providing you with knowledge about them is not meant to scare you, but rather to empower you. No one should have to be frightened into taking control of his sexual health. Rather, with this information, I hope being safe and careful becomes a matter of self-respect. Without protection, there just isn't an excuse good enough to participate in a sexual relationship with someone whose health you're not 100 percent sure about.

Choosing a Condom

There are many different condoms to choose from, but not all of them are made with quality. The chart on page 364 can give you the wide range of styles, sizes, textures, and other features of condoms. However, before purchasing, you may want to consider the following information.

> ➤ Condoms break. Any condom can break during
> intercourse, for many different reasons. Breakage is
> almost invariably the result of improper handling,
> such as using teeth to open the foil or keeping
> condoms in wallets or car glove boxes, where heat will
> eventually break down the latex in the condom,
> making it easier to burst. Also, the compressed

rectangular packaging some brands use reduces the longevity of the condoms themselves.

➤ Any lubricant with an oil or petroleum base (e.g., Vaseline) will also break down and destroy latex condoms. During a study conducted by Dr. Bruce Voeller, founder of the Mariposa Foundation, men who were chronic condom "busters" were discovered to have been using everyday hand lotion as a lubricant. A lubricant must be water based, and most hand lotions contain some form of oil. Oil is a latex condom's mortal enemy because it immediately begins to erode the latex. Therefore, it is imperative that you check the ingredients of a lotion carefully before using it with a latex condom. Better still, use a water-based lubricant intended for this purpose, such as Astroglide, Sensura, or Liquid Silk. (There is more complete information on lubrication in chapter 12.)

➤ The most often-heard excuse from men who have had unprotected sex is that they don't like condoms because they diminish the pleasure factor. That isn't the question here: It's a matter of safety. However, after you both have been tested and waited the six-month period to make sure you're both healthy, during which you have had no risk factors or sex with anyone else, and then are tested a second time, you will be free and clear to use other methods of birth control.

➤ One of the excuses I hear from men in my seminars is that they are too big to fit into any of the condoms currently available. In my seminars, I usually open a regular-size condom, shape my fingers into a bird's beak, and, watching my nails, unroll the condom over my hand and stretch/pull it down so that it covers my entire forearm past my elbow (it fits, trust me). How much bigger can you be than that? Try it yourself if you don't believe me.

➤ For those gentlemen who have thick, broad penises, there are condoms specifically manufactured with this in mind. These men find regular condoms fit a little too snugly at the base of the shaft and/or at the head. There are two large-size condoms available, Magnum and Trojan-Enz. Field researchers definitely prefer the Magnum. They say the Trojans smell awful and have a "yucky" texture. There is also a larger-head condom coming back onto the market under the name Pleasure Plus. This condom has a baggier head that allows for more friction and stimulation and is completely different in sensation. A similar sensation can be achieved with a regular condom by putting a jelly-bean size dollop of lubricant into the end of the condom before putting it on.

SECRET FROM LOU'S ARCHIVES

Because the herpes and human papilloma viruses can affect skin not covered by a condom, the efficiency of condoms is not as good as it might be for HIV or chlamydia, which are generally contracted from body fluids. However, you can add to your protection if you avoid contact when lesions are active and use condoms religiously at other times.

(continued on page 366)

CONDOM BRANDS	Box Description/Type of Lubrication*	Size in mm (Metric)**
LATEX		
Kimono MicroThin	Dark Blue/Silicone	170 x 49 mm
Trojan-Enz Lubricated	Blue/Silicone	185 x 52 mm
Paradise Super Sensitive	White/Black/Silicone	180 x 52 mm
Crown Skin Less Skin	White/Blue/Silicone	180 x 55 mm
Contempo Exotica	Blue/Woman/Silicone	180 x 49 mm
Vis-a-Vis Ultra Thin	Multi-Colored/Silicone	165 x 49 mm
Trojan Ultra Thin	Grey/Silicone	185 x 52 mm
LifeStyles Ultra Sensitive	Light Grey/Silicone	180 x 52 mm
InVigra	Royal Blue/Silicone	185 x 52 mm
Contempo Wet n' Wild	Woman/Thong/Silicone	180 x 52 mm
Paradise Extra Large	Black/purple	190 x 56 mm
Magnum	Black/gold/Silicone	180 x 56 mm
Pleasure Plus	Metallic/Silicone	175 x 52 mm
Lifestyle Discs	Individual Blister Pack	N/A
NATURAL		
Naturalamb Skin Kling Tite	Black/Jelly-Type	165 x 55 mm
POLYURETHANE		
Avanti for Men	Black with Swirl/Silicone	N/A
Supra	Gold/Silicone	N/A
Reality for Women	Pouch/Silicone	175 mm-7"
FLAVORED		
Kiss of Mint condoms	Green/Non-lubricated	180 x 52 mm

Best-seller in grocery stores: Trojans.
Best-seller in Adult Stores: Contempo RoughRider. (The name sells this product, as the little bumps do nothing for the lady.)

Condom Features 1. Thickness 2. Surface Feel 3. Slim/Wide Fit 4. Size Variation	Where to Purchase: Drugstore, Supermarket, Mail Order, Internet, Adult-Novelty Store	Field Researchers Comments & F.Y.I.
1. Ultra Thin 3. Slimmer	D/S/M/I/A	Light and strong
4. Oversized available in green box	D/S/M/I/A	Leading condom in sales at retail
1. Ultra Thin and Pinky Sheer	D/S/M/I/A	Similar to Crown condoms
1. Ultra Thin 3. Slimmer	D/S/M/I/A	So sheer and invisible, used in porn films
3. Slim Fitting	M/I/A	Nice and snug for the slimmer man
1. Ultra Thin	D/S/M/I/A	Really sheer
4. Baggy shape for greater friction	D/S/M/I/A	Known name
1. Ultra Thin	D/S/M/I/A	Identical condom to Contempo Bareback
1. Regular	D/S/M/I/A	Similar to Lifestyle Lubricated and Trojan-Enz Lubricated, but cost less
2. Generous lubrication	M/I/A	Identical condom to Lifestyles Lubricated
3. Wider Fit	D/S/M/I/A	
3. Wider Fit	D/S/M/I/A	Best for Italian Method/ Sheerest of larger condoms
4. Oversized end & slight ribbing heightens sensation	D/S/M/I/A	Similar to InSpiral & LifeStyles Extra Pleasure
4. Separate pack per condom	D/S/M/I/A	Clear instructions
2. Most natural feel	D/S/M/I/A	Does not protect against STDs
N/A	D/S/M/I/A	Too much breakage
N/A	D/S/M/I/A	Available ONLY with nonoxynol-9
N/A	D/S/M/I/A	Protection women can control
Real flavor not just fragrance	D/S/M/I/A	Best of all the "flavored"

* At time of original publication. All latex condom packages describe those WITHOUT nonoxynol-9. All male
  latex condoms available with or without nonoxynol-9.
** Condom widths—49 mm slim fit, 52 mm average width, 56 mm wider fit.

➤ As the only manufactured spermicidal in the United States, nonoxynol-9 was introduced into the United States in 1920 as a cleaning solution in hospitals. This very irritating substance is found in any diaphragm gel, contraceptive foam, contraceptive sheets, cervical caps, or condoms that contain spermicide. As a spermicidal (i.e., it kills sperm), it breaks down the lipid (fat) layer of the sperm. If it sears this outer layer of sperm, can you imagine what it does to the surface of *her* skin? On contact, this substance can literally burn her. Imagine taking detergent and rubbing it on the most delicate area of the woman you love. I have also heard from many women who have been exposed to nonoxynol-9 that they have experienced bladder and vaginal infections. If you or she is experiencing any irritation, you may want to avoid this nasty substance. As one seminar attendee told me, "My wife and I started using a diaphragm with foam after our son was born a year ago. She had constant vaginal infections, which never seemed to go away. She was in constant pain, and we eventually stopped having sex. Sure enough, when I learned from your seminar about nonoxynol-9, we discovered that had been the culprit. Within a week of our stopping using the foam, everything cleared up." In addition, nonoxynol-9 reduces the average five-year shelf life of condoms by two years.

➤ Although you may hear differently, spermicides containing nonoxynol-9 were created to help reduce the risk of unwanted pregnancy, *not* sexually transmitted diseases. Nonoxynol-9 has proved to be effective at killing *only* HIV and herpes in laboratory tests. There are *no* studies showing nonoxynol-9 has a risk-free effect on human beings. There are *no* studies showing it interferes with the transmission of HIV in normal activity. It has been shown to kill HIV and STDs in test tubes, but there is no clinical evidence to suggest it is a safe measure for disease prevention.

➤ There are long-term research projects under way for other microbicidal products, but they are not near completion. The best protection against HIV, gonorrhea, and pregnancy is a latex condom used properly and correctly every time you have sex. But keep in mind that 10 percent of the population is allergic to latex.

SECRET FROM LOU'S ARCHIVES

"My fiancée used to use those contraceptive sheets, the kind that are inserted like a tampon. Well, I started to get this awful burning sensation in my penis in the middle of sex. Finally, I figured out it was the contraceptive sheet with nonoxynol-9 that was getting rammed into the end of my penis. I would be sore for days and peeing was really painful."

➤ Spermicides should be used only in addition to condoms, never in place of them.

➤ Beware of condoms labeled as "novelty" condoms, such as "glow-in-the-dark." These are not intended to provide pregnancy or STD protection.

➤ The "ribbed for her pleasure" condoms do nothing for women. They were designed so men would buy them thinking they did something—they don't.

> French ticklers are best for their laugh factor, not the pleasure factor. Why? Because up in the nether reaches of the vaginal barrel most women only have an awareness of pressure sensation, not little hats on condoms.

> If you're shy about purchasing condoms, there are several mail-order catalogs available. See the resource section in the appendix.

> As of June 1999 the major manufacturers of condoms in the United States, Ansell and Carter-Wallace, had pretty much shut down domestic production and now manufacture products in offshore plants. The plants here were old, with dated equipment from the 1960s and 1980s, which wasn't adaptable to the needs of the contemporary market. Ansell makes Lifestyles, Contempo, and Prime; Carter-Wallace makes Trojans, Class Act, and Magnums.

SECRET FROM LOU'S ARCHIVES

The FDA allowable failure rate for condoms is 4 in 1,000, picked randomly.

Techniques for Safe Sex

Putting on a condom doesn't have to interrupt the momentum or excitement of your sexual experience; instead, by sharing the procedure with your partner, you can actually increase the play or erotic factor. Let her put the condom on you, for instance, or put it on together, using both your hands to roll it down. For more adventurous women, there is the Italian Method, which involves the woman putting a condom on using her mouth.

Another fun trick to try is placing a dollop of condom-safe (water-soluble, latex-safe) lubricant the size of a jelly bean in the nipple end of the condom before you put it on. This will enhance sensation by reducing that "stuck-on" feeling.

Resources

Safety is essential, but it doesn't have to undermine the sensuality of your lovemaking. Being aware of the risks and taking preventive measures will only increase your connection with your partner and maintain the honesty of your relationship. The following is a list of resources you can contact for further information.

Free Information and Referrals about Sexually Transmitted Diseases (STDs)

Centers for Disease Control and Prevention
www.cdc.gov

**CDC National HIV/AIDS
and Sexually Transmitted Disease Hotline**
800-342-AIDS or 800-227-8922
(24 hours a day, 7 days a week)

Hepatitis Hotline
888-443-7232

American Liver Foundation
800-223-0179

National Herpes Hotline
919-361-8488

About Sexuality

**American Association of Sex Educators,
Counselors and Therapists (AASECT)**
www.aasect.org
Can provide a list of AASECT-certified
therapists in your area.

Society for the Scientific Study of Sexuality
www.ssc.wisc.edu/ssss

American Board of Sexology
www.sexologist.org
Can provide referrals to Diplomates
and Clinical Supervisors in your area.

**Sex Information Education Council
of the United States (SEICUS)**
www.seicus.org

A Final Note

In my years of working with and listening to men and women about their sexuality, I have learned that having great sex is tied to being an artful, fearless, and adventurous lover. Therefore, while the techniques, positions, and hints I have provided in this book will make you technically proficient, being an expert lover is much more about your attitude. It's about feeling confident and trusting yourself. It's about wanting to please your lover. It's about really caring.

I have also learned in my years of working with men and women that the deepest and most satisfying sex usually comes when two people are open, honest, and respectful in their communication. Once these principles are in place, there are no bounds to the passion, spontaneity, and wonderful, soul-merging sex you and your partner can experience. And I offer you this book in hopes that it brings you to that joyful, fun place with your lover. Enjoy!

Resources

Where You Can Get the Toys

In collecting the best sources for toy products, I asked store owners several questions in order to verify their commitment to high quality and an open, encouraging attitude: Did they have a positive sex attitude? Would a woman be comfortable going into the store by herself or ordering over the phone? How big was its selection? Did they sell their mailing list? Was their e-mail site secure?

Catalogs are a great, safe way to introduce tools into the relationship. The very act of choosing a toy can be a bonding, intimate experience. It's a gentle way to suggest what you'd like to try. By looking at the pictures together, you and your partner can feel each other out about what might seem like fun, what might seem too risky, and so on. Initially, making suggestions can make you both feel vulnerable. Women especially fear being rejected. Remember, gentlemen, they don't want to risk being perceived as "loose," if they suggest using a sex toy.

Essentially, the catalogs I am recommending are tasteful. A couple of these outfits are more oriented toward women, provide wonderful support staff to answer questions via an 800 number, and have careful explanations in the catalogs themselves. Other catalogs are a bit more edgy and less pristine.

Condomania

www.condomania.com

Order line: 800-9CONDOMS (926-6366)

This Web site and phone/mail order service is one of the best non-retail sources for condoms. Has a ROAD TEST chart on the site based on published articles. They offer a selection of over three hundred different condoms. The e-mail site uses SSL encryption when placing an order.

WEST COAST

SEATTLE

Toys in Babeland

707 East Pike Street, Seattle WA 98122

206-328-2914 / Catalog: 800-658-9119

E-mail: biglove@babeland.com / Web site: www.babeland.com

This is a female-run store, originally created as a place for women and their comfort. It now carries some male-oriented products. Workshops and seminars.

SAN FRANCISCO

Good Vibrations

Retail stores:

1210 Valencia Street, San Francisco CA 94110

2502 San Pablo Avenue, Berkeley CA 94702

Mail order:

938 Howard Street, Suite 101, San Francisco CA 94103

415-974-8990 / 800-289-8423 (in the U.S.)

Fax: 415-974-8989 / E-mail: customerservice@goodvibes.com
Web site: www.goodvibes.com

Good Vibrations is one of the best all-around store/catalog combinations. Their specialty is vibrators—and they have an endless supply and selection. They also offer a vast array of lubricants, special massage oils, and videos and books. The selection of toys and leather goods is also of high quality, durability, and inventive styling. All their products have passed customer satisfaction tests. The staff is known for its courteous, nonjudgmental, sex-positive attitude, offering sensitive, knowledgeable, and helpful service.

LOS ANGELES

The Pleasure Chest

7733 Santa Monica Boulevard, West Hollywood CA 90046
323-650-1022 / Order line: 800-753-4536
Fax: 323-650-1176 / Web site: www.thepleasurechest.com

This Pleasure Chest targets a primarily gay male clientele, with a strong leather focus, though straight men and women will find many products for them, including videos and apparel.

Glow

8358 1/2 West 3rd Street, Los Angeles CA 90048
323-782-9080 / E-mail: glowspotLA@aol.com

Glow offers an outstanding selection of aromatherapy products. Custom blending available.

The Love Boutique

18637 Ventura Boulevard, Tarzana CA 91356
818-342-2400
2924 Wilshire Boulevard, Santa Monica CA 90403
310-453-3459 / Toll-free ordering: 888-568-4663

The two stores are female owned and operated and are open seven days a week. While they offer a small selection of items, the customer is treated with care by a knowledgeable staff. The staff seems uniquely focused on making women feel more at ease and comfortable with their sexuality.

Paradise Specialties

7344 Center Avenue, Huntington Beach CA 92647
714-898-0400

Refined, comfortable environment.

SAN DIEGO

F Street Stores

751 Fourth Avenue, San Diego CA 92101 / 619-236-0841
2004 University Avenue, San Diego CA 92104 / 619-298-2644
7998 Miramar Road, San Diego CA 92126 / 619-549-8014
1141 Third Avenue, Chula Vista CA 92011 / 619-585-3314
237 East Grand, Escondido CA 92023 / 619-480-6031

The stores in this chain offer a wide range of male and female products; it was also one of the first to create a women's novelty section.

Condoms Plus

1220 University Avenue, San Diego CA 92103
619-291-7400

This is a store "with a woman in mind." It is a general-license store for all sorts of gifts, as well as condoms. In other words, you can buy a stuffed animal for your child as well as an adult novelty item for your partner. The novelties, however, are in their own section of the store.

MIDWEST

CHICAGO

The Pleasure Chest

3155 North Broadway, Chicago IL 60657

773-525-7152 / Catalog sales: 800-316-9222

The majority of customers are women and couples. This is the store that defines what an adult store should be like: clean, bright, tastefully presented, with nonjudgmental salespeople who look like you and me. This and the New York store (see page 378) show the benefit of being run and operated by the owner, who focuses on taking good care of the customer.

Frenchy's

872 North State Street, Chicago IL 60611

312-337-9190

This store has undergone a major renovation in appearance and size. It is now three times larger and offers a range of products for men and women.

MINNEAPOLIS/ST. PAUL

Fantasy House Gifts

709 West Lake Street, Minneapolis MN 55408

612-824-2459 / Web site: www.fantasygifts.com

There are eight Fantasy House stores in the area, including Bloomington, Bernsville, St. Louis Park, Crystal, Fridley, Coon Rapids, and St. Paul—and two stores in New Jersey (Marlton and Turnersville). Adult material and novelties presented with a comfortable midwestern environment and attitude. They recently added the Condom Kingdom store in Minneapolis to their operation.

OKLAHOMA

Christies Toy Box

1184 North MacArthur Boulevard, Oklahoma City OK 73127

405-942-4622

Christies is part of a chain of adult stores, ranked number one in the state of Oklahoma; stores also exist in Texas.

WISCONSIN

A Woman's Touch

600 Williamson Street, Madison WI 53703

888-621-8880 or 608-250-1928 / Website: www.touchofawoman.com

A newsletter is posted on the site, listing seminars and workshops. Carries prescreened books and videos so that they are female friendly. The site is encrypted. Run by an M.D. and M.S.W. (social worker), and therefore the information is current.

EAST COAST

NEW YORK

The Pleasure Chest

156 Seventh Avenue South (between Charles and Perry)

New York NY 10014

212-242-2158 / Toll-free: 800-316-9222

E-mail:pleasurechestny@aol.com / Web site:www.apleasurechest.com

The New York store and its Chicago sister store are both popular, classy, and well stocked, with a range of products for both men and women.

Eve's Garden

119 West 57th Street, Suite 1201, New York NY 10019

212-757-8651 / Orders: 800-848-3837

Web site: www.evesgarden.com

This is a female-owned-and-operated store. What the Pleasure Chest did in 1972 for gay male consumers Eve's Garden did for women in 1974. Located in the heart of midtown Manhattan, Eve's Garden is in the least likely of areas. It is known far and wide as the matriarch of feminine-focused, sex-positive merchandising.

Toys in Babeland
94 Rivington Street, New York NY 10002
212-375-1701 / E-mail: comments@babeland.com
Web site: www.babeland.com

THE SOUTH

NORTH CAROLINA

Adam & Eve
PO Box 800, North Carrboro NC 27510
800-765-ADAM (2326) / Customer service: 919-644-8100

This is the biggest mail-order adult-products company in the United States. It offers a full range of products. Please be aware that Adam & Eve sells the names in their customer database.

TEXAS

Forbidden Fruit
108 E. North Loop Boulevard, Austin TX 78751
512-453-8090 / Orders and information: 800-315-2029
Web site: www.forbiddenfruit.com

Three locations in Austin. Very female-friendly atmosphere. Seminars. The site is secure.

CANADA

BRITISH COLUMBIA

Womyn's Ware Inc.

896 Commercial Drive, Vancouver, British Columbia V5L 3Y5

888-996-9273, order desk; 604-254-2543, store.

Web site: www.womynsware.com

CALGARY

The Love Boutique

9737 MacLeod Trail South, Calgary, AB T2J 0P6

403-252-1846

Just For Lovers

Store #1: 920 36th Street NE, #114 / 403-273-6242

Store #2: 4014 MacLeod Trail South / 403-243-2554

Store #3: 1415 17th Avenue SW / 403-245-9505

Store #4: 4247 Bow Trail SW / 403-282-7125

NOVA SCOTIA

Venus Envy

1598 Barrington Street, Halifax, Nova Scotia B3J 1Z6

902-422-0004 / Web site: www.venusenvy.ca

ONTARIO

Venus Envy

110 Parent Avenue, Ottawa, Ontario K1N 7B4

613-789-4646 / Web site: www.venusenvy.ca

TORONTO

Seduction

577 Yonge Street, Toronto, ON M4Y 1Z2

416-966-6969

This recently opened retail operation is the largest adult-novelty store in North America, measuring 15,000 square feet on three floors. The customers are well taken care of by young, fresh-faced college-age women who know what they are selling.

Come As You Are
701 Queen Street West, Toronto, ON M6J 1E6
877-858-3160 / Web site: www.comeasyouare.com

"Good sex is a cooperative effort." Only cooperative-run sex store in Canada.

VANCOUVER

Love Nest
Store #1: 119 East 1st Street, North Vancouver, BC V7L 1B2
604-987-1175
Store #2: 102-4338 Main Street, Whistler, BC V0N 1B4
604-932-6906
Web site: www.lovenest.ca

Any of the listed products in the book can be purchased through The Sexuality Seminars/FRANKLY SPEAKING, INC. All transactions are confidential and we do not sell our mailing list. To purchase products, inquire about my seminar schedule, book a seminar, be placed on the FRANKLY SPEAKING mailing list, or to get more information, contact:

Frankly Speaking, Inc.
11601 Wilshire Boulevard
Suite 500
Los Angeles CA 90025

310-556-3623
1-877-SexSeminars (1-877-739-7364)
E-mail: LouPaget@aol.com / Web site: www.LouPaget.com

Purchases can be made by Visa/MasterCard, cash, or check. FRANKLY SPEAKING, INC. shows on all bank statements and is the name under which all correspondence is sent. All products are discreetly packaged and shipped Priority Post unless otherwise requested. The Speciality Sophist-Kits™ gift boxes can arrive in presentation style (open) or closed— for a bigger surprise. They are delivered UPS or Federal Express and are shipped through Artfull Baskets.

Bibliography

Anand, Margot. *The Art of Sexual Ecstasy: The Path of Sacred Sexuality for Western Lovers.* Jeremy Tarcher, Los Angeles. 1989.

————. *The Art of Sexual Magic: Cultivating Sexual Energy to Transform Your Life.* Tarcher/Putnam, New York. 1995.

————. *Sexual Ecstasy: The Art of Orgasm. Exercises from the Art of Sexual Magic.* Tarcher/Putnam, New York. 2000.

Bakos, Susan Crain. *What Men Really Want: Straight Talk from Men about Sex.* St. Martin's, New York. 1990.

Barbach, Lonnie. *For Each Other: Sharing Sexual Intimacy.* Anchor Press/Doubleday, New York. 1982.

Barrows, Sydney Biddle. *Mayflower Manners: Etiquette for Consenting Adults.* Doubleday, New York. 1990.

Bechtel, Stefan. *The Practical Encyclopedia of Sex and Health.* Rodale, Emmaus, Pa. 1993.

————. *Sex: A Man's Guide.* Rodale, Emmaus, Pa. 1996.

Bell, Simon, Richard Curtis, and Helen Fielding. *Who's Had Who.* Warner Books, New York. 1990.

Birch, Robert. *Oral Caress: The Loving Guide to Exciting a Woman. A Comprehensive Illustrated Manual on the Joyful Art of Cunnilingus.* PEC Publications, Columbus, Ohio. 1996.

Bishop, Clifford. *Sex and Spirit: Ecstasy and Transcendence, Ritual and Taboo. The Undivided Self.* Little, Brown and Company, New York. 1996.

Blank, Joani. *Good Vibrations: The Complete Guide to Vibrators.* Down There Press, San Francisco. 1989.

Block, Joel D., and Susan Crain Bakos. *Sex Over 50.* Rewar Books, Paramus, N.J. 1999.

Boteach, Shumley. *Kosher Sex: A Recipe for Passion and Intimacy*. Main Street Books, Doubleday, New York. 1999.

Brame, Gloria. *Come Hither: A Commonsense Guide to Kinky Sex*. Fireside Books, New York. 1999.

Caine, K. Winston. *The Male Body: An Owner's Manual*. Rodale, Emmaus, Pa. 1996.

Chalker, Rebecca. *The Clitoral Truth: The Secret World at Your Fingertips*. Seven Stories Press, New York. 2000.

Chang, Dr. Stephen T. *The Tao of Sexology: The Book of Infinite Wisdom*. Tao Publishing, Reno, Nevada. 1986.

Chesser, Eustace. *Strange Loves: The Human Aspects of Sexual Deprivation*. William Morrow and Company, New York. 1971.

Chia, Mantak, and Douglas Abrams. *The Multi-Orgasmic Male: How Every Man Can Experience Multiple Orgasms and Dramatically Enhance His Sexual Relationship*. Harper, San Francisco. 1997.

Chia, Mantak, and Maneewan Chia. *Cultivating Female Sexual Energy: Healing Love through the Tao*. Healing Tao Books, Huntington, New York. 1986.

Chia, Mantak, and Michael Winn. *Taoist Secrets of Love: Cultivating Male Sexual Energy*. Aurora Press, Santa Fe. 1984.

Chichester, B., ed. *Sex Secrets: Ways to Satisfy Your Partner Every Time*. Rodale, Emmaus, Pa. 1996.

Chu, Valentin. *The Yin-Yang Butterfly: Ancient Chinese Sexual Secrets for Western Lovers*. Tarcher/Putnam, New York. 1993.

Cohen, Angela and Sarah Gardner Fox. *The Wise Woman's Guide to Erotic Videos: 300 Sexy Videos for Every Woman—and Her Lover*. Broadway Books, New York. 1997.

Comfort, Alex. *The Joy of Sex: A Gourmet Guide to Love Making*. Fireside/Simon & Schuster, New York. 1972.

———. *The New Joy of Sex: A Gourmet Guide to Lovemaking for the Nineties*. Crown, New York. 1991.

Danielou, Alain. *The Complete Kama Sutra: The First Unabridged Modern Translation of the Classic Indian Text*. Park Street Press, Rochester, Vt. 1994.

Deida, David. *The Way of the Superior Lover: A Spiritual Guide to Sexual Skills*. Plexus, Austin, Texas. 1997.

Dick & Jane. *Erotic New York: A Guide to the Red Hot Apple*. City & Company, New York. 1997.

Dodson, Betty. *Sex for One. The Joy of Selfloving*. Crown, New York. 1996.

Douglas, Nik, and Penny Slinger. *Sexual Secrets: The Alchemy of Ecstasy; 10th Anniversary Issue*. Destiny Books, Rochester, Vt. 1989.

Eichel, Edward, and Philip Nobile. *The Perfect Fit: How to Achieve Mutual Fulfillment and Monogamous Passion through the New Intercourse*. Signet, New York. 1993.

Ellison, Carol Rinkleib. *Women's Sexualities: Generations of Women Share Intimate Secrets of Sexual Self-Acceptance*. New Harbinger, Oakland, Calif. 2000.

Estes, Clarissa Pinkola. *Women Who Run with the Wolves: Myths and Stories of the Wild Woman Archetype*. Ballantine, New York. 1992.

Fisher, Helen. *Anatomy of Love; The Natural History of Monogamy, Adultery and Divorce*. W. W. Norton, New York. 1992.

———. *The First Sex: The Natural Talents of Women and How They Are Changing the World*. Random House, New York. 1999.

George, Stephen C. *A Lifetime of Sex: The Ultimate Manual on Sex, Women and Relationships for Every Stage of a Man's Life*. Rodale, Emmaus, Pa. 1998.

Gerstman, Bradley, Christopher Pizzo, and Bradley Seldes. *What Men Really Want: Three Professional Men Reveal to Women What It Takes to Make a Man Yours*. Cliff Street Books/HarperCollins, New York. 1998.

Goldstein, Irwin and Larry Rothstein. *The Potent Male*. Regenesis CyclePress, (no city given). 1995.

Gordon, Sol. *The New You*. An Ed-U Press, Fayetteville, NY. 1980.

Gray, John. *Mars and Venus in the Bedroom: A Guide to Lasting Romance and Passion*. HarperCollins, New York. 1995.

———. *Men, Women and Relationships: Making Peace with the Opposite Sex*. Beyond Words Publishing, Hillsboro, OR. 1993.

Griffin, Gary. *The Condom Encyclopedia*. Added Dimensions, Los Angeles. 1993.

Harris, Marvin. *Our Kind: Who We Are, Where We Came From and Where We Are Going*. Harper & Row, New York. 1989.

Hatcher, Robert A. *Contraceptive Technology*, 16th ed. Irvington Publishers, New York. 1994.

Heimel, Cynthia. *Sex Tips for Girls*. Simon & Schuster, New York. 1983.

Hite, Shere. *The Hite Report: A Nationwide Study on Female Sexuality*. Dell, New York. 1976.

———. *The Hite Report: On Male Sexuality*. Ballantine, New York. 1981.

Hollander, Xaviera. *The Happy Hooker*. Dell, New York. 1972.

Holstein, M.D., Lana L. *How to Have Magnificent Sex: The Seven Dimensions of a Vital Sexual Connection*. Crown, New York. 2001.

Hutton, Julia. *Good Sex: Real Stories from Real People*. Cleis Press, San Francisco. 1995.

J. *The Sensuous Woman*. Dell, New York. 1969.

Janus, Samuel and Cynthia Janus. *The Janus Report on Sexual Behavior: The First Broad-Scale Scientific National Survey Since Kinsey*. John Wiley & Sons, New York. 1993.

Joannides, Paul. *The Guide to Getting It On: A New and Mostly Wonderful Book About Sex*. 368 pp. Goofy Foot Press, Los Angeles. 1996.

Kahn, Alice, Beverly Whipple, and John Perry. *The G Spot: and Other Recent Discoveries About Human Sexuality*. Dell, New York. 1982.

Kahn, Sandra. *The Kahn Report on Sexual Preferences*. Avon, New York. 1981.

Kaplan, Helen Singer. *The New Sex Therapy: The Active Treatment of Sexual Disorders*. Brunner/Mazel, New York. 1974.

Keesling, Barbara. *Sexual Pleasure: Reaching New Heights of Sexual Arousal & Intimacy*. Hunter House, Alameda, Calif. 1993.

———. *How to Make Love All Night (and Drive a Woman Wild). Male Multiple Orgasm and Other Secrets for Prolonging Lovemaking*. Harper Perennial, New York. 1994.

Kline-Graber, Georgia, and Benjamin Graber. *Woman's Orgasm: A Guide to Sexual Satisfaction*. Popular Library, New York. 1976.

Kronhausen, Phyllis and Eberhard Kronhausen. *The Complete Book of Erotic Art*, vols. 1 and 2. Bell Publishing, New York. 1978.

Knutila, John. *Fit for Sex: A Man's Guide to Enhancing and Maintaining Peak Sexual Performance*. Reward Books, Paramus, N.J. 2000.

Ladas Kahn, Alice, Beverly Whipple, and John Perry. *The G-Spot: and Other Recent Discoveries about Human Sexual*. Dell, New York. 1982.

Legman, G. *The Intimate Kiss: The Modern Classic of Oral Erotic Technique*. Warner, New York. 1973.

Lewinsohn, Richard. *A History of Sexual Customs*. Harper & Brothers, New York. 1958.

Locker, Sari. *Mindblowing Sex in the Real World: Hot Tips for Doing It in the Age of Anxiety*. 258 pp. HarperPerennial, New York. 1995.

Love, Brenda. *Encyclopedia of Unusual Sex Practices*. Barricade Books, New York. 1992.

M. *The Sensuous Man*. Dell, New York, 1971.

Mann, A. T., Jane Lyle. *Sacred Sexuality*. Element Books Limited, Shaftsbury, Dorset, England. 1995.

Massey, Doreen. *Lovers' Guide Encyclopedia: The Definitive Guide to Sex and You*. Thunder's Mouth Press, New York. 1996.

Masters, William, and Virginia Johnson. *Human Sexual Response*. Little, Brown and Company, Boston. 1966.

Masters, William, Virginia Johnson, and Robert C. Kolodny. *Heterosexuality*. HarperCollins, New York. 1994.

McCary, James Leslie. *Sexual Myths & Fallacies*. Schocken, New York. 1973.

McCutcheon, Marc. *The Compass in Your Nose and other Astonishing Facts about Humans*. Jeremy P. Tarcher, Los Angeles. 1989.

Meletis, Chris D. *Better Sex Naturally: Herbs and Other Natural Supplements That Can Jump Start Your Sex Life*. The Philip Lief Group, (no city given). 2000.

Milsten, Richard, and Julian Slowinski. *The Sexual Male: Problems and Solutions: A Complete Medical and Psychological Guide to Lifelong Potency*. W. W. Norton and Company, New York. 1999.

Mooney, Shane. *Useless Sexual Trivia: Tastefully Purient Facts about Everyone's Favorite Subject*. Fireside, New York. 2000.

Morris, Hugh. *The Art of Kissing*. 1936.

Muir, Charles, and Caroline Muir. *Tantra: The Art of Conscious Loving*. Mercury House, San Francisco. 1989.

Neret, Gilles. *Erotica Universalis*. Benedikt Taschen, Verlag, Germany. 1994.

O'Connell, Helen E., et al. "Anatomical Relationship Between the Urethra and Clitoris." *Journal of Urology*, 159 (1998): 1892.

Ogden, Gina. *Women Who Love Sex: An Inquiry into the Expanding Spirit of Women's Erotic Experience*. Womanspirit Press, Cambridge, Mass. 1999.

Otto, Herbert A. *Liberated Orgasms: The Orgasmic Revolution*. Liberating Creations, Inc. Silverado, Calif. 1999.

Oxford English Dictionary, Second edition. Oxford University Press, Oxford. 1989.

Panati, Charles. *Sexy Origins and Intimate Things: The Rites and Rituals of Straights, Gays, Bi's, Drags, Trans, Virgins and Others*. Penguin Books, New York. 1998.

Parsons, Alexandra. *Facts & Phalluses: A Collection of Bizarre and Intriguing Truths, Legends and Measurements*. St. Martin's, New York. 1989.

Patterson, Ella. *Will the Real Women . . . Please Stand Up!* Knowledge Concepts, Texas. 1993.

Penney, Alexandra. *The Sexiest Sex of All*. Dell, New York. 1993.

Purvis, Kenneth. *The Male Sexual Machine: An Owner's Manual*. St. Martin's, New York. 1992.

Ramsdale, David, and Ellen Ramsdale. *Sexual Energy Ecstasy. A Practical Guide to Lovemaking Secrets of the East and West*. Bantam, New York. 1993.

Rancier, Lance. *The Sex Chronicles: Strange-But-True Tales from Around the World*. General Publishing Group, Los Angeles. 1997.

Reinsch, Judith. *The Kinsey Institute New Report on Sex: What You Must Know to Be Sexually Literate*. St. Martin's, New York. 1990.

Rilly, Cheryl. *Great Moments in Sex*. Three Rivers Press, New York. 1999.

Sacks, Stephen. *The Truth About Herpes*, 4th ed. Gordon Soules Publishers, Vancouver, Canada. 1997.

SARK. *Succulent Wild Women: Dancing with Your Wonder-full Self!* Fireside/Simon & Schuster, New York. 1997.

Schnarch, David. *Passionate Couples: Love, Sex and Intimacy in Emotionally Committed Relationships*. W. W. Norton, New York. 1997.

Schwartz, Bob, and Leah Schwartz. *The One Hour Orgasm: How to Learn the Amazing "Venus Butterfly."* 3rd ed. Breakthru Publishing, Houston. 1999.

Scoble, Gretchen, and Ann Field. *The Meaning of Flowers: Myth, Language and Lore*. Chronicle Books, San Francisco. 1998.

Smith, David, and Mike Gordon. *Strange but True Facts about Sex: The Illustrated Book of Sexual Trivia*. Meadowbook Press, Minn. 1989.

Smith, Richard. *The Dieter's Guide to Weight Loss During Sex*. Workman Publishing, New York. 1978.

Stoppard, Miriam. *The Magic of Sex: The Book That Really Tells Men about Women and Women about Men*. Dorling Kindersley, New York. 1991.

Stubbs, Kenneth Ray, and Louise-Andrée Saulnier. *Erotic Massage: The Touch of Love*. Secret Garden, Larkspur, Calif. 1993.

Tannahill, Reay. *Sex in History*. Scarborough House, Briarcliff Manor, New York. 1980.

Tannen, Deborah. *You Just Don't Understand: Women and Men in Conversation*. William Morrow, New York. 1990.

Taormino, Tristan. *The Ultimate Guide to Anal Sex for Women*. Cleis Press, San Francisco. 1998.

Taylor, Timothy. *The Prehistory of Sex: Four Million Years of Human Sexual Culture*. Bantam, New York. 1996.

Tepper, Mitchell Steven. "Attitudes, Beliefs, and Cognitive Process That May Impede or Facilitate Sexual Pleasure and Orgasm in People with Spinal Cord Injury." *Dissertation in Education*. Presented to the Faculties of the University of Pennsylvania in Partial Fulfillment of the Requirements for the Doctorate of Philosophy. 1999.

Trager, James. *The Women's Chronology: A Year-by-Year Record, from Prehistory to the Present*. Henry Holt, New York. 1994.

Tuleja, Tad. *Curious Customs: The Stories Behind 296 Popular American Rituals*. Harmony Books/Crown, New York. 1987.

Waggoner, Glen, and Kathleen Moloney. *Esquire Etiquette: The Modern Man's Guide to Good Form*. Collier Books, New York. 1987.

Walker, Barbara G. *The Woman's Encyclopedia of Myths And Secrets*. Harper & Row, New York. 1983.

Walker, Morton. *Foods for Fabulous Sex: Natural Sexual Nutrients to Trigger Passion, Heighten Response, Improve Performance & Overcome Dysfunction*. Magni Group, McKinney, Tex. 1992.

Wallace, Irving. *The Nympho and Other Maniacs: The Lives, the Loves and the Sexual Adventures of Some Scandalous and Liberated Ladies*. Simon & Schuster, New York. 1971.

Watson, Cynthia Mervis. *Love Potions: A Guide to Aphrodisiacs and Sexual Pleasures*. Tarcher/Putnam, New York. 1993.

Welch, Leslee. *Sex Facts: A Handbook for the Carnally Curious*. Carol Publishing, New York. 1992.

Wildwood, Chrissie. *Erotic Aromatherapy: Essential Oils for Lovers*. Sterling, New York. 1994.

Worwood, Valerie Ann. *Scents & Scentuality: Aromatherapy & Essential Oils for Romance, Love and Sex*. New World Library, Novato, Calif. 1999.

Zacks, Richard. *History Laid Bare: Lover Perversity from the Ancient Etruscans to Warren G. Harding*. HarperCollins, New York. 1994.

Zilbergeld, Bernie. *Male Sexuality*. Bantam, New York. 1978.

———. *The New Male Sexuality: The Truth about Men, Sex, and Pleasure*, Rev. edition. Bantam, New York. 1999.

Zimet, Susan, and Victor Goodman. *The Great Cover-Up: A Condom Compendium*. Civan, Inc., New York. 1988.

Zimmerman, Jack, and Jaquelyn McCandless. *Flesh and Spirit: The Mystery of the Intimate Relationship*. Bramble Books, Las Vegas. 1998.

Index

Underscored page references indicate boxed text. **Boldface** references indicate illustrations.

A

Aaberg, Phillip, 78
AASECT, 370
Abs, intercourse and, <u>230</u>
Abstinence, 346
Acquired immune deficiency
    syndrome (AIDS). *See*
    HIV/AIDS
Action spots, <u>93</u>, 101, 102,
    171–73, 197. *See also*
    Manual sex
Addison's disease, 328
AFE zone, 160–61
A-frame effect, 162
Aging, effects of, on
  sexual desire, 112
  sexual functioning, <u>33</u>, 34,
    325–26, <u>326</u> , 333
AIDS. *See* HIV/AIDS
Alcohol consumption,
    333–34
Alpha males, 13

American Association of Sex
    Educators, Counselors
    and Therapists
    (AASECT), 370
American Board of Sexuality, 370
American Liver Foundation, 370
Anafranil, 337
Anal beads, 140–41, 284–85
Anal orgasms
  female, 166
  male, 125, 138–39, <u>139</u>
Anal sex
  attitudes about, 252–53
  female orgasms and, 166
  male orgasms and, 125,
    138–39, <u>139</u>
  myths about, 252
  oral sex and, 218
  pornography and, 11
  tips for, 253, 276
  toys for, 140–41, 284–85
Anand, Margot, <u>292</u> , 299, 317
Anemia, 328

Anilingus, 138–39
Anorexia nervosa, 329
Anorgasmic women, 44
Anterior fornix erotic (AFE) zone, 160–61
Aphrodisiacs, 262–63
  aromatherapy oils, 260
  Ecstasy, 263
  genital kissing, 87–88
  myths about, 262
  oysters, 263
Arbour Zena, 79
Arch position, 215, **215**
Arms, 95–96
Aromatherapy, 75, 258–59, 260 , 261
Arousal. *See also* Foreplay
  indicators of, 180, 197, 223, 275
  myths about, 111–12
  sexual response and
    female, 38–42, **38**, **40**
    male, 32–33, **32**
Athletic sex, 233, 246
Attitudes, sexual, 115, 119, 121, 122
Attraction, female, 238

B

Backdoor sex. *See* Anal sex
Back massages, 94–95
Bacterial vaginosis (BV), 201
Baker, Chet, 79
Baker-Riskin, Anita, 151
Bakos, Susan Crain, 41
Barbach, Lonnie, 156, 165
Barry, John, 79

Basket Weave technique, 131–33, **132**
Bathing, 72
Beards. *See* Facial hair, male
Behavior modification, 336
Belly button massages, 93–94
Benzocaine, 142
Better Than Sex (BTS) position, 247–50, **249**
Big Draw technique, 311–12, **312**
Birth control, 56 , 343, 344, 367
Bladder infections, 201, 218, 269
Blended orgasms, 142, 156, 166–67
Block, Joel, 41
Blue balls, 112
Body awareness, 23–24
  female physical changes and, 37–45, **40–41**
    arousal, 38–42, **38**, **40**
    ejaculation, 44–45, 168–69
    genitalia, **37**
    orgasms, 43–44
    resolution, 45
  male physical changes and, 29–37, **30–31**
    arousal, 32–33, **32**
    ejaculation, 35–36
    erection, 33–34, 332
    genitalia, **29**
    resolution, 36–37
  sexual response cycles and, 24–29, **25**, **26**
Body glides, 268
Body odor, 75
Body stimulation, all-over, 167
Bondage, 286
Boredom, sexual, 51, 55
Brain, as sex organ, 47, 60

Breakfast, in bed, 65
Breast exams, 100
Breast-feeding, orgasms during, 164
Breast orgasms
    female, 163–64
    male, 140
Breasts, 99–100
Breathing
    arousal and, 180, 197, 223, 275
    Tantric, 296–97
Britton, Bryce, 289
BTS position, 247–50, **249**
Buddhist Tantra. See Tantra
Bungee jumping harness, 287
Burning sensations, 250
Buttocks massages, 95
Butt plugs, 140, 284
BV, 201

C

Calluses, 174
Candles, scented, 259
Carrying woman's belongings, as courtly behavior, 63–64
CAT, 162, 233
CDC National HIV/AIDS Hotline, 340, 369
Cervical orgasms, 161–62
Chair Therapy position, 218, **219**, 220
Chang, Stephen, 307
Cheese, as seductive food, 77
Chia, Mantak, 333
Chinese Taoism, 293
Ching-Chi, 294, 295
Chin pressure, 222

Chlamydia, 348–49, 349
Chlamydia trachomatis, 349
Chocolate, as seductive food, 76
Cholesterol, 338
Chua Chee Ann, 160
Circulatory system, 333
Cirrhosis, 329
Clap, 349–50, 349
Cleanliness, 69, 73
Climax. See Orgasms
Clitoral orgasms, 156, 157, 158, 162
Clitoris, **42**, 158, 173, 178, 179, 190
    dildo/vibrators for, 276
    flicking problem and, 203–4
    pathway for, 161–62
    stimulating (see also Manual sex, performed on female)
    tips for, 207, 221–24
Cocaine, 334
Cock rings, 141, 281–83
Cohen, Angela, 12
Coital alignment technique (CAT), 162, 233
Cold sores, 353
Commitment, 21–22
Communication, 48–57
    compatibility and, 51–52
    gender differences in, 14, 16–20
    sexual desire and, 56–57
    sexual preferences and, 52–53
    sharing and, 48–50
    spontaneity and, 54–55
Compatibility, 51–52
Conception
    Caribbean belief about, 115
    during orgasm, 239

Condoms
  best brands of, 364–65
  failure rate of, 368
  latex, 364–65, 367
  natural, 364–65
  polyurethane, 364–65
  putting on, 368–69
  safe sex and, 367
  spermicides and, 366–67
  STDs and, 347
  tips for choosing, 269, 361–69,
    363
Condyloma, 353–54
Congestive heart failure, 329
Copulation, duration of, 27
Cosmopolitan, 114
Counseling, 336
Courtly behavior, 60–66, 66
  kissing as, 86–88
Cradle and Diamond Tip
    technique, 221
Crystal wand, 285, 285
Cultural barriers, 118–19,
    203
Cushing's syndrome, 329

D

Death, during orgasm, 49
Deep throating, 11, 135
Delayed ejaculation, 335
Depression, 329, 337
Desensitizing sprays, 141–42
Desire, sexual
  low, 326–28
  stress and, 56–57
Diabetes, 332
Diaphragms, 154

Dildos, 274
  Chinese, 285
  tips for using, 275–76
  types of, 230, 276–81, 277,
    278, 279, 280
  vibrating features of, 275
Dip-Test, 196
Dirty words, 19
Discharge fluid. See Ejaculation,
    female
Doggy style position, 242–44,
    243
Doing Your ABCs technique, 220
Double Duty position, 189, 189
Douching, 181, 200
Downward Dog position, 213
Drug addiction, 329, 334
Dry orgasms, 142–43
Dynamic position, 194–95, 194

E

Ears, 91–92
Ecstasy, 263
Ejaculation
  female
    myths about, 110, 160
    sex research on, 116–17, 161
    sexual response and, 44–45,
      168–69
  male
    ancient beliefs about, 113
    delayed, 335
    premature, 155, 155,
      334–37, 336
    sexual response and, 35–36
Elevator technique, 220
Embrace, 268

Emotions
  feeling safe, 49
  honesty, 49–50
  performance anxiety, 47–48,
    113–14, 148–49
  rejection, 51–52
  vulnerability, 52
*Encyclopedia of Unusual Sex
  Practices*, 262
Enhancers, pleasure, 141, 257–58
  aphrodisiacs, 87–88, 262–63
  aromatherapy, 75, 258–59, 260 ,
    261
  desensitizing sprays, 141–42
  Kegel exercise, 288–89
  lubricants, 264–70, 265
  sex toys
    anal beads, 140–41, 284–85
    bungee jumping harness, 287
    butt plugs, 140, 284
    cock rings, 141, 281–83
    crystal wand, 285, **285**
    dildo/vibrators, 230, 274–81,
      277, 278, 279, 280
    Pearl Necklace, 131, 281
    shaft sleeves, 283–84
    Sportsheets™, 286
    surgical procedures, 287–88,
      288
  vacuum pumps, 273
  Viagra, 142, 327
Enya, 78
Epididymitis, 349, 350
Erectile dysfunction, 326 ,
  330–34, **331**, 335
Erections
  arousal and, 142
  difficulties achieving, 144, 326,
    330–34, **331**, 335

  in elephants, 114
  myths about, 111
  sexual response and, 33–34
  during sleep, 34
Erogenous zones, female, 81–83
  kissing, 83–88
  men's fascination with, 89
  Sensual Massage and, 100,
    101–2
  Swirl technique and, 100–101
  touching, 88–89
    back, 94–95
    belly button, 93–94
    breasts, 99–100
    buttocks, 95
    ears, 91–92
    face, 91
    feet, 96–99, **98**
    head, 88–89
    limbs, 95–96
    neck, 92–93
    shoulders, 92–93
Erotic Mind, The, 292
Essential oils, 259, 260, 261
Essential Tantra, The, 307
Estrogen, 262
Etiquette, 61–64
Excuses, overcoming, 56–57
Exercise, 230, 288–89, 311
Eye contact, 17
Eyegasm, 127

F

Face, 91
Facial hair, male, 104, 206–7,
  225
Facial massages, 261

Fantasies
of married women, <u>50</u>
masturbation and, 140
pornography and, 10
sources for, 103, 140
Fantasy orgasms
female, 167
male, 139–40
Feet, 96–97, **98**
Fellatio, <u>134</u>. *See also* Oral sex,
performed on male
Femme Productions, 12
Fertilization, 152–55
Figs, as seductive food, 76
Finger insertions, for manual
stimulation, 182–83,
<u>195</u>
Classics, 183–87, **184**, **186**
position 2, 187–88, **187**
position 3, 188–91, **188**, **189**,
190, **191**
position 4, 191–96, **191**, **192**,
193, **194**, **195**, **196**
Fingernails, 174, <u>175</u>
Finger Vibe vibrator, 280, **280**
Fisher, Helen, <u>110</u>
Flesh and Spirit, 293
Flowers, 65–66, <u>66</u>
Follicular phase, 153–54
Foods, seductive, 76–77
Foot massages, 96–97
erotic trigger points for, 97–99
reflexology chart for, **98**
Foot reflexology, **98**
For Each Other, 156
Foreplay
checklist for, 104–5
erotic, 226
as essential to woman, 151

mental arousal and (*see* Mental
arousal)
myths about, 111–12
physical arousal and (*see*
Physical arousal)
sexual response and, <u>43</u>, 223
Fountains, relaxation and, 79
Fox, Sarah Gardner, 12
Fragrances, <u>64</u>
French kiss, 85, 86
French ticklers, 368
Freud, Sigmund, <u>111</u>, 116
Frog Prince position, 196
Frustration, sexual, 112
Full moon, sex during, <u>67</u>
Fusion orgasms, 166

G

Gag reflex, 135
Gender differences, in
communication, <u>14</u>, 16–20
genitalia, 176
orgasms, 155–56
relationships, 67
Genital herpes, 342–43, 351–53
Genitalia
differences between male and
female, 176
female, **37**, 175–76
G-spot, 181–82
vagina, 179–81
vulva, 176–79, **177**
hygiene of, 204–5
female scent and, 201–2, 205
pubic hair and, 205–6, <u>205</u>
male, **29**
Genital warts, 354

Gloves, latex, 346
G-Man position, 195–96, **195,
    196**
Goldstein, Irwin, 333
Gonorrhea, <u>349</u>, 349–50
Graaf, Regnier de, 44
Grafenberg, Ernst, 181
Grapes, as seductive food, 76
G-Spot, The, 159
G-spot stimulation
    best positions for, 160, 187–88,
        187, 195, 195–96, **196**
    clitoral orgasms and, 156, 157,
        158, 162
    female ejaculation and, 110,
        116, 160
    guide to, 159–60, 181–82
    sex toys for, 279, **279,** 285, **285**
G-Spotter, 279, **279**

H

Hair
    male facial, 104, 206–7, 225
    pubic, <u>90</u>, 205–6, <u>205</u>, 226
    touching female's, 89–90
Hand assist position, 209, 225
Hands
    herpes and, 346
    holding, 63
    kissing, 86
    touching, 95–96
    washing, 174
Headaches, <u>235</u>
Head massages, 89–90
Hearing, 77–79, <u>78</u>
Hemochromatosis, 329
Hepatitis B, 354–55

Her Leg over His Shoulder
        position, 212, **212**
Hernia surgery, 332
Herpes
    causes of, 351
    cold sores and, <u>353</u>
    safe sex and, 342–43
    symptoms of, 351–52
    testing for, 352–53
    transmission of, 346–47
Hessel, Lasse, 27, 28
Hip Harness vibrator, 280–81
Hitachi Magic Wand vibrator, 279,
        279
HIV/AIDS, 356–61. *See also* STDs
    resources about, 348, 369–70
    safe sex and, 342, 367
Holding hands, as courtly
        behavior, 63
Holiday, Billie, 79
Honesty, 49–50
Hormones, male, <u>33</u>, 89, 176,
        337–38
Hot Sensual Massage Lotion, The,
        267–68
Hot spots, 229. *See also* Action
        spots
Hovering Butterfly position, 215,
        216, **216**
HPV. *See* Human papilloma virus
Human immunodeficiency virus.
        See HIV/AIDS
Human papilloma virus (HPV),
        346, 353–54, <u>354</u>
Human Sexual Response, 24
Hygiene
    of female genitalia, 201–2,
        204–5
    male body odor and, 75

Hygiene (cont.)
  male facial hair and, 104,
    206–7, 225
  of pubic hair, 205–6, <u>205</u>, 226
Hypothyrodism, 329

Interruptions, minimizing,
    69–70
Italian Method, 369
It Takes 3 position, 185–87,
    186

I

Ice cubes, 221
Imagery-induced orgasms, 167.
    See also Fantasy orgasms
Impotence, 325, <u>326</u>, 330–34,
    331
Incense, 259
Infinite cycle technique, 317–18,
    317
Intercourse
  anal penetration, 138–39, <u>139</u>,
    252–53
  attitudes about, 227–28
  at night, <u>115</u>
  penis size and, <u>228</u>, 230–31,
    <u>231</u>
  positions for, 231–50
    Better Than Sex (BTS),
      247–50, **249**
    man from behind (doggy
      style), 242–44, **243**
    man superior (man on top),
      232–35, **234**
    during pregnancy, 251
    side by side, 239–42, **240**
    sitting/kneeling, 247, **248**
    standing up, 244–47, **245**
    woman superior (woman on
      top), 236–38, **237**
  thrusting during, <u>126</u>, 229–30
  tips for, 250

J

Jarrett, Keith, 79
Jellogasm, <u>127</u>
Johnson, Virginia, 35
*Journal of the American Medical
    Association*, 148
Joy of Sex, The, 3
Jr. Dreidel position, 189, **189**

K

Kabazzah technique, 309, 311
Kallmann's syndrome, 329
Kama Sutra, 3
Kaplan, Helen, 335
Kegel exercise, 288–89, 311
Kenny Rankin Album, The, 79
Kivin Method, 216–17, **217**
Kidney failure, 329
Kinsey, Alfred, 25
Kissing
  courtly types of, 86–88
  mouth orgasms during, 165
  nasal problems and, <u>88</u>
  power of, 83–85, <u>84</u>
  Tantric, <u>308</u>
  tips on, 85, 221
Klinefelter's syndrome, 329
Kneeling/sitting position, 247,
    248

L

Labia majora, 176
Labia minora, 177
Ladas, Alice Kahn, 110, 159
Latex condoms, 269, 364–65,
    367
LDL cholesterol, 338
Legs, 95–96
Legs Together position, 209, **211**
Liberated Orgasm, 292
Libido, female, 110
Lighting, 72
Limbs, 95–96
Lips, 84, 165
Lipstick, 9
Liquid Silk, 268
Listening skills. *See*
    Communication
Liver function, 338
Lotion, hand, 174
Lotus position, 316
Love, Brenda, 262
Love Muscle, The, 289
Love Potions, 263
Loving the Prize position, **212**,
    213, 223
Lubricants, 264–70
    guide to, 265–69, 266
    tips for choosing, 268, 269–70,
        362
    tips for using, 145, 264, 265,
        265, 269
Lubrication, natural
    during arousal, 38–39, 180,
        197, 208, 213, 264
    during sleep, 264
    taste of, 205
Luteal phase, 154–55

M

Mammograms, 100
Man from behind position,
    242–44, **243**
Manners, good, 61–64
Man superior (man on top)
    position, 160, 232–35,
    234
Manual orgasms, male, 128–33
    techniques for
        Basket Weave, 131–33, **132**
        Ode to Bryan, 128, 129–31,
        130
        Penis Samba, 131
Manual sex
    performed on female, 171–97
        action spots for, 93, 101, 102,
            171–73, 197
        female genitalia and, 175–82,
            177
        lubricants for, 265
        positions for, 182–83
            Classics, 183–87, **184**,
            186
            position 2, 187–88, **187**
            position 3, 188–91, **188**,
            189, **190**, **191**
            position 4, 191–96, **191**,
            192, **193**, **194**, **195**,
            196
        tips for, 171–73, 196–97
    performed on male
        techniques for
            Basket Weave, 131–33, **132**
            Ode to Bryan, 128,
            129–31, **130**
            Penis Samba, 131
MAO inhibitors, 263

Marijuana, 334
Massage oils. *See also* Lubricants
    Embrace, 268
    Liquid Silk, 268–69
    Maximus, 269
    Midnite Fire, 267–68
    Sensura/Sex Grease, 267
    Very Private Intimate
        Moisturizer, 266–67
Masters, William, 35
Masturbation
    female, 99–100, 173
    male
        myths about, 112
        orgasms and, 127, 143–45,
            155
        reasons for, 144
        techniques for, 144–45
Maximus, 269
McCandless, Jaquelyn, 292
McCutcheon, Marc, 262
Media, power of, 13, 113–16
Medications, 181, 324, 338–39
Meditation techniques, 296–97
Menopausal women, 181, 197
Menstrual cycle, 152–55
Menstrual flow, 153
Mental arousal, 59–60. *See also*
        Aromatherapy
    courtly behavior and, 60–64
    engaging woman's senses and,
        73–80
    relaxation and, 66–72
    romance and, 64–66
Mercy sex, 150
Microtickler vibrator, 279, **279**
Midnite Fire, 267–68
Milsten, Richard, 27, 33, 112,
        325, 335

Missionary position, 112, 232
Monoamine oxidase inhibitors,
        263
Mons pubis, 176, 222
Mood for sex, *See* Mental arousal;
        Physical arousal
Mood swings, 153
Morin, Jack, 292
Mouth Magic technique, 136,
        137
Mouth orgasms, 164–65
Moviola, 79
Mr. Hoover technique, 220–21
Muir, Caroline, 301, 308
Muir, Charles, 301, 308
Multiorgasmic women, 39, 113
Multiple sclerosis, 332–33
Music, 78–79
Myotonic dystrophy, 329
Myths, about
    anal sex, 252
    aphrodisiacs, 262
    arousal, 111–12
    erections, 111
    female ejaculation, 110, 160
    foreplay, 111–12
    masturbation, 112
    oral sex, 202
    orgasms
        controversy over, 116–17,
            123
        media's impact on, 113–16
        misleading statements and,
            109–12, 111
        nature of pleasure and,
            119–21
    performance anxiety, 47–48,
            113–14, 148–49
    pornography, 9–12

sexiness, 114–16
sin/pleasure, 118–19

N

Nasal problems, kissing and, 88
National Herpes Hotline, 370
Neck, oral sex and man's, 224
Neck massages, 92–93
Negligee, 68
Neonatal herpes, 352
New Male Sexuality, The, 25, 144
New York Times, 148
NGU, 349
Nipple orgasms
    female, 163–64
    male, 125, 140
Nongonococcal urethritis (NGU),
    349
Nonoxynol-9, 201, 270, 270,
    366–67
Nonsexual contact, 82–83, 83. *See
    also* Touching
Not-on-the-Mouth kiss, 87
Nutritional deficiencies, 329
Nuts, as seductive food, 77

O

Obsessive-compulsive disorder,
    337
O'Connell, Helen, 178
Ode to Bryan technique, 128,
    129–31, 130
Olives, as seductive food, 77
Opening door, as courtly behavior,
    61–62

Oral orgasms, male, 133–38, 137
Oral sex
    performed on female, 199–226
        attitudes about, 133–34, 200
        clitoral stimulation and
            flicking problem and,
            203–4
        tips for, 207
        cultural references about,
            203
        female genitalia and,
            200–202, 201
        illegality of, 204
        myths about, 202
        positions for, 207, 208–21
            Arch, 215, 215
            Chair Therapy, 218, 219,
                220
            Classics, 209–13, 210,
                211, 212
            Hovering Butterfly, 215,
                216, 216
            Kivin Method, 216–17,
                217
            Rear Approach, 217–18,
                219
            Side by Side, 213–14, 214
            Sit on My Face (SOMF),
                215–16, 215
            69, 213–14, 214
        power of, 199–200
        special moves for, 220–21
        tips for, 221–24
        troubleshooting solutions for,
            224–26
    performed on male, 133–38
        deep throating, 11, 135
        fellatio, 134
        gagging and, 135

Oral sex (cont.)
   performed on male (cont.)
      Mouth Magic technique,
         136, **137**
      swallowing and, 11, 136, 138
Orgasmic fingerprinting, 122, <u>165</u>
Orgasms, 46
   female, 147–69
      average length of, <u>128</u>
      conception during, <u>239</u>
      foreplay and, 151
      new approach to, 149–52
      sexual response and, 43–44,
         168–69
      types of, 157–58
         AFE zone, 160–61
         anal, 166
         blended, <u>156</u>, 166–67
         breast/nipple, 163–64
         clitoral, 156, 158, 162
         fantasy, 167
         G-spot, 159–60
         mouth, 164–65
         U-spot/urethral, 163
         vaginal/cervical, <u>111</u>, 114,
            116, 156, 161–62
         zone, 167
      uncertainty about, 14–15
      uniqueness of, 122–23, <u>165</u>
   gender differences in, 155–56
   male, 125–45
      average length of, <u>128</u>
      enhancers for, 141–42
      masturbation and, 143–45
         reasons for, 144
         techniques for, 144–45
      types of, 126–27, <u>127</u>
         anal, 138–39, <u>139</u>
         breast/nipple, 140

fantasy, 139–40
manual, 128–33, **130,
   132**
oral, 133–38, **137**
prostate, 138
toys, 140–41
myths about
   controversy over, 116–17, 123
   media's impact on, 113–16
   misleading statements and,
      109–12
   nature of pleasure and,
      119–21
   sin/pleasure and, 118–19
   vaginal, <u>111</u>
   timing issues and, <u>151</u>, 152–55
   uncertainty about, 14–15
Otto, Herbert, 24, 165, 195, 292
Out of the Frame, 78
Overstimulation, 223
Ovulatory phase, 154
Oxytocin, <u>54</u>
Oysters, as seductive food, 77, 263

P

Pain, during sex, 250
Paraurethral glands, 110, 168
Parkinson's disease, 329
Partners, number of, 347–48
PC muscles, <u>168</u>, 181, 288, 289,
   <u>289</u>, 311
Pearl Necklace, 131, 281
Pedicures, 72
Pelvic nerve system, **32**, 155–56
Pelvic rocking, 229, 313
Pelvis inflammatory disease (PID),
   <u>201</u>

Penis
  of elephant, 114
  enhancers (see Enhancers,
      pleasure)
  enlargement, 287–88, 288
  manual stimulation of, 128–33,
      130, 132
  orgasms, 125, 127
  size, 228, 230–31, 231
Penis Samba technique, 131
Performance, sex as, 12, 13–14
Performance anxiety, 47–48,
      113–14, 148–49
Perineum, 179
Period, menstrual, 153
Perry, John D., 110, 159, 181
Pharmacological drugs, 336–37
Pheromone, 202
Physical arousal, 81–83
  foot reflexology and, 98
  kissing and, 83–88
  orgasms without (see Fantasy
      orgasms)
  teasing and, 102–3
  touching and, 88–102
Physical response cycles, 25, 26
  aging and, 39
  female, 37–45, 40–41
    arousal, 38–42, 38, 40
    ejaculation, 44–45
    genitalia, 37
    orgasms, 43–44
    resolution, 45
  male, 29–37, 30–31
    arousal, 32–33, 32
    ejaculation, 35–36
    erection, 33–34, 332
    genitalia, 29
    resolution, 36–37

Picasso kiss, 87–88
Picasso technique, 221
PID, 201
Plant extracts, 263
Playboy, 10
Playful Wave technique, 314–16,
      315
Pleasure
  avenues of, 56
  cultural barriers to, 118–19
  nature of, 119–21
Plums, as seductive food, 76
PMS, 153, 155
Pornography, myths about, 9–12
Positions, for
  anilingus, 138–39
  G-spot stimulation, 160
  intercourse, 231–50
    Better Than Sex (BTS),
        247–50, 249
    man from behind (doggy
        style), 242–44, 243
    man superior (man on top),
        232–35, 234
    during pregnancy, 251
    side by side, 239–42, 240
    sitting/kneeling, 247, 247
    standing up, 244–47, 245
    woman superior (woman on
        top), 236–38, 237
  manual sex, 182–83
    Classics, 183–87, 184,
        186
    position 2, 187–88, 187
    position 3, 188–91, 188,
        189, 190, 191
    position 4, 191–96, 191,
        192, 193, 194, 195,
        196

Positions, for (cont.)
 oral sex, 207, 208–21, 222–23
  Arch, 215, **215**
  Chair Therapy, 218, **219**, 220
  Classics, 209–13, **210**, **211**,
   212
  Hovering Butterfly, 215, 216,
   216
  Kivin Method, 216–17, **217**
  Rear Approach, 217–18, **219**
  Side by Side, 213–14, **214**
  Sit on My Face (SOMF),
   215–16, **215**
  69, the, 213–14, **214**
  Stand and Deliver, 218, **219**,
   220
 Tantric, 301–6
  Completing the Circuit, 301,
   305, 306
  horizontal (man on top),
   303–4, **303**, **304**, **305**
  horizontal (woman on top),
   304–5
  man behind the woman, 305,
   306
  Yab Yum, 301–3, **302**
Postmenopausal women, 181
Potent Male, The, 333
Preferences, in
 penis size, <u>228</u>, 230–31, <u>231</u>
 relationships, 52–53
Pregnancy, positions during, 251
Premature ejaculation, 155, <u>155</u>,
  334–37, <u>336</u>
Premenstrual syndrome, 153, 155
Prepuce, 178
Pressure sensitivities, 221–22, 229
Priapism, 142
Prolapsed disk, 332

Prostate gland, 284
Prostate orgasms, 125, 138–39,
  156, 284
Prostate specific antigen (PSA),
  168, 338
Prostatitis, 330
Prozac, 336–37
PSA, 168, 338
Pubic hair
 abundance of, <u>90</u>
 straight, <u>119</u>
 shaving female, 205–6, 226
Pubococcygeal (PC) muscles, <u>168</u>,
  181, 288, <u>289</u>, 311
Pudendal nerve system, 155–56,
  162
Pulsa Bath vibrator, 280, **280**

R

Rabbit Pearl vibrator, 278–79, **278**
Ramsdale, David, 318, 319
Rankin, Kenny, 79
Rear Approach position, 217–18,
  219
Rear-entry sex, 242–44, **243**
Reflexology, **98**
Rejection, fear of, 51–52
Relaxation, female, 68–71, <u>71</u>
 importance of, 66–67
 indicators of, 180, 197, 223, 275
 tips for, 72
Remote-controlled vibrators, 277,
  277
Replacement hormones, 338
Reproductive cycle, female, 153–55
Resolution, sexual response and,
  31, 36–37, **41**, 45

Ring and Seal technique, 135
Riskin, Michael, <u>151</u>
Romance, 60–66, <u>66</u>. *See also*
    Courtly behavior;
    Mental arousal
Rose Petals technique, 138–39
Roses, 65–66, <u>66</u>
Rushing, 222

S

Safe sex, 341–45, <u>344</u>
  birth control, 343
  condoms, 347, 361–68, <u>363</u>
  hepatitis B and, 354–55
  HIV/AIDS and, 342, 356–61
  resources about, 340, 369–70
  sexually transmitted diseases
    and (*see* STDs)
  techniques for, 368–69
Saliva, as lubrication, 265
Santamaria, Francisco Cabello,
    44, 168
Scalp massages, 89–90
Scent, female, 201–2, 205
Scents and Scentuality, 97
Scheduling sex, 55, <u>60</u>
Science magazine, <u>172</u>
Sculptor position, 193–95, **193,**
    194
Secretions, vaginal, 181
Seduction. *See* Mental arousal;
    Physical arousal
SEICUS, 370
Self-consciousness, 70–71
Self-lubrication. *See* Lubrication,
    natural
Self-pleasuring. *See* Masturbation

Senior citizens, 112
Senses, engaging woman's
  hearing, 77–79, <u>78</u>
  sight, 73–74
  smell, 74–77, <u>74</u>, <u>75</u>, <u>262</u>
  taste, 76–77
  touch, 79–80
Sensual Massage, 100, 101–2
Sensuous Woman, The, 3
Sensura/Sex Grease, 267
Sex drive, female, <u>110</u>, 154
Sexiness, myths about, 114–16
Sex Information Education
    Council of the United
    States (SEICUS), 370
Sexual desire
  low, 326–28
  stress and, 56–57
Sexual dysfunction, female,
    148–49, 332. *See also*
    Sexual functioning
Sexual Ecstasy, 299
Sexual energy, 294, <u>295</u>
Sexual Energy Ecstasy, 318
Sexual frustration, 112
Sexual functioning, 323–24
  aging and, 325–26, <u>326</u>
  dysfunction and, <u>324</u>
  female, 148–49, 332
  health considerations affecting,
    328–30
  chronic prostatitis, 330
  impotence/erectile
    dysfunction, <u>326</u>,
    330–34, **331**, <u>335</u>
  premature ejaculation, 155,
    <u>155</u>, 334–37, <u>336</u>
  prostatitis, 330
  low desire and, 326–28

Sexual functioning (cont.)
 medications and, 338–39
 sexually transmitted diseases
  and (*see* STDs)
 testosterone and, <u>33</u>, 337–38
Sexuality
 goal-oriented, 121–22
 nature of pleasure and, 119–21
 physical side of, 23–24
  genitalia, **29**, **37**
  sexual response cycles, **25**, **26**
   female, 37–45, **38**,
    40–41, **42**
   male, 29–37, **30–31**, **32**
   phases in, 24–29
 pleasure-directed, 122, 149–50
 resources about, 370
 self-consciousness and, 70–71
 sin/pleasure and, 118–19
 spiritual, 291–94, 319
 STDs and, 339–40
Sexually Transmitted Disease
  Hotline, 340, 369
Sexually transmitted diseases. *See*
  STDs
Sexual Male, The, 27, 325
Sexual nerve arrangements, **32**,
  38, 155–56
Sexual response cycles, **25**, **26**
 aging and, <u>39</u>
 female, 37–45, **40–41**
  arousal, 38–42, **38**, **40**
  ejaculation, 44–45, 168–69
  genitalia, **37**
  orgasms, 43–44
  resolution, 45
 male, 29–37, **30–31**
  arousal, 32–33, **32**
  ejaculation, 35–36

 erection, 33–34, 332
 genitalia, **29**
 resolution, 36–37
 phases in, 24–29
Shaft sleeves, 283–84
Sharing, 48–50
Shoulder massages, 92–93
Side by Side position, for
  intercourse, 239–42, **240**
 performing oral sex on female,
  213–14, **214**
Sight, 73–74
Silk, 144, 222
Sinus problems, kissing and, <u>88</u>
Sit on My Face (SOMF) position,
  215–16, **215**
Sitting/kneeling position, 247,
  248
69 position, 213–14, **214**
Skin, 100–101, 197
Slowinski, Julian, 27, 33, 111,
  325
Smell, 74–77, <u>74</u>, <u>75</u>, <u>262</u>
Smoking, <u>35</u>, 333
Society for the Scientific Study of
  Sexuality, 370
Softgasms, 111, 142
SOMF, 215–16, **215**
Spermicides, 201, 270, <u>270</u>,
  366–67
Spiritual sex, 291–319
 Tantra and
  ancient Indian, <u>297</u>
  benefits of, 299, 301
  male orgasmic potential in,
   300
  orgasm and, 318–19
  positions for, 301–6, **302**,
   303, **304**, **305**, **306**

practice of, 294–98, <u>295</u>
techniques for, 307–18, **309,
310, 312, 315, 317**
Spontaneity, 54–55, 119
Sportsheets™, 286
Squeeze technique, 141
Stair kiss, 87
Stand and Deliver position, 218,
219, 220
Standing for a woman, as courtly
behavior, 63
Standing up position, 244–47,
245
Static position, 193–94, **193, 194**
STDs, 201, 339–40, 345–46
common types of
clap, 349–50, <u>349</u>
chlamydia, 348–49, <u>349</u>
epididymitis, <u>349</u>, <u>350</u>
gonorrhea, 349–50, <u>349</u>
herpes, 346–47, 351–53
human papilloma virus
(HPV), 346, 353–54,
<u>354</u>
syphilis, 350–51
resources about, 348, 369–70
safe sex and, 342–43, <u>363</u>, 367
transmission of, 346–48
Stereotypes, female, 18
Stimulation, types of
female, 157–58
male, 126–27
Straight On position, 209, **210**
Strawberries, as seductive food, 76
Stress, 56
Strumming the Frenulum
technique, 220
Stubbs, Kenneth Ray, 307
Suckling orgasms, 164

Surgical enhancements, 287–88,
<u>288</u>
Swallowing, 11, 136, 138
Swirl technique, 100–101
Swoon kiss, 86
Syphilis, 350–51

T

Table manners, 64
Tactile sensations, 122, 144
Tantra, 293–94
ancient Indian, <u>297</u>
benefits of, 299, 301
male orgasmic potential in, **300**
orgasm and, 318–19
positions for, 301–6
Completing the Circuit, 301,
305, 306
horizontal (man on top),
303–4, **303, 304, 305**
horizontal (woman on top),
304–5
man behind the woman, 306,
306
Yab Yum, 301–3, **302**
practice of, 294–98, <u>295</u>
techniques for, 307–18, **309,
310**
Big Draw, 311–12, **312**
Kabazzah, 309, 311
Wave of Bliss, 313–18, **315,
317**
Tao of Sexology, 307
Taormino, Tristan, 252
Taste, 76–77
T-Cross position, 209, **211**
Teasing, 102–3

Tepper, Mitchell, 118, 120
Testosterone, 33, 89, 176, 337–38
Three Finger Draw technique,
      312
Thrusting, 126, 229–30
Tightness, vaginal, 181
Time for sex, 70, 71, 73
Timing issues, orgasm and, 151,
      152–55
Tobacco, 35, 333
Tongue
   flicking, 203–4
   power of, 199–200
   sucking, 84, 85. See also
         Kissing; Oral sex
Touching. See also Manual sex
   genitals, 171–73, 196–97
   mental arousal and, 79–80
   nonsexual, 82–83, 83
   physical arousal and, 88–100,
         258
   Sensual Massage, 100, 101–2
   Swirl technique, 100–101
Touring the Dance Floor position,
      190, **190**
Toys, 271–73, 273
   anal beads, 140–41, 284–85
   bungee jumping harness, 287
   butt plugs, 140, 284
   cock rings, 141, 281–83
   crystal wand, 285, **285**
   dildo/vibrator
      choices of, 274
      tips for using, 275–76
      types of, 276–81, **277**, **278**,
         279, **280**, 285
      vibrating features of, 275
   Pearl Necklace, 131, 281

shaft sleeves, 283–84
Sportsheets™, 286
vacuum pumps, 273,
Tuberculosis, 329
Tumors, 329

U

*Ultimate Guide to Anal Sex for
      Women, The*, 252
Up-Against-the-Wall kiss,
      87
Urethra, 163, 168, 179
Urethral orgasms, 163
Urinary tract infection, 179
U-spot/urethral orgasms, 163
Uterus, 161

V

Vagina, 179–81
   blowing into, 221
Vaginal cup, 154
Vaginal dryness, 154
Vaginal infections, 201, 201, 218,
      265
Vaginal orgasms, 111, 114, 116,
      156, 157, 161–62
Vaginal secretions, 181
Venus Butterfly position, 192–93,
      193
Verve Jazz Round Midnight series,
      79
Very Private Intimate Moisturizer,
      266–67
Viagra, 142, 327

Vibrators
    basics of, 274–75
    tips for using, 178–79, 275–76
    types of, 276–81, **277**, **278**,
        279, **280**
Visual stimulation, 10
Vitamins, 205
Vulnerability, 52
Vulva, 176–79, **177**

W

Waermark, 78
Wand style vibrator, 277, **277**
Waterproof vibrators, 278
Watson, Cynthia Mervis,
    262–63
Wave of Bliss technique, steps in
    connecting breath to breath,
        316
    cultivating arousal, 313–14
    infinite cycle, 317–18, **317**
    opening to your inner light,
        316–17
    pelvic rocking, 313
    playful wave, 314–16, **315**
Waxing, pubic hair, 206
Webster, Ben, 79

Whipple, Beverly, 110, 121, 122,
    159
Windham Hill Retrospective, 79
Wine, 77
*Wise Woman's Guide to Erotic
    Videos, The*, 12
Woman superior (woman on top)
    position, 160, 236–38,
        237
Woodhull, Victoria, 117
Woody Woodpecker kiss, 85, 86
World Is Your Oyster position,
    192, **192**
Worwood, Valerie Anne, 97
Wrists, 95–96

Y

Yab Yum position, 301–3, **302**
Yeast infections, 201
Y-Knot position, 190–91, **191**

Z

Zilbergeld, Bernie, 25, 36, 144
Zimmerman, Jack, 292
Zone orgasms, 167